THE AUSTRALIAN ABORIGINES

A. P. ELKIN is one of the founders of anthropology in Australia. Educated at the University of Sydney and the University of London, from which he received his Ph.D. in 1926, he returned to Australia and began his field-work among the Aborigines.

In 1933 he became the second chairman of the Department of Anthropology at the University of Sydney, a post he held for 23½ years, retiring in 1956. During this period, his field-work took him to all parts of Australia, as well as New Guinea, and other areas in Oceania.

The recipient of numerous awards and a member of many scientific organizations, Dr. Elkin has also been editor of *Oceania*, an anthropological journal, since 1933 and has written widely on the Australian Aborigines and other anthropological matters. His influence on the growth of Australian anthropology is widely recognized and his contributions to the welfare of the Aborigines as well as the native people of New Guinea are often acknowledged.

The Australian Aborigines

BY

A. P. ELKIN

Professor Emeritus of Anthropology,
University of Sydney
Editor of *Oceania*

PUBLISHED IN CO-OPERATION WITH
THE AMERICAN MUSEUM OF NATURAL HISTORY

THE NATURAL HISTORY LIBRARY
ANCHOR BOOKS
DOUBLEDAY & COMPANY, INC.
GARDEN CITY, NEW YORK

The Australian Aborigines was originally published by Angus &
Robertson Ltd., in 1938. A second edition was published in
1943 and a third edition in 1954. The Natural History Library
edition is published by arrangement with Angus & Robertson
Ltd.

Natural History Library edition: 1964

FOREWORD

PROFESSOR ELKIN, retired chairman of the Department of Anthropology at the University of Sydney and a lifelong student of the Australian Aborigines, presents in this revised edition of his book a fascinating, human, and modern treatment of one of this planet's most interesting, isolated, and primitive peoples. Earlier accounts of this aboriginal people informed the theories of anthropologists and the analogies of psychoanalysts and stocked the image bank from which the lay reader draws when he comes upon such words as *savage*, *primitive*, and *aboriginal* or *totem* and *boomerang*. These are the people found by the early explorers of the seventeenth century, living as hunters and food gatherers, stark naked, their hair matted over their eyes against the hot and brilliant sun. The Aborigines took the light-skinned Europeans for ghosts and, to the horrified eyes of the men sent to Australia as criminals and as guards, they appeared to exemplify the degradation of man made in God's image.

The Australian Aborigines lived in widely dispersed groups in the great inhospitable continent, warming themselves by carrying firebrands in their hands, building no permanent buildings and, with no knowledge of agriculture, often surviving incredible hardships in their search for food in the years of drought that plague all living things in Australia. Through the long centuries, in religious and ritual systems that recognized a spiritual rather than a biological paternity and that emphasized the power of the old men over the newly initiated, they re-enacted in paint and feathers, dance and mime, the conditions

of their continuing existence as peoples. Poor and crude
as their weapons and utensils were, in their social organization and their articulate relations with their environment, their cultures were complex and beautiful. They are
perhaps the outstanding example in the world of how a
people who remained at a very simple technological level
could still develop a poetic and artistic approach to life,
expressed in long liturgies that were closely bound up
with the special country in which each tribe lived:

Now the New Moon is hanging, having cast away his
    bone:
Gradually he grows larger, taking on new bone and flesh.
Over there, far away, he has shed his bone: he shines on
    the place of the Lotus Root, and the place of the
    Dugong,
On the place of the Evening Star, of the Dugong's Tail,
    of the Moonlight clay pan. . . .

Early contacts between European settlers and Aborigines were sad and destructive. The white settlers put
bounties on the heads of the Aborigines, treating them
like pests to be eliminated; the Aborigines found little in
the white way of life to understand or incorporate into
their own. Only where population was very scarce and
the white man was dependent on the Aborigine for an
understanding of some trackless waste, was there some
temporary matching of needs and skills. Not recognizing
physical paternity as important, the Aborigines accorded
white men a type of sexual hospitality that produced a
mixed blood population without evoking respect or understanding from either group. Then, for a time, it seemed
that this remote race might die out altogether. But the
population has rallied, and the Australian conscience has
stirred.

Professor Elkin writes with tremendous sympathy for
the Aborigine, combining an anthropologist's grasp of his
culture, a field worker's vivid knowledge of the way in

which the aboriginal people really lived, and a lifetime of interpreting the Aborigines to contemporary Australians. He knows which aspects of aboriginal life seem most incomprehensible to modern man—and explains them. He knows how difficult it has been for the white Australian to understand and to treat as fully human—like himself— a people who look so different and who live such a different way of life. As a result, this book is time binding, bringing our records of a contemporary Stone Age man together with the most modern struggles for human dignity and the inclusion of all members of the human species in one human race. After a lifetime of work, Professor Elkin feels that "we face the future confidently."

Margaret Mead

The American Museum of Natural History
New York 1964

PREFACE TO THIRD EDITION

THE fifteen years which have passed since the first edition of this book was published have seen great advances in our knowledge of the Australian Aborigines. Systematic field-work, begun in 1926, has been carried on almost con-tinuously, though some restrictions were imposed by the conditions and calls of war. This research has been in the spheres of social and physical anthropology, linguistics and psychology, and amongst part-Aborigines as well as full-bloods. The areas ranged from the vicinity of the Trans-continental Railway in the south to the farthest tip of Arnhem Land in the north, and from the Indian Ocean in the west to the Pacific shores in the east.

Probably few people realize how slender was our knowledge of the Aborigines until well into the second quarter of this century. Many articles had been written by missionaries, police and other persons who were in contact with the natives. A few books of collected essays, and others based on questionnaires, have been published. But this information, though useful, was superficial and scrappy. The valuable contributions on, and analyses of the social organization and marriage laws, made by such investigators as L. Fison and A. W. Howitt, R. H. Math-ews and A. R. Brown (later Professor Radcliffe-Brown), while of much theoretical interest, were based on recon-structed and indeed, well-articulated, skeletons from which most of the flesh had disappeared. This was inevi-table because the first-hand experience of these writers was limited to tribal remnants in settled regions, whose indigenous culture was already a thing of shreds and patches. The slight, though very acceptable books by Mrs J. S. Smith, Mrs Langloh Parker and John Mathew were limited in the same way. And Dr W. E. Roth's work, though based on experience of tribes in different stages of contact, was for the most part dry as dust, suffering from the form of presentation as government bulletins. The social skeletons were not even articulated, though the collected bones were solid.[1]

There was, however, one outstanding exception. Baldwin Spencer, Professor of Zoology in the University of Melbourne, after an expedition into Central Australia in the early 1890s as biologist, turned his scientific training in observation, description and classification into the field of Australian anthropology. He devoted three field expeditions of a year or more each to this research, being helped in the first two by Mr F. J. Gillen, Sub-Protector of Aborigines at Alice Springs, who had sound personal knowledge of the local natives. *The Native Tribes of Central Australia* (1899) was correctly hailed as something new in anthropological research. It dealt almost solely with one tribe—the Arunta—and no such complete, detailed, yet controlled and balanced description of an Australian tribe has appeared since. It showed a sound appreciation of the social structure in relation to behaviour and, in particular, presented an extraordinarily rich account of Arunta ritual and mythology. It revealed that a tribe was really a dynamic social phenomenon. An excellent sequel was provided in *The Northern Tribes of Central Australia* (1904), particularly in its record of the Warramunga tribe, and in its classification of tribal cultures. In 1914 *The Native Tribes of the Northern Territory* appeared, breaking new ground in Melville Island and the Alligator rivers region, where contact with Europeans was still at a minimum.

These books revealed the importance of anthropologi-

[1] See Appendix at the end of this book, on "Additional Reading".

cal research by scientifically trained persons amongst
tribes whose way of life was not seriously disturbed. Such
research showed the way to understanding the Aborigines, and also to interpreting the less satisfactory accounts
which could be obtained from tribal remnants. This,
however, required money and personnel. However, it was
necessary to "redeem the time", for tribal cultures were
changing rapidly and tribes dying out. The Pan-Pacific
Science Congress of 1923, which met in Australia, urged
that this research be done before it was too late, and that
a University Department of Anthropology be established
for the purpose. Through the representations of the Australian National Research Council the Department was
founded at Sydney University in 1925 and funds were
obtained from American Foundations for research.

From 1926 to about 1946 planned research was carried out in Aboriginal Australia under the direction of
the Research Council, through its Committee on Anthropology of which the Professor of Anthropology was Chairman. Since 1946 research has been continued on a limited
scale with grants from the University of Sydney and other
sources. Fourteen social anthropologists, one psychologist,
and five linguists have worked in the field for periods of
from one to four years each, and totalling forty-two years
between them. In addition a number of expeditions,
consisting of several specialists each, have gone into the
field from the Universities of Adelaide and Sydney for
short periods of research; the University of Melbourne
has maintained one Research Fellow; nine anthropologists,
and one psychologist from abroad, have collaborated with
the Research Council or with one of the Universities;
and finally, the Anthropological Departments in the Mu-
seums have done a lot of research, particularly in the
fields of archaeology and physical anthropology. As a result a dozen and more important books and monographs
have been published, and articles by the score in learned
journals.

This wealth of material has been kept in mind in preparing this new edition, although no attempt is made to summarize it. We are concerned with the general appreciation of Aboriginal society and culture, not with detailed descriptions.

I have also had the opportunity both of collaborating with other field-workers, and also, especially since 1944, of again doing regular periods of field-work myself in both eastern Australia and in Arnhem Land and its neighbourhood, so that I can still write of people whom I know—not just know about.

Important revisions have been made in Chapters I and II and additions to Chapters VII and VIII. The latter are made possible by our increased knowledge of the women's sacred and secret life, and of the fertility-mother cult. Three new chapters have been included. New chapters IX and X have arisen mainly out of recent research into Aboriginal visual art, music and dancing; and the new final chapter deals with the Aborigines as Australians —citizens and citizens-to-be. When the first edition was written we were only turning our minds as an act of faith towards that goal. Indeed, we then doubted whether, when and if we reached it, there would be any but part-Aborigines remaining. Now we face the future confidently. With mutual behaviour more and more based on understanding and good-will, we are justified in looking forward to the time, not so far ahead, when the Aborigines, full-bloods and mixed-bloods, will share proudly with us all in an Australia which they have helped to enrich.

A. P. Elkin

University of Sydney,
September, 1953.

PREFACE TO SECOND EDITION

ADVANTAGE has been taken of the issue of a second edition to make some minor alterations, to bring up to date the appendix on "Additional Reading", and to enlarge the index.

A. P. Elkin

March, 1943

PREFACE TO ORIGINAL EDITION

INTEREST in the Australian Aborigines as human personalities has increased during the past few years, and nowadays there is a growing desire not only to treat them
justly, but also to help them rise culturally—if only we
knew how. We realize that we have done them much
wrong and injury during the past one hundred and fifty
years, through ignorance even more than through cal-
lousness and indifference. Our great need, therefore, is
to understand them and the cultural problems which
confront both them and ourselves. Given a right understanding, governments, administrative officers and missionaries would be qualified to formulate policies and
methods designed to assist the Aborigines in the task of
adjusting themselves to the great changes which have
come upon them. Australia should still be theirs, even
as it is ours. Their very presence in the country imposes
on us a dual mandate to seek their good as well as our
own, the unwritten but human terms of which we should
endeavour to fulfil.

This book is offered as a contribution to that understanding which should inspire our attitude to, treatment
of, and work for, the Aborigines. It is intended for three
types of readers: those of the general public who would
like to know more of this interesting but unfortunate people; administrative officials and missionaries who have to
work amongst the Aborigines or to deal with matters
concerning them; and University students and scientists.

The chapter headings show that the book is in no
sense superficial or merely descriptive. It seeks to understand Aboriginal tribal and social organization, law, belief,

ritual and philosophy. I do not regard the Aborigines as interesting survivals of man's early ancestors, nor their customs as cultural curiosities—noble, barbarous or amusing. I am concerned with their culture as a means of life worked out during the past centuries—a culture which is being strained to breaking point by contact with ourselves. Some passages of the book are not simple, for an understanding demands more than an elementary introduction. It is not easy to write simply about the intricacies of a people's law, philosophy and religion, especially when that people occupies a whole continent and is divided up into tribes with many variations in social organization and belief. We are apt to make the mistake of thinking that because a people is primitive and poor in material possessions, it has a very elementary form of social order and religious life. Some folk carry the metaphor of child-race too far. A child-race is so called because it has not attained to the stature of our civilization; its grown men and women, however, are adults; they do not think as children but as social personalities who are responsible for the development and maintenance of the social, economic and religious life of their community. Therefore, we should not expect the understanding of that life to be a matter for the kindergarten; it is a subject worthy of our best efforts. But difficult as some aspects of my task have been, I hope that what I have written is, at least, clear.

I suggest that most readers will do well to pass lightly over the second parts of Chapters III and IV until they have finished the book, after which they might care to learn more about the relationship systems and social groups which prevail amongst the Aborigines. Needless to say, those persons whose work lies amongst them, must master those sections.

The substance of this book has been given at various times in lectures to Tutorial Classes organized by the Department of Tutorial Classes and by the Extension Board of the University of Sydney. It is based on a full knowledge of the literature on the Aborigines, but it could not have been written apart from the field-work I have been able to do at various times during the past eleven years, under the auspices of the Australian National Research Council; I spent twelve months in the Kimberleys (1927–8) and nearly twelve months in the southern and central parts of the continent in 1930, and have paid several visits to the remaining groups of Aborigines on the North Coast of New South Wales. This experience enables me to write of a people whom I know, and of persons who have helped me to understand their "way of life". I thank them for their help and their friendship, and hope that those few of them who hear of this book will realize that it was written to help the white man understand the Aborigine.

On one occasion, a good old native asked me why I wanted to know so much about their custom and belief. In the course of my answer, I mentioned the lack of understanding of native life which exists amongst those white persons (police, missionaries and employers) who have most to do with Aborigines, and which explains many unfortunate happenings; I added that I desired to gain an understanding of native life so that I might pass it on to these very people in the hope that they would then be able to adopt a different and a wiser attitude toward native custom and the Aborigines in general. The old man thought, and then replied, "That is good; but you have come too late." I answered, "Yes, too late for your tribe" (it was completely broken down), "but perhaps not too late to help some other tribes not so far away." I hope it is not, even yet, too late.

I wish to express my thanks to Miss M. Collier and Miss M. Ravenscroft of the Department of Anthropology for their great help with the typing and with the reading of the typescript and proofs.

A. P. Elkin

July, 1938

CONTENTS

division. (viii) Arnhem Land. Bark-paintings. Carvings and composite figures. Doctrine in art. Variety of Aboriginal visual arts.

present picture. The process of assimilation.
The group aspect of assimilation. Aboriginal citizenship the goal.

LIST OF ILLUSTRATIONS

eastern Arnhem Land. *Bottom,* mission girls "dancing" at burial ritual. Goulburn Island.

17. *Top,* tree-stage burial, with inquest stones underneath. North-western Australia. *Bottom,* painting-up in pipe-clay: initiation ritual. Southern Arnhem Land.
18. Bone-pointing. Central Australia.
19. Preparing coffin for bones. Goulburn Island.
20. Warramunga and Wailbri tribes, decorated for totemic ceremony. North-central Australia.
21. *Top,* recording Nyindi-yindi corroboree at Delissaville. Northern Territory. *Bottom,* the anthropologist learns. Far North-eastern Arnhem Land.
22. Raising four visiting young men after being painted with local clan designs. Arnhem Land.
23. Casting spears at fish from a tree.
24. Facing the future.

KINSHIP TABLES

Chapter I

THE ABORIGINES AND THEIR MANNER OF LIFE

MOST people who think at all of the Aborigines are concerned not so much with understanding their social, religious and mental life, as with gaining information about their human classification and place of origin. How are they grouped amongst the peoples of the world? Are they the lowest race in existence? Where did they come from? Such are the usual questions asked, and though this book is not a study in physical anthropology, some indication of the answers to these questions will be given before passing on to its real subject matter.

WHO ARE THE ABORIGINES?

Broadly speaking, there are four main divisions of human beings. First of all there is the *European,* which is itself subdivided into three main types or groups: the Nordic, characterized by tall stature, fair hair, blue eyes and long head, and found in its purest form in parts of Scandinavia; the Alpine type with its broad head, short stature and medium coloured hair and eyes, which predominates in Switzerland; and the Mediterranean, with its sallow to dark, and even brown or black skin, long head, short stature, and dark hair and eyes; this third group includes the Southern Europeans, Egyptians, peoples of Palestine, the so-called Aryans of India, and also the Abyssinians who are sometimes quite black. The Polynesians, too, are generally classified in part with this group, because of the Indonesian element in their physical constitution. These three subdivisions are in most regions very mixed with one another, and in Africa and the Pacific with other main types.

The Australian Aborigine differs from the various groups which are included in the European division, in skin colour, form of the nose, shape of the head, face and mouth, thickness of the bones of the brain-case and in the average amount of brain matter or size of the brain cavity which is, on the average, about twenty per cent less than in the case of Europeans.

The second main division is the *Mongoloid,* which includes the Chinese, Japanese, Siamese, Malays, American Indians and the predominant element in the Micronesians. All readers are familiar with the general type —the yellowish skin, straight black hair of the head, the comparative absence of hair from the face and body, the high cheek-bones and, in some subdivisions, the broad head. The Australian Aborigine differs in skin colour, shape of the head which is narrower and has a retreating forehead, shape of the face with its absence of high cheek-bones, and in the greater amount of hair on the body; the eyes, too, are different and the appearance of an eye-slant, caused by the epicanthic fold in the corner of the eye, which is frequent in some Mongoloid groups, is never found amongst the Aborigines.

The third great division, the *Negroid,* needs little description; the skin is brown to black, the hair woolly or frizzy, the lips frequently everted, the forehead bulging, head narrow, and stature tall to medium. There are, however, many variations in a division which includes the peoples of Africa south of the Sahara, such as the Bushmen, Hottentots, Zulu, Bantu, and Ashanti. In addition, though separated by the Indian Ocean, the Andaman Islanders, Papuans, Melanesians and Tasmanians, on the basis of external characteristics, have been included in the same division. The Australian Aborigine differs in skin colour, which is generally less dark than in the case of the Negroid groups, and in the form of his hair which is curly or wavy but not woolly. He also has more body hair, while his lips are much less everted.

The Aborigine, therefore, is neither Negroid, Mongoloid nor European. But it is sometimes argued that he is really a primitive European or Caucasian (as this division is sometimes called). The argument is in part negative in character. The Aborigine is obviously neither Mongoloid, nor Negroid, and as there are only three great divisions, or so the argument seems to imply, he must belong to the third. Moreover, the form of his hair and the hairy nature of his body are similar to that of the average European. True, there are differences, for example, the smaller quantity of brain matter, a retreating forehead, frequently heavy eyebrow ridges and prognathic jaws; but these, it may be said, only show that he is a primitive relation of ours; they do not disprove the relationship. But let us be careful; these very features which distinguish the Australian Aborigine from ourselves have been held to justify his being grouped with the strange Neanderthal man, extinct these 20,000 years, with his beetling eyebrow ridges, stooping gait, short shins, retreating forehead, prognathic jaws, teeth with great pulp cavities but short roots, and other massive and primitive features. A careful examination of the features, however, shows that the Aborigine is neither Neanderthaloid, nor is he European. It is not surprising to find in him some features European or Neanderthal in character, for all human types must resemble one another in some, or indeed many, features, seeing that all have in common a very extensive ancestry. Sir Arthur Keith has suggested that the Australian Aborigine represents the type from which all modern races have sprung, and Sir Grafton Elliot Smith regarded him as the representative of Aurignacian man; the latter was the first human being of definitely modern type to appear in Europe—the people whose coming apparently caused the extinction of their Neanderthaloid predecessors.

In view of the differences which exist between the Aborigine and the other great divisions of mankind, be they Nordic, Alpine, Mediterranean, Negroid or Mongoloid, and in view of the expert opinions of such scientists as those just mentioned, who would regard him as representing a generalized though primitive modern type, the Australian Aborigine is now classified in a special group, the Australoid.

PHYSICAL CHARACTERISTICS OF THE ABORIGINE

There are many individual variations between Aborigines—in stature, head-form, face and general appearance —those variations which contribute to individuality; but no one could mistake an Aborigine. The following is a general description: chocolate-brown skin which appears black when sunburnt and unwashed; wavy to curly hair; a plentiful growth of hair on face and body; usually a low or retreating forehead and a narrow head which is sometimes keel-shaped on top; eyes deep set; eyebrow ridges sometimes very heavy, but not made of a solid piece of bone as in Neanderthal man; nose, depressed at root and fairly wide at the nostrils; jaws sometimes prognathous, or projecting in the region of the mouth; the chin sometimes retreating; mouth wide, skullcap very thick;[1] hands very slender; legs also slender and buttocks slight; very erect carriage of the body; average height about five feet five or six inches, with variations from short to tall, some individuals being over six feet. In most of these features the Australian Aborigine differs from ourselves, the Mongol and the Negro, and therefore is rightly classed, as already stated, in a special human division.

[1] This affords great protection to the brain in case of blows with clubs and axes in fights or when mourning. The temporal region is avoided; it is just as thin as in European skulls.

Are There Any Other Australoid Groups?

The answer to this question is yes; that is, there are other human groups sufficiently like the Australian Aborigine to be classified with him in the Australoid division. These groups are found as small remnants in the lands from Australia to southern India. Evidence suggests that there have been some Australoid folk in New Guinea and the Celebes, and archaeology points to their former presence in Java. The Sakai of the Malay Peninsula, the Veddas of Ceylon and the aboriginal hill-tribes of southern India are regarded as variants within this division. The impression some of these make on a person who is familiar with the Australian Aborigine, is that they are fundamentally the same stock; thus during a visit to Suva, Fiji, I was struck by the appearance of an Indian in the street; without expressing my thoughts, I asked my companion who had studied the Aborigines in the field, to look at this Indian; he said Australian Aborigine. Such impressions are borne out by careful observations.

The Origin and Migrations of the Aborigines

Until recently all we could say with any degree of certainty was that the Aborigines came from the north, and that they had a common origin with other Australoid groups. Now, thanks to further palaeontological evidence and to an increasing understanding of human variations and relationships, the following is a reasonable theory: man's immediate ancestors or else the very earliest generalized type of man spread from a common centre to those regions which are especially associated with the main divisions of mankind, and where the peculiar characteristics of those divisions were gradually developed. One such region consisted of the islands north of Australia, especially Java. Here from very early types Australoid man was differentiated and spread north to Malaya and India, and south to New Guinea and Aus-

tralia. Moreover, the Australoid type in its turn, sub-
jected to varied environments and through variations
selected in lines of descendants, gave rise to the many
sub-races which are known as Papuan and Melanesian.[2]

The Australoid migrations must have been a slow
process covering many centuries, for they were but food
gatherers, moving now here, now there, in search of
fresh and better "hunting-grounds"; they were probably
urged on by the pressure of population, more particularly
of a people with a higher culture. The pockets, remnants
and traces which can still be recognized—as in Ceylon,
Malaya, the East Indies and New Guinea—suggest that
small groups have managed to survive in the less desirable localities, in the mountains or jungle, while the
rest have been absorbed, extinguished or forced to move
on. At last some Australoids came to Australia where for
a long period they were able to work out their adjustment
to its environment undisturbed, for it was not until 1788
that any other people thought Australia worth invading
and settling.

This immigration involved the crossing of water spaces,
for no matter how far back in human history it occurred,
or how different the relative amounts of land and water
were then in that region, there were at least two
stretches of water to be traversed; these were the straits
between Borneo and Celebes and Bali and Lombok,
known as Wallace's line, and either the Timor Sea or
Torres Strait. We do not know in what sort of craft the
Aborigines crossed these waters but there is no reason
for doubting their ability to make the necessary cross-
ings. We must judge them in this regard by the feats of
those along the northern coasts. For example, a light
double craft of mangrove logs is used for crossing to the
islands of the Buccaneer Archipelago, King Sound, north-

---

[2] R. Ruggles Gates, *Human Ancestry* (1948), Chapters VI, X.
Arthur Keith, *A New Theory of Human Evolution* (1948),
Chapters XXIV–XXVI.

western Australia where the tide rises thirty-four feet and the tidal rips are very dangerous. But by skilful navigation in a zigzag course, a native paddles to the middle of the strait with the outgoing tide and reaches the other shore with the incoming tide. Along the northern shores, they are adept with dug-out canoes, and incidentally, they are good long-distance swimmers and feel quite at home in the water. This makes them very useful on <u>luggers</u> and also in "naked" diving for pearl-shell. So we may picture them reaching Australia finally by raft or canoe, bringing with them the dog (or dingo) which is not <u>indigenous</u> and had to rely on man for its transport to its new home.

The Aborigines landed in northern Australia, probably on Cape York Peninsula, and perhaps also at different times on other parts of the coast. From there they gradually spread across the continent, though we cannot speak with certainty about the routes followed. They probably spread around the north and down the east and west coasts; down the Queensland rivers on to the Diamantina and Cooper and so into South Australia; from the Queensland coast on to the headwaters of the Barwon and along the Darling River system and on to the Murray right to its mouth; and gradually across the deserts from north to south until the Bight was reached.

It is difficult to get satisfactory evidence for such hypotheses, but there is some: the geographical conditions made these routes fairly obvious, while movements since white occupation show the spread along two of them—namely, along the Darling River system, more especially up its eastern tributaries, and into the Hunter Valley, and across the deserts of western South Australia to the Bight. Trade routes, too, are suggestive of natural roads of expansion—for example, down the Diamantina and Cooper and on to Spencer Gulf. Mythology may also refer to movements of groups, especially in eastern Australia; the myth of the migration of Nurunderi and his people down the Lower Murray to its mouth is the best example. Often, however, mythological history refers to the movements of culture and culture-heroes rather than to a people's movement over part of the continent and we must not confuse cultural with racial history.

THE ANTIQUITY OF MAN IN AUSTRALIA

We do not know, even approximately, when the Aborigines came to Australia or what length of time they took to spread over it. Archaeological research has not made much progress in Australia. Some years ago Professor J. W. Gregory came to the somewhat surprising conclusion that the Aborigines had only been in Victoria about four hundred years. The finding of a stone axe deep in an alluvial deposit tells us little, for very quick changes are apt to occur in the great alluvial localities, like the Lower Hunter, New South Wales. The immense size of shell mounds, especially in northern Australia has been quoted as proof of a great antiquity of human occupation; I have seen a cockle-shell mound forty-five yards in circumference and three feet six inches high and there are larger ones. But the formation of such a heap does not imply thousands of years. A few score natives spending a few weeks occasionally in the locality would make a large refuse heap in the course of a century. The Talgai fossil skull found in 1884 in the Darling Downs, southern Queensland, is also indecisive, for we do not know the rate of mineralization in this region, and there was no geological evidence for determining its relative age. Uncertainty also surrounds the geological age of the Cohuna and Keilor skulls found in Victoria in 1925 and 1940 respectively; but, like Talgai, they are definitely Aboriginal. Each of them, however, exhibits some exceptionally large, powerful or rugged traits, and though these traits can be matched individually in present-day Aborigines, their collective presence in any one skull is, at least, unusual. Therefore, though these skulls do not prove antiquity they do suggest an Australian type, somewhat different from the modern Aboriginal. Moreover, their likeness to the Wadjak skull found in Java in 1889 does no more than confirm a northern hiving-off ground for the Aborigines since the Ice Age. It does not determine the period of their arrival in Australia. Similarly, methodical archaeological work at two sites on the Lower Murray in 1929 lead to the conclusion that "these occupational records are at least of some antiquity.[3] Nothing more definite can be said at present. The spread of a food-gathering people over the continent, the settlement of the various groups, as population increased, in separate tribal territories and the development of distinct languages and dialects require a long period of time but not necessarily a great antiquity. There was very little, if any, opposition to the spread of the invaders. Moreover, isolation during the dispersion, followed by continued isolation during the greater part of each year, of the tribal and sub-tribal groups once they had settled, must have soon led to dialectal variations. One or two thousand years gives scope for many changes, as exemplified by the history of Britain or of Polynesia. However, the results of recent archaeological research together with the new dating techniques suggest that the continent has been occupied for over ten thousand years.

This question is connected with another: was there a preceding race in Australia, namely, the Tasmanians? The latter were related to the Melanesians and Papuans, but possessing a much simpler culture than these. A few of their words, customs and implements have been shown to

[3] H. M. Hale and N. B. Tindale, "Notes on some Human Remains in the Lower Murray Valley, South Australia" Records of the South Australian Museum, vol. iv, no. 2, 1930. N. W. G. Macintosh, Reader in Anatomy, University of Sydney, kindly assembled for me in digest the latest material bearing on the Talgai, Keilor and Cohuna skulls, and on other finds. At present there is no factual evidence of antiquity.

be the same as those of the Australians, but, as far as we
know, the latter had many customs, beliefs and advanced
types of implements which the Tasmanians lacked. If the
Tasmanians were living in parts of Australia at the time
the Aborigines commenced their invasion, they must have
been either conquered and absorbed, or extinguished, or
else forced to seek a new home across Bass Strait which
may have been much less formidable then than now. It
is also possible that the Tasmanians were already in their
island home as well as on the mainland at the time of
the Australoid invasion and that they were not joined by
any of their folk who were north of the strait. In either
case, the evidence suggests that those who survived in
Tasmania were very little, if at all, influenced by the invaders' culture.

The Rev John Mathew in his interesting book, *Eagle-
hawk and Crow*, suggests that the moiety system in eastern and south-western Australia reflects and records an
historical conflict between two distinct peoples, one being
lighter in colour than the other. In these regions, the two
social and ceremonial groups into which each tribe is
divided are distinguished by names (eaglehawk and
crow, white and black cockatoo, light-blooded and dark-
blooded) denoting contrast in colour, and Mr Mathew
interprets the ceremonial opposition which exists between
the moieties as a survival of the struggle between the
lighter coloured Australians and the darker Tasmanians.
But a wide survey of the dual organization throughout
Australia, and outside of it, does not permit us to find its
origin in such a racial conflict in Australia, if it did occur.
In spite of this, however, students are re-examining the
archaeological material, and also the linguistic and mythological evidence to which Mr Mathew drew attention,
before accepting the theory of a non-mainland route for
the Tasmanians. Indeed, in the opinion of one writer (in
1937), "the only conclusion which seems to be tenable is
that the Tasmanians formerly inhabited Australia and

reached Tasmania from the continent". According to another hypothesis, however, the Tasmanians came from New Caledonia and, without settling on the mainland of Australia, moved slowly, mainly in simple boats or rafts, down its eastern coast and then from island to island in Bass Strait until at last they reached Tasmania. More recently a careful student of the subject has shown the possibility of a voyage in simple vessels from the New Hebrides to Tasmania and that Tasmanoid people exist in the former. He has also shown the improbability of such craft crossing from Wilson Promontory to Tasmania.[4]

AUSTRALIAN TRIBES AND LANGUAGES

Whenever it was, and whatever were their relations with the Tasmanians, the Australian Aborigines took possession of Australia, spread over its surface and by 1788 numbered, as far as we can calculate, about 300,000. This comparatively small number—not more than the population of one of our smaller capital cities—may surprise

[4] Readers interested in this question should refer to N. W. G. Macintosh, "A Survey of Possible Sea Routes Available to the Tasmanian Aborigines", *Records of the Queen Victoria Museum*, Launceston, 1948, pp. 123–44, and to D. S. Davidson's "The Relationship of Tasmanian and Australian Cultures", a short essay of fifteen pages in vol. i of the Publications of the Philadelphia Anthropological Society published in 1937. Other references are: John Mathew, *Eaglehawk and Crow* (1899); A. W. Howitt, *The Native Tribes of South-East Australia* (1904), Chapter I; and John Mathew, *Two Representative Tribes of Queensland*, (1910), Chapter I, in which he replies to Dr Howitt's and other criticisms of his view. Howitt and Mathew also deal with the origin of the Australian Aborigines. For this, reference should also be made to G. E. Smith, *Human History*, Chapter IV. A recent theory, put forward by J. B. Birdsell and based on a field survey, but not yet satisfactorily established, is that the Aborigines are racially tri-hybrid, consisting of Tasmanoid, Archaic Caucasoid (mainly represented in South-East Australia) and pre-Dravidian or Carpentarian (the real Australoid). For this, see *The Australian Encyclopaedia*, 2nd Edition, under "Aborigines: Early Man; Physical Features".

many. But it was only arrived at after a very careful examination of all references to native population made since 1788, and as far as the unsettled or relatively unsettled areas are concerned, on the basis of field research. In the course of the latter work, genealogies of as many individuals as possible are recorded, and note is made of the membership of local subdivisions of the tribes. This research has been proceeding since 1926, and there is so far no reason for suggesting that the number 300,000 is very far wrong.

This does not mean that the Aborigines were only in Australia long enough to increase to that figure, for we know that in many tribes, even in good country, a balance between numbers and food-resources is maintained by infanticide and sometimes by abortion. In times of severe drought in the drier parts of the continent, infanticide is apt to be practised temporarily in the interests of the adults without any thought of the future of the group. In any case, we cannot assert that the Aborigines were followers of Malthus and consciously watched and kept the population total within predetermined limits. Convenience of the mother and the age of the previous child, for children are suckled until they reach the age of two and over, are the usual considerations. But a more intimate acquaintance with the thoughts and social principles of tribal leaders may show that an intelligent and traditional interest is taken in the population problem.

The 300,000 were divided into about 500 tribes, some of which were possibly only sub-tribes or well-marked local divisions of large tribes. The membership of a tribe varied from about 100 to 1500, and averaged about 500 or 600. There were as many languages or distinct dialects as tribes. It is true that the same words and sounds appear in very many of the languages, even in those far apart, though very often the meanings of the same words differ. This may well imply a common origin of the words in one language. In addition, the general principles of the language, both as regards its syntax or structure, and its part in native culture, are the same all over the continent. They are precision, brevity of expression, an emphasis on concreteness and an endeavour to express in one word or in as few as possible, a complete picture of the situation or desire; this is done by the inflexions of the word or words used. The languages, too, are all related to the culture and cannot be understood or satisfactorily mastered without a knowledge of tribal thought, belief and custom. In grammar, too, there is a wide-spread similarity in word order; in poverty of conjunctions; in absence of relative pronouns; in richness of the forms of the verb; in the use of the dual; in the use of phrase-order for expressing comparison and similarity; in distinguishing by suffixes between the nominative subject as a name and as an active agent; in the wealth of inflexions for the noun and pronoun; and in the significance of some of the case affixes. Finally, there is something about the form and sound of the words and sentences used all over the continent which suggests to the person working amongst the Aborigines, that there is no fundamental difference between their languages. I found this in places so far apart as north-western Australia, Laverton District of Western Australia, western and north-eastern South Australia and the north-east of New South Wales.

But there are differences, more particularly regional differences, and it is possible to place a text of reasonable length in its region both by its word sounds and grammatical variations. Thus, *v* is rare in Australia, but is found in the Flinders Range, South Australia; initial *mb* is typical of the Aranda of Central Australia, though also found in Cape York Peninsula; *th* and *dh* are used mainly in parts of New South Wales and Victoria; modified *u* (*u*) is not common but is used in the Nyul-Nyul, north of Broome, while the heaviest and ugliest language is found in north-central Victoria. In some languages every word ends in a vowel, even in one vowel, *a*, whereas in others, various consonants, here *n* and *m*, and there *k* or *g* or *t* as well as vowels, may form the last letter.

With regard to grammar, the most complicated types are found in Northern Kimberley, where there are four noun classes (instead of the three genders in English), and the verb is very difficult because it incorporates pronoun objects as well as subjects. The Central Australian languages are relatively simple because the verb is as a rule invariable for both person and number and there is none of the noun-class complication such as exists in the far north-west. Taking grammar and phonetics into consideration, Australian languages are at present classified into five groups, plus an extensive region about which we know nothing. They are:

(i) North-western Australia, (ii) South-eastern Australia (from the mouth of the Murray east), (iii) Central Australia (from Laverton in Western Australia to south-western Queensland), (iv) North and Central Queensland, and (v) New South Wales north of the Lachlan. As an example of the differences between languages, we may compare the word for man (and its declension) in three languages taken respectively from regions (ii), (iii) and (v):

	Narrinyeri		*Aranda*		*Yualayi*
Nom.	ko:ni		atua		ure
Agen.	——		atula		ureu
Gen.	konald		atuka		uregu
Dat.	konang		atuna		uremo
Acc.	kon		atuna		ure
Voc.	koninda		atu		ure
Abl.	konil		atunga		uremi
Exat.	konanmant	Instrum.	atualela	Instrum.	ureu
		Locative	atula		

As an illustration of the conjugation of verbs and of the difference in the word and form of conjugation, even in tribes a comparatively short distance apart, we may take the present tense of "to come" in the Bunaba language between the Fitzroy River and the King Leopold Ranges, and in the Ungarinyin just north of these ranges.

			Bunaba	Ungarinyin
Sing.	1.		*wadngira*	*ngialu*
	2.		*wad(a)nggira*	*bralu*
	3.		*wadira*	*bealu*
Dual	1.		*wadjirage*	*ngaiariwalu*
Plur.	1.		*wadwarage*	*ngaialu*
	2.		*wadgurage*	*kwialu*
	3.		*wadwurage*	*bialu*

In addition to the difference in the stem (*wad*-and-*alu*), person and number are denoted in Bunaba by suffixes and in Ungarinyin by prefixes.

I have referred briefly to the matter of language because there are still a number of folk who underestimate the wealth of vocabulary, the variety of grammatical forms and the power of expression of Australian languages. Some attribute only a few hundred words to a language, whereas the names for all the phenomena and objects with which the Aborigine is familiar, and the verbs, adverbs, adjectives and pronouns which are necessary for the description of activities, situations, conditions and plans, would soon run past the two thousand mark. I mention this number because a missionary prepared a vocabulary of the Aranda, Central Australia, of almost this length over sixty years ago and said that expressions were constantly turning up for notions that he did not think the Aborigines possessed; moreover, experience since his day has shown how inadequate his dictionary was. Such a list, of course, does not include the numerous forms made by declension and conjugation of nouns, adjectives, adverbs and verbs according to the rules of the particular language—by prefixes, suffixes, infixes and phonetic changes; there are in some instances up to 900 forms of the verb. In addition, there are regular mechanisms for forming parts of speech from one another (verbs from nouns etc.), and even in some languages at least, for making abstract nouns. Incidentally, though these languages tend towards the concrete and particular, they do possess and use general terms, for example, a word for fish as well as for various kinds of fish, for tree as well as for different kinds of trees.

Such facts as the above, even without further elaboration, suggest that an Australian language is an adequate means of expressing thought in Aboriginal life. This does not mean that thought processes are expressed by them in the same way as in English, or that a literal translation of their texts is satisfactory. Their languages belong to their own cultural world and the words, phrases and methods of expression derive their meaning from it. The corollary is that knowledge of the language and an understanding of thought, belief and custom must proceed together.[5]

THE ABORIGINES' MEANS OF LIVELIHOOD

Nomadic Food-gatherers. The Aborigines are food-gatherers. They do not practise any form of gardening or animal husbandry. Opportunities were, of course, unfavourable, especially with regard to the latter, but although they were quite familiar with the seeds of many food-providing plants, they did not realize that those plants grew from the seeds. Incidentally, as we shall see when discussing totemism, their spiritual interpretation of nature and its associated efficacious ritual would not encourage

[5] Those who desire to go further in the study of Australian languages are recommended to read *Studies in Australian Linguistics, Oceania* Monographs, no. 3, edited by A. P. Elkin. The first two chapters deal respectively with "The Nature" and "The Structure" of Australian languages. For a survey of Northwestern Australian languages (including Arnhem Land), see A. Capell, "Languages of North and North-west Australia", and of "Arnhem Land" in *Oceania*, vol. x, nos. 3 and 4; vol. xii, no. 4; and vol. xiii, no. 1. Other important works are T. G. H. Strehlow, *Aranda Grammar and Phonetics*, and W. E. Smythe, *Elementary Grammar of the Gumbainggar Language*, (N.S.W.), *Oceania* Monographs, nos. 7 and 8.

thought to work along such lines. The food-gathering life is parasitical; the Aborigines are absolutely dependent on what nature produces without any practical assistance on their part. They must, therefore, seek their food wherever it can be found. In other words, they are compelled by circumstances to be nomadic. This point requires emphasis; the nomadic aspect of Aboriginal life is not biologically founded, but is culturally, in short, economically, determined. If the means of gaining a livelihood be changed, then the characteristic of nomadism will be changed. Pastoralism in arid conditions—as in Arabia—accentuates it and indeed leads to true nomadism, whereas agriculture puts an end to it. Therefore, one way for the Aborigines to lose their nomadic habits, would be to adopt a gardening and agricultural life where such is possible. This, however, will not come to pass quickly. The hunting life has its attractions, to say nothing of the ritual which is associated with it. Moreover, the gardening life will only be embraced in so far as understanding of its processes (tilling, sowing, fertilizing, tending and waiting) are grasped, and for the time being, at least, are correlated with ritual and animistic belief. Education and religion have an important part to play in this change.

In one north Queensland mission, near Cooktown, the Kokoyimidir tribesmen are literate in their own language and in English. They are also capable agriculturalists, and make good use of the proceeds of their work. Usually, however, attempts to teach literacy have been half-hearted, and gardening has consisted only of carrying out instructions about digging, weeding and watering. Indeed, gardens have existed mainly for the benefit of the mission or station kitchen. Consequently, it has not become part of the social and economic life of the tribe. In spite of this, settled life is being slowly adopted by Aborigines through association with European settlers or pastoralists in their tribal country. Not being able to eject the white man and his cattle, they gradually accept both as part of the situation. They "sit down" near the homestead; supply the labour which the settler can get nowhere else; and in return obtain food, tobacco, clothes and other articles for which they develop a taste.

Pastoral work is a logical step for the semi-nomadic Aborigines to take in the advance to food-production and a settled life. It combines periods of camp-life, at the homestead, with periods of "nomadism". Mustering, branding and droving cattle, and horse-riding, provide plenty of movement, and the excitement of the chase. In addition, they see a parallel to their native respect for class and tribal boundaries in the pastoralist's recognition of the country and herds of his neighbours. For Aborigines do not wander anywhere and everywhere in search of food, contesting the rights of others who may forestall them, but in visiting the countries of other local groups, even of the same tribe, they must observe relationship and visiting rules. Such rules, incidentally, prevent clashes and preserve social cohesion.

Needless to say, a people which depends absolutely on hunting, fishing and food-gathering within limited areas for its food develops great skill in those pursuits. The Aborigines can live in parts of the bush for considerable periods, where a white man would die of thirst and hunger. But we must remember that this skill in the food-quest is not the only manifestation of their mental powers; indeed, an over-emphasis on it may lead to lack of appreciation of their intelligence. Animals are skilful at getting their food, even at learning tricks if this will help them. In order, therefore, to avoid such an error, we should concentrate not so much on the powers of finding food, as on the implements and weapons used—boomerangs, spears, clubs, nets, traps, stone axes, chisels and firesticks, noting not only the remarkable precision with which these objects are made, but also their decoration. This will take us into the sphere of ritual and belief, with which the designs engraved or painted on the weapons are associated; indeed, the craft of making the various articles has been handed down from the great culture-heroes who are now important figures in the cult-life. Moreover, the designs are usually the same as those depicted on the sacred symbols used in the secret religious life, and can only be worked by those fully initiated men who know the songs or chants connected with them, and these designs—consisting of circles, wavy lines, and herring-bone patterns—duly "sung", endow the instrument or weapon with a potency which comes from the world of spirits, culture-heroes and magic. A boomerang so marked is not just beautified; but, through its artistic decoration, it has become a perfect, sure and never-failing boomerang.

Religion and magic, however, not only enter the hunting life through this "sanctifying" of the weapons and implements used in it; they are also directly brought into operation. The hunter may take with him a secret bull-roarer, which will ensure unerring accuracy of aim, but the game obtained with its aid can only be eaten by fully initiated men. More important, however, is the performance at prescribed times of the year by definite groups of men, of totemic ceremonies designed to ensure the increase of those species and phenomena on which man, the hunter and food-gatherer, depends for his life. This ritual is the logical application and expression of the Aborigines' totemic view of the universe.[6] Thus, there is a necessary sequence from the food-quest, to the weapons used in it, to the designs on these, to the sphere of mythology and ritual and to Aboriginal philosophy. Economics, art and religion are mutually interdependent, and to understand the hunting and food-gathering activities demands also an understanding of these other aspects of life.

Material Possessions. In material possessions, the Aborigines are undoubtedly poor, though the degree of poverty varies in different regions. The western tribes of South

[6] This will be explained in Chapter VI.

Australia (Aluridja) are probably the poorest. Living in a desert region, foraging over large areas for food, and continually searching for better country, they have managed with the minimum of equipment. Their possessions consist of a barbed wooden spear; a spear-thrower and a hitting-stick, both of which are converted into chisels by fastening a piece of sharp stone on to one end with gum; a stone axe (until recently); a wooden dish; grinding-stones; a digging-stick and firesticks; a few sacred and magical objects. Other tribes have these and in addition boomerangs, shields, fishing-nets, baskets, and some sort of huts. Generally speaking those with the most possessions are most given to the adornment of their weapons and implements. The Aluridja are an example of material poverty and a lack of art, whereas some tribes of Cape York Peninsula have a much richer material culture and at the same time take much pains to beautify their work, chiefly by painting. As the former live in a desert environment and the latter in a comparatively fertile region, we might be tempted to correlate interest in art with the easier, and its absence with the more severe, conditions of life. But the correlation is not straightforward. The Aranda, who live in a semi-arid region, relieved by permanent waters, decorate their boomerangs, shields and sacred churinga (bull-roarers and totemic symbols), axe-handles, knife-sheaths and clubs with painted and also incised designs. On the other hand, the Ungarinyin and Worora in the Northern Kimberley, who live in ideal "blackfellow" country, hardly decorate any of their few material goods. The latter paint their well-made bark buckets, but not their soft-wood shields; and the designs which I saw on their locally-made bull-roarers were very crude indeed. The Ungarinyin are even poorer in worldly possessions and in their decoration. On the other hand, these tribes have the most remarkable cave-paintings in Australia and also are experts in making stone spear-points by pressure flaking, a highly technical process only practised in its true form in Northern and

Eastern Kimberley. Such a spear-point is itself a work of art. The cave-paintings, to which reference will be made in Chapter VIII, belong to the religious life, and this reminds us that even the Aluridja decorate their own bodies for secret ceremonies, and that the tribes of the deserts east of Laverton (Western Australia) make and wear remarkable decorations around their necks and on their heads in some of the totemic rituals.

It is difficult to generalize. In some cases, at least, the absence of suitable material is the reason for not making various weapons and articles. Further, shields and boomerangs obviously lend themselves most to adornment, and therefore tribes who do not possess them lack a favourable secular medium for artistic expression. But the Melville and Bathurst islanders, ignorant of these two weapons, have developed the single-piece many-barbed wooden spear into a really fine work of art in shape and colour, though probably making it less serviceable as a weapon. On the other hand, the coastal Arnhem-Landers, who also lack the shield and boomerang, have not made the spear an expression of beauty in anything like the degree found on Melville and Bathurst islands, and indeed have almost lost whatever urge they had to do this; but they are the most advanced of all Aboriginal "schools" of art, whether we think of painting on rock, bark, wooden and composite objects, or on the human body, or of moulding and "carving" in the round. Their art, however, is almost wholly connected with the sacred life. Indeed, it may be that all Aboriginal art stems from the latter. Certainly, art, ceremony and religion are inter-related; indeed, in Australia they form one whole. Moreover, since, as previously suggested, the artistic designs are associated with myths and chants, the spread of the former depends upon the diffusion of the latter. A tribe which does not decorate its weapons and implements is not necessarily inartistic, but, most likely, does not possess a myth sanctioning or requiring a design. This subject repays careful research.

A very interesting and surprising fact is the number of tribes which do not make or possess boomerangs and shields. We are apt almost to equate Australian Aborigine and boomerang, but this weapon is absent from the west of South Australia, the Northern Kimberley and north-eastern Arnhem Land, while the shield is lacking in the first of these regions, and from the second with the exception of the Worora tribe.

Huts are rare in Australia. Beehive-shaped structures well made of saplings and mud may still be seen in the north-east of South Australia, and similar huts made of grass and saplings are used on the Northern Kimberley coast. These huts are used mainly as a means of escape from mosquitoes—the very small opening which serves as a door can be closed up, or a smoke fire may be lit near it. In parts of northern Queensland, sleep is sometimes taken on a stage over a smoke fire which keeps the mosquitoes away. The usual type of native hut is simply a wurley of saplings and branches or a mere lean-to. In any case, the natives prefer to sleep in the open, even in very cold weather, with a fire between each person. This preference is manifested by many Aborigines, even civilized ones, on missions, government settlements and stations. Though houses are provided, the natives sleep, and indeed, almost live, outside. Perhaps it should be stated that these houses are seldom suited to the climate, or to the number and the past experience of those who are supposed to live in them.

On the other hand, some Aborigines do learn to build huts more substantial than the native type; they are an adaptation of our structures. Amongst the best I have seen were some made of light timber and paper-bark, square in shape, fastened where necessary with wire. It appears that a type of building, intermediate between the indigenous type (where there is one) and simple "white" structures, is required until the Aborigines desire houses and have learnt to use them and keep them in order.

Clothes, in our sense of the term, that is for the purpose

of concealing parts of the body or for keeping it warm, are not worn, though in a few tribes a kangaroo skin was sometimes used as a protection from the cold. In many regions both sexes go completely naked, while in some a pubic tassel made of fur string is worn, though it is not an effective covering. Indeed, in the case of the men, this tassel or the pearl-shell pubic pendant is really a sign of having reached a prescribed stage in initiation. It corresponds to a "lodge apron". Girls who wear these fur tassels have reached the age of marriage. Taking Australia as a whole, we may say that anything worn on the body almost always serves as personal decoration, especially in connexion with the ceremonial life, or to mark the attainment of "adulthood".

Position of the Aborigines amongst the Peoples of the World

The question "Are the Aborigines the lowest race of mankind?" is not easily answered. Physically, they have some primitive features, for example, the thickness of the skullcap, the shape of the face, the retreating nature of the forehead and the comparatively small brain. But the Negroid peoples also possess some primitive features, and anatomists have pointed out that Europeans are not lacking in this regard. Psychologists, too, have been trying to devise satisfactory intelligence tests to show that along some lines the Aborigines are higher than some human groups and lower than others, for example, in the capacity to adapt themselves to our civilization. But so far, this research is only in the experimental stage.[7] Nor is the question easier if it refers to culture. As far as material possessions are concerned, they are very poor, but so too are the Bushmen of South Africa, and other food-gathering peoples, and indeed, some of the gardening groups also. All we can say is that with regard to material culture,

[7] S. D. Porteus, *Primitive Intelligence and Environment.* O. Klineberg, *Race Differences.*

the Aborigines, being food-gatherers, living perforce in semi-nomadic fashion, are lower than most horticultural and village peoples. But even so, we must remember that their lowliness is not to be equated to a primeval state or one just above that reached by the animals. The fine workmanship of many of their weapons, implements and sacred objects and the artistic decoration of these, show that a food-gathering people is capable of a high standard of craftsmanship and quite praiseworthy artistic expression. Moreover, as we shall realize, their social organization, marriage rules, taboos, philosophy and ceremonial life are, in some respects, no lower nor less complicated than our own. True, some of the Aborigines' customs and beliefs are crude, but the same is true of some of ours, or was true in many white communities not so long ago.

From the practical point of view, however, the question of the relative cultural position of the Aborigines is not important. They have evolved a working adaptation to their geographical and social environment, and in applying or even modifying their plan of economic, social and spiritual life, they show as much intelligence as does the average European with regard to the cultural adaptation of his own group. The problem is the extent to which the Aborigines are capable of working out a fresh adaptation to the changed conditions which have come upon them as the result of the settlement of their country by whites. The change has been sudden and all-pervading, going right to the roots of their religious and mental adjustment. This, however, was not understood by us, whether we were cabinet ministers, officials, missionaries or settlers. Indeed, until the results of intense anthropological research, carried on since 1927, were thoroughly studied, we neither understood nor appreciated Aboriginal social and religious life, nor the significance of that cultural and social clash which arose, and which still arises, from the invasion of a primitive food-gathering people's country by a civilized, agricultural and industrial people. The purpose of this book is to contribute towards this understanding. It will not be concerned any further with the Aborigine's appearance, with his food or its acquisition. We must know the fundamentals of his tribal, local and social organization; his conception of relationship not only to his fellows, but also to the land which is his home; his philosophy of life; his religion and magic; his ritual and mythology; and that general pattern of life which has been made by, even as it has moulded, him and his ancestors down the centuries. In gaining this knowledge, we shall at the same time understand the significance of some of the changes wrought by the coming of the white man.

Postscript. In the earlier editions of this book the last paragraph of this chapter included the statement that "neither governments, missionaries nor educational authorities have yet planned and put into operation policies designed to help the Aborigines tackle the tremendous task of readjustment which confronts them". That was written in 1937. Following on several years of representations, based on increasing knowledge of the problems, enlightened advances in policies and administrative methods were gradually but surely brought into being from 1938 onwards, especially after the war. The above statement, therefore, can be omitted. But the need for more and deeper understanding remains.

Chapter II

THE LAND AND THE ABORIGINES

The Tribe

The Aborigines are divided into tribal groups of which there were in 1788 possibly 500. A tribe is a group of people related by actual or implied genealogy, who occupy and own a definite area of territory and hunt and gather food over it according to rules which control the behaviour of the smaller groups and families within the tribe. The tribal boundaries are usually fairly clearly defined by natural features; sometimes there is a kind of no-man's-land between two tribes, and occasionally it is difficult to know to which tribe certain territory belongs, for the simple reason that it is of little value or interest, and so no one cares. Examples of this uncertainty are the Gournditch-mara of Victoria, the Chepara of south-eastern Queensland and the Murngin of north-eastern Arnhem Land.[1] The area of the tribal territory varies, for the most part, with the nature of the country, more especially according to its fertility and food-supply. Thus, on the north coast of New South Wales in a narrow strip of country, roughly 300 miles long by sixty to ninety miles in width but well watered by rivers and a good rainfall, there were several tribes on each river, numbering altogether about twelve with several sub-tribes, whereas in the drier interior of the State the Wiraduri alone occupied more territory than all these small tribes put together. Likewise, along the Queensland coast, the country along the Daly, Fitzmaurice and Victoria rivers

[1] A. W. Howitt, *Native Tribes of South-East Australia*, pp. 249, 86. W. L. Warner, *A Black Civilization*, p. 15.

of the Northern Territory, and in the Upper Murray River region in Victoria and New South Wales, the tribal areas were comparatively small, whereas the Aranda of Central Australia occupied a large tract of country stretching from about Hermannsburg eastwards well beyond Alice Springs and south-east right down the whole course of the River Finke for a distance of 400 miles.

In the case of some groups of small tribes, it is difficult to know whether we are dealing with distinct tribes, or with sub-tribes and local groups of one tribe. For example, the Djukan, Ngormbal and Djabera-Djaber between Broome and Carnot Bay in north Western Australia might well have been local groups of one tribe; possibly this was also true of a number of the small "tribes" on the Murray River with doubled names, such as the Laitu-Laitu, Baraba-Baraba and others, and also of many of the *-bara* or *-bura* tribes of eastern Queensland, such as the Wakel-bura, Mutabura, and many others.[2] This indecision arises, of course, from the fact that groups of these tribes or sub-tribes share a number of features in common, features which find a place in a working definition of a tribe. Such a definition is the following: a tribe is a grouping of Aborigines who (i) inhabit and own a usually definite area of country; (ii) use a language or dialect peculiar to themselves; (iii) know themselves, or are known, by a distinct name, though sometimes it is difficult to learn what this is, and indeed, it may not exist; (iv) possess customs and laws which often vary in some degree from those of neighbouring tribes; and (v) have their own rites and beliefs which frequently differ from those practised and held respectively by the peoples around.

The Tribe, a Linguistic Group. Every tribal group, however, does not fulfil the implications of each part of the definition. The first part is generally true, allowing for in-

[2] Neither Dr A. W. Howitt nor his informants could decide whether these Queensland communities were tribes or sub-tribes. Op. cit., p. 62.

definiteness here and there. The linguistic test is also a
fairly safe one, for, as we saw in Chapter I there are real
differences between languages and dialects in Australia.
But the possession by a group—even a large one—of a dialect distinct from some neighbouring groups, does not
alone constitute it a tribe. Within the one tribe there may
be several dialects; thus there are four or five in the large
Aranda tribe—the northern (Bond Springs), the western
(Hermannsburg), the eastern (Alice Springs and east with
probably a subdivision) and the southern (Macumba) dialects. In one dialect words may usually begin with the
vowels *a* or *i*, which are just as consistently dropped in the
neighbouring part of the tribe; or in one the ending of the
word to mark the genitive or possessive case is *-kona*, but
in the next is *-ka* only; or it may be that there is a change
in an internal vowel of a verb, so that for example the *a*
in one is *u* in the other; thus *mara* in Western Aranda is
mura in Northern Aranda. It is quite common to be told
by members of one part of a tribe that they speak "light",
while those in another part speak the tribal language
"heavy". For example, at Innamincka the Yantruwanta
say *mädra mädra* for stone, whereas the local groups
around Nappamerrie, farther up Cooper's Creek, say *mada
mada*.

But while allowing for such variations of a common
language within a tribe, we sometimes find that the differences in speech between two tribes are of the same order.
For example, the Bard language at the north of Dampier
Land differs from the Nyul-Nyul on its south for the most
part in the omission of initial effort in the pronunciation
of words: compare *alabel* and *wolabel* (wife's brother),
alor and *yürmor* (wife's mother), *ainman* and *wainman*
(wife's mother's parents); apart from this, however, the
dialects are the same, the Bard appearing to be a soften-
ing of the Nyul-Nyul. But though in some other cases such
a dialectal difference—and indeed a greater difference—is
found in sub-groups of a tribe, the Nyul-Nyul and Bard

must be regarded as distinct tribes for other reasons which, of course, receive support from the dialectical difference; these reasons are territorial and social.[3] Reference will be made to the latter a little farther on.

Significance of Tribal Territory. In spite of this, however, the linguistic test of tribal grouping is a sound one; in most cases, a tribe is a territorial and linguistic group with some other characteristics peculiar to itself. But in referring to a tribe as a territorial group, we must remember that this aspect is not really important politically or economically. In other words the tribe seldom, if ever, functions as a whole in warfare or food-gathering. These are matters which concern local groups or clans. There are no wars for territorial aggrandizement, though just as the present arrangement of tribal territories must have come into being at some time or other, so some change and rearrangement does still occur. For example, the tribes on the east of the Macumba which runs towards the north end of Lake Eyre, have been working south, as the natives on the Cooper either themselves moved farther south or have died out; thus, the Wongkonguru and Ngameni have come down from the Mikari sandhill desert to their present localities. In the same way, the Auanbura of central Queensland took the country of their neighbours, the Bithelbura, when these died out. Likewise, groups from the Musgrave and Everard Ranges region have migrated and are migrating south and east either to take up unoccupied country, or to fill up the vacuums caused by the dying out of the tribes formerly living in those parts. The natives of the Warburton Ranges, too, in Western Australia have moved in towards the Laverton-Mount Margaret district, taking the place of the local tribes which have almost ceased to exist. In this way, through migration and separation, differences of dialects and social organization arise such as we find characterizing the various groups speaking

[3] There may also be some difference in totemic conceptions.

similar dialects in western South Australia. Of course, these days, there is an attraction exercised by the white man and his goods, but strangely enough, it does not cause natives of a distant tribe to pass through the territories of intervening tribes so as to reach these apparently delectable associations, but only to fill up tribal and territorial gaps; moreover, these movements and changes in tribal boundaries were in progress quite apart from our influence. No doubt, the urge was chiefly economic.

But here is an important point: until a mythology grows up, or is transplanted, linking the migrating group to its new tribal home, it regards itself as a sojourner only, for the true tribal home is the territory in which the old-time mythical tribal heroes or ancestors travelled and performed exploits and instituted rituals. Moreover, the Aborigines believe that the spirits of the people yet unborn have existed since that heroic age, possibly reincarnated from time to time, and that the spirit-homes of the members of a tribe and also the spirit- or life-centres of natural species are usually situated along the routes followed by those heroes and ancestors. Therefore, the future of the tribe is only assured so long as its members remain in tribal territory. This will be discussed further when dealing with the local groups within the tribe and with totemism.

It is quite clear then, that apart from the sentiment which grows up around one's ancestral home, and apart too from the fact that every prominent feature in the country is a memorial of the activity of the great culture-heroes, tribesfolk would have no desire to forsake their own territory, for it is the home of their own spirits and the source of life of the natural species on which they depend for sustenance; certainly, they would not feel an urge to take the country of another tribe, for it is not their spirit-home.

When they do leave, it is by a process of drift, perhaps in the hope of reaping some economic benefit and with the intention of returning to their own tribal territory from time to time, especially for ceremonial purposes. With regard to the past, in the course of long periods, fresh mythological ties have grown up in the new land, or the mythological lines and "paths" have been lengthened to link their present home with the old one, and so no disaster has come. To-day, however, matters are different, for the mythological process is thwarted by contact with us in station and town life, and on missions. The result is that the group becomes like a ship without compass or anchor; social disintegration and depopulation follow. This justifies and, indeed, demands the setting up not merely of reserves but also of institutions or settlements in the territories of tribes which are about to be attracted towards our townships, stations and mining-centres. Such institutions should present to the natives the best of the attractions which they find in the latter—attractions associated with work, pleasure, food, and possibly religion. In other words, we must make it possible for them to obtain in their own tribal country such new interests as will prevent them from wandering away to their doom. Missionary organizations and governments have sometimes set up "institutions" in such outposts though not necessarily from the motive mentioned here; but missions do usually endeavour to keep the natives from other forms of white contact. However, much more needs doing, and the governments and missions should work together to prevent the depopulation of tribal areas through the attraction of the natives to centres of settlement.[4]

Inter-tribal Gatherings. A tribe usually consists of several localized groups which are the real political and economic units, and it is they which tend to make one tribe dovetail, as it were, into its neighbours. This is mainly the effect of the kinship system, for all persons with whom

[4] Since this sentence was written in 1937, much greater co-operation has grown up between governments and missions—especially since World War II. The latter are more and more regarded as agencies—in some cases almost irreplaceable, to be assisted to perform prescribed functions. See Chapter XIII.

any person comes into contact must be brought into the kinship system and therefore given a place in a common life of economics and general behaviour. Indeed, language apart, border hordes of two tribes are more interested in one another than are distant hordes within one tribe. Moreover, inter-tribal gatherings are held for ceremonial purposes in which the fundamental unity of purpose of two or more tribes is made manifest, namely, the search for life through initiation, burial and totemic rituals. At such gatherings, quarrels between groups of the one or different tribes are openly settled, and corroborees or public entertainments shared. Such meetings are organized and controlled by the old men of the various local groups, not of the tribes as such. In the same way, when several local groups of one tribe meet, common business is directed by the elders of these groups.

Inter-tribal Meetings and Culture Contact. It is through such meetings that customs and modifications in social rules are spread or made, as the case may be; such new customs and changes may, for example, affect the kinship system, methods of grouping relations, the totemic organization and ritual, initiation and burial rites and customs. If different tribes are to meet together, and they do, they must understand their various methods of grouping relations so that mutual behaviour can be organized and respected during the time of meeting; likewise, they must become conversant with each other's important customs and rites so that they can all take part in them. In this way, many social forms and ritual customs and beliefs become widespread—a process which we have been able to watch and record during the past sixty years. Thus the division of the tribe into four sections or groups of relations for certain social purposes has spread from about the Broome area right down to Laverton and across the desert to the Warburton Ranges and also up the Fitzroy River to Fitzroy Crossing. The division into eight groups has spread from about the south-eastern portion of the Kimberleys, north towards Wyndham, west to Fitzroy Crossing, east and north-east to the Daly River—and on to north-eastern Arnhem Land, as well as south-east to Central Australia. The similarity of terms as well as actual observation of the diffusion makes such generalization possible.

To take an example of another type: circumcision has spread from the Kimberley Division in a fan-wise manner south, south-east, east and finally north-east, to the Great Australian Bight, to Innamincka and the far west of Queensland and through north-eastern Arnhem Land. Since the occupation of Australia by whites, it has spread farther south-west and north-east in areas where there was little or no settlement; there is no doubt that if we had not come to Australia, this ritual operation and the mythology associated with it would have spread all over Australia, and comparatively quickly, for its diffusion was expedited by the mechanism of the secret society; whatever be the difference between tribes, the general patterns and object of their initiation rites are the same—and in every case the authority of the headmen, the "masters" and "past-masters", is complete. Moreover, general approval of the whole community has not to be considered, for a change in initiation ritual only concerns the men as members of a secret society.

New burial customs have also spread in Australia but apparently not so fast or wide as changes in initiation practices, possibly because general opinion and conservativeness were somewhat of a hindrance. A type of mummification spread down parts of eastern Australia only; and "burial" of the corpse in a tree stage as part of a method of inquest leading up to a later mourning ceremony and final disposal of the bones, seems to have spread east from the Kimberleys to the Queensland border, but no farther south than in the vicinity of a line joining the De Grey River and Tennant's Creek. Generally speaking, too, such innovations in burial ritual were kept for the benefit of initiated men only, or in some cases only for headmen or medicine-men. Perhaps in time, they would have become the privilege of all men and women in the tribe.

In some cases the spread of customs and social rules implied no small degree of ability on the part of the men concerned. The most striking example is the combination of the subsection system of classifying relations, that is, everybody in the tribe, into eight groups, with a marriage rule which permits or even encourages marriages between cross-cousins,[5] whereas such a system seems designed to prevent these marriages and normally functions in tribes where such marriage is strictly forbidden; indeed, it has been held that the subsection system could not function in a tribe which allowed such marriages. But in two parts of the Northern Territory, the Daly River and north-eastern Arnhem Land, the system has been adopted from their neighbours by tribes which practise cross-cousin marriage, and they have adjusted the two institutions in a most ingenious way. Normally, in the subsection system, a man and his son's son belong to the one group, but these tribes have found that if cross-cousin marriage be practised regularly, a man's descendant in the male line will not be in his own subsection group until the generation of his son's son's son's son has been reached—that is, two generations farther off than in most tribes. This can be worked out by us from a diagram, but the natives concerned show that it is fact by giving the names of the subsections of father, mother and child in order until the complete cycle has been accomplished. A real appreciation of what these Aborigines have done in this adjustment will not be fully understood until we have studied the kinship system and social groupings, but at least, we can realise that they possess no small degree of intellectual ability, and that they can cope with the problems that arise through the contact of tribes and culture.

This point should not be lightly passed over. The Abo-

---

[5] That is, marriage with mother's brother's daughter or father's sister's daughter. See Chapter III.

rigines have in the past adopted changes in their social, religious and economic life—they have successfully solved problems arising from culture contact—and they are doing so to-day. Where, however, they are successful in this, the changes are not being pushed on them in an overwhelming manner, but are discussed, understood and adopted. Of course, this takes place within their own tribal and inter-tribal life. In addition, the civilized Aborigines are modifying some of their own old customs and rites, because these interfere with the work in which they are engaged or the life which they now live.[6] Such facts give hope for the future of the Aborigines if we are prepared to help them understand the new problems which confront them, and find solutions which, even though sometimes unsatisfactory to us, would be their own solutions. This should be the objective of all policies of native education and indeed of native administration. In the meantime we must try to realize the full implication of the fact that the natives have successfully managed tribal and inter-tribal affairs for untold ages and have solved the cultural problem arising out of cultural and inter-tribal contact.

Inter-tribal Meetings and Language. There is also a mixing of dialects at the borders of tribes; to use the phrase of a native, a "pidgin" language is developed. But in any case, almost every Aborigine can "hear" or understand two if not three languages, even though he may only speak his own. As a result, conversation can be carried on at gatherings of an inter-tribal nature. This fact should be borne in mind by missionaries and administrative officers who, though convinced that a knowledge of the native language is essential for the effectiveness of their work, are unable to decide which language to learn; there are often several languages in their area or on their mission, and a knowledge of one would appear to give direct contact only with the few who speak it. They therefore conclude that

[6] A. P. Elkin, "Civilized Aborigines and Native Culture", *Oceania*, vol. vi, no. 2, pp. 125–9.

the effort is not worth while and learn none, but use a form of "pidgin" which is useless for the conveying of any but the most concrete of directions; or else they take for granted that the Aborigines possess some remarkable power of learning, unaided, a foreign language, namely English, which is very different in form and construction from their own. Incidentally, such persons miss an unrivalled means of getting to understand their native charges. The principle is: learn the language of the local or largest tribe concerned.

The mixing of tribes at meetings is no doubt responsible for the diffusion of what we might call international words; these are a few essential words, such as those for camp, water, fire, foot, revenge-expedition and bull-roarer. The word for camp, *ngura*, with little dialectal variation, is found right across Australia from Lagrange via South Australia to the coast of New South Wales. The words for foot (*djina*) and eye (*mil*) are as wide-spread, while I have found the one word for water (*kapi*) used over half the continent from the west into South Australia; for revenge-expedition, *wormala*, from north-central Australia to the Bight; and for bull-roarer *madagi*, from Northern Kimberley to the Musgrave Ranges.

Tribal Sentiment. But in spite of the inter-tribal distribution of many social laws and ritual practices, the blending or mutual understanding of neighbouring languages, the friendship of neighbouring local groups of adjacent tribes, and the holding of inter-tribal gatherings, there is a tribal sentiment centring round the tribal territory, language and social customs; moreover, this is strengthened by the differences in custom and speech manifested by other tribes, and also by the fear of the unknown. Though members of one tribe are on friendly terms with, and possibly married to, members of the next tribe, yet they are apt to pride themselves on their differences from it and even to attribute to it dastardly practices. Thus, men of the Nyul-Nyul tribe at Beagle Bay, eighty-five miles north of Broome, Western Australia, who had been associated with the mission there all or most of their lives, assured me that the Bard tribesmen, their northern neighbours, had no laws and were really inferior—and this in spite of the fact that there was intermarriage between the two tribes. I later found that the lack of law amongst the Bard, which enabled the Nyul-Nyul men to shake their heads in superior fashion, was the absence of the section system; this is the grouping of relations into four named divisions—a grouping which, incidentally, was not of great practical use to the Beagle Bay folk seeing that cross-cousin marriage was prohibited by them, and that the absence of sections made little difference to the Bard who had the same marriage laws and kinship system as the former.[7]

Fear of the Unknown. A more striking manifestation of the tribal sentiment is seen in the attribution of "evil" practices to other tribes, an attribution which increases with distance. Thus the cannibals and the savage treacherous natives are always those of the next tribe or the next but one, though when the investigator visits and studies them, he finds them quite as peaceable and courteous as those he just left, but now it is the latter who are credited with savage attributes. Of course, natives may be desirous of parrying inquiries into any of their own customs of which they think their questioner may not approve, and may do so by attributing their practice to another tribe. But in this way they are possibly admitting the existence of the customs in their own tribe. There is, however, more in it than that, namely the fear of the unknown. Not infrequently a local group sets out full of vim and boastfulness to go some distance away to attack another tribe, but some days later returns in "ones" or "twos" and "threes"

[7] The function of these sections and their relation to kinship and marriage will be discussed in Chapter IV. The section system is not in itself of much practical advantage for marriage regulation unless cross-cousin marriage is allowed. Incidentally the Bard have since adopted the section system.

and so on, without having sighted the group in the other tribe whom they set out to annihilate. Had they met the latter, they would have been brave enough, performed the preliminaries and had the fight—or if their heart had kept up, might have successfully attacked the "enemy" camp at dawn. But as they got away from their own tribal territory, they passed into country of unknown totemic heroes and spirit-centres some of which might be lethal to those who did not know how to approach them. Moreover, they were in a region where the forms of magic, being unknown, were endowed by their imagination with special potency, and might cause them disaster. And so, one by one, in face of the terrors of the unknown, they gave in and turned back. It may be hard for us to appreciate this belief in magic and fear of the unknown, and yet it should not be so; most of us are still afraid to break with old customs and tradition; we feel that our welfare depends partially, if not wholly, on the observance of certain religious rules and are apt to attribute strange, if not evil, motives to people of a different religious or national grouping. But with us, these practices and beliefs are very much overlaid with scientific views and complicated social and economic organization, whereas amongst the Aborigines they are the very warp and woof of life; for them so much of life and knowledge is still unexplored and unknown country; the causes of natural phenomena and human changes and disasters are not known as we know them; instead, explanation is found in magic, itself a power of which man stands in awe, for it is but partially understood. Its dangers can be averted by ritual, and the contingencies of life met in the same way. Thus, revenge expeditions can be protected from the enemy's magic by magical observances, and so courage can be maintained, but distance and delay raise doubts regarding the efficacy of this ritual; fears arise and courage goes.

This point is of importance in our dealings with the Aborigines. Explorers have often told us that their native guides forsook them at the borders of their tribal country, afraid to go on—and if they did not turn back, they remained close to their white leaders. But we still take natives accused of certain offences or crimes, and witnesses through what are to them foreign lands to be tried and examined in a foreign place (Darwin, etc.), in a foreign language (English) and in a setting marked by strange taboos and powers (jail, court, police, judge, rules). Have we ever tried to realize what this means to a people so afraid of the unknown and its magical terrors? The journey through the unknown is bad enough, but at its end they are put in the jail with natives speaking strange tongues, and in the court they are surrounded by the paraphernalia of powerful magic. Needless to say, such a system should be discontinued wherever and whenever possible because it is the cause of very real and great psychological damage; this is, of course, quite apart from the obvious disadvantage from which the native prisoner and witnesses suffer in our court procedure and through the use of the white language.

Tribal Names. The tribal sentiment is often symbolized by the recognition of a tribal name, that is, recognition and use by the members of the tribe concerned. Thus a member of the Ungarinyin, Worora, Nyul-Nyul, Karadjeri or other tribe of north-western Australia, the Aranda or Warramunga of Central Australia, the Yantruwanta, Wailpi or Arabana of South Australia, and the Wikmunkan, Kabi, Kamilaroi, Kattang, Wiraduri or Woiworung of the eastern states, will say "I Ungarinyin" or "I Arabana" and so on. But in some cases, it seems to be impossible to obtain a tribal name, or indeed a general name of the language spoken. There are names of the local groups within the tribe, but that seems to be all, and so we find an ethnographer taking one of these local names and using it for the whole tribe. I did this for the Forrest River Mission people, the Yeidji, and Dr Warner did it for a group in north-eastern Arnhem Land, the Murngin. It is also diffi-

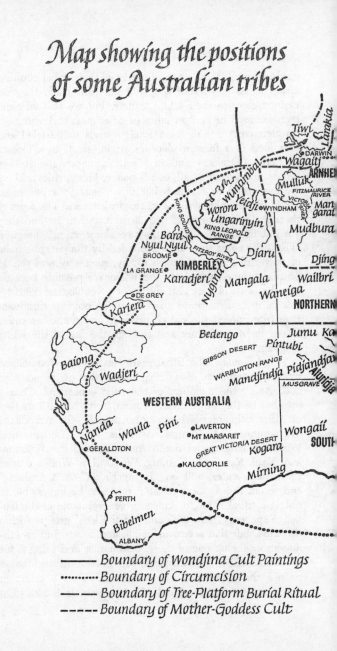

Map showing the positions of some Australian tribes

Tiwi

Laiakia

DARWIN

Wagaiti

ARNHEM

Wunambal

Mulluk

FITZMAURICE
RIVER

Worora

Yeidji

VICTORIA RIVER

Man garai

Ungarinyin

WYNDHAM

KING LEOPOLD
RANGE

Mudbura

Bard

Nyul Nyul

FITZROY RIVER

Djaru

Djing

BROOME

KIMBERLEY

Djaru

LA GRANGE

Karadjeri

Nyigina

Mangala

Waneiga

Wailbri

DE GREY

NORTHERN

Kariera

Bedengo

Jumu Ka

Pintubi

GIBSON DESERT

Baiong

WARBURTON RANGE

Wadjeri

Mandjindja

Pidjandja

Aurtjta

MUSGRAVE

WESTERN AUSTRALIA

Nanda

Waula

Pini

LAVERTON

MT MARGARET

Wongaii

SOUTH

GREAT VICTORIA DESERT

GERALDTON

Kogara

KALGOORLIE

Mirning

PERTH

Bibelmen

ALBANY

—————— Boundary of Wondjina Cult Paintings

·············· Boundary of Circumcision

— — — Boundary of Tree-Platform Burial Ritual

‐ ‐ ‐ ‐ Boundary of Mother-Goddess Cult

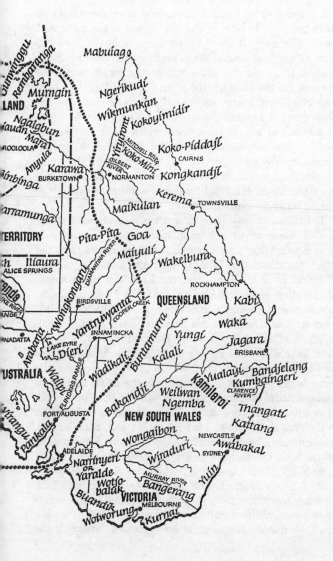

cult sometimes to ascertain from one tribe the names of other tribes, or to be sure that the answer is the real tribal name. The reply is often a term for a compass direction, such as north or south. Thus, north of the Forrest River Mission is the Bemba tribe—but *bemba* means north; on the east are the Nalamo—the word for that direction; likewise Nyul-Nyul means south, and the name given for the people east of Laverton, Kogara, means east. But the tribes so designated are, in cases with which we have become more or less acquainted, known by those names. So the Bemba are the north people, and the Nyul-Nyul the south people. Such words, however, in some cases lose their primary meanings; the Nyul-Nyul are so-called even by the people on their south.

Tribal names may have interesting derivations in addition to the cardinal points: in many cases, especially in New South Wales and Victoria, the name comes from the tribal negative; the Wongaibon from *wongai*, no; the Wiraduri from *wirai*, no, and the Kamilaroi, from *kamil*, no. In other cases, it is derived from the local pronunciation or word for something or other; the Didjitara of northwestern South Australia are so-called from *didji*, a small child; in other words, they are the people, *tara*, who say *didji* for child, while farther south are the Madutara, the people who say *madu* for truth. In other parts again, the name is derived from some feature in the tribal country or some plentiful article of food. The name of the Tongaranka in north-western New South Wales means hillside, while Wakelbura in Queensland is from *wakel*, eels. Some names, too, appear to be really nicknames; the name Koko-piddaji of northern Queensland means "speech-poor devils", and *koko-baldja*, "speech abrupt", while the Kokata in south-central South Australia are the flesh-eaters, or cannibals. In many cases, however, we have not yet found the source or meaning of the tribal name. When preceded by such a word as *wong-*, *koko-*, or *nangi-* meaning "speech", the term refers to the language rather than to the people, thus Wongaranda, is the language of the Aranda.

Tribal Customs and Mythology. Tribes, or more usually, groups of tribes can be distinguished from one another by differences in customs, laws and myths. These differences vary in degree, being comparatively slight between tribes of the one group, and more marked between groups. Thus, in north-western Australia, in the Derby-Broome-Lagrange region, there are a number of tribes with a form of social organization known as the section system;[8] the names of the four sections in each tribe are the same and they are arranged in the same ideal order of marriage, descent and generation level. As a result, members of any of this group of tribes have a common method of ordering social and ceremonial behaviour, that is, in its outlines. There are, however, some differences in the details of totemic and mythological thought between those south of Broome and those north of that town. But when we pass from the Nyul-Nyul tribe of Beagle and Pender bays to the Bard tribe just north of the latter, we find that the absence of the section system until quite recently, was associated with a significant difference in the kinship system and in one of the marriage rules. The Djaui, a small tribe of the Buccaneer Archipelago, resembles the Bard and with it forms a small group. Across King Sound and the King Leopold Range are the tribes of Northern Kimberley, which are characterized by the possession of patrilineal moieties and a totemic cult centring around remarkable cave-paintings. But there are differences within the group, more particularly with regard to the marriage law. The Forrest River tribes allow marriages with certain types of first cousin, while those around Walcott Inlet and Port George IV forbid these. Passing to Eastern Kimberley, we see another feature, the subsection system which divides each tribe into eight social and totemic groups.

[8] The tribe is divided socially into four groups which function in marriage and ceremony. See Chapter IV.

If now we travel south of Lagrange to the De Grey region, we find the four-section system again, and with names the same as, or dialectal variants of, those to the north, but here they are arranged in a different order of marriage and descent. East of Laverton and throughout the western half of South Australia, there are no such divisions, and the kinship system is remarkably different from that found in most parts of Australia. Farther east again, in north-eastern South Australia, we find matri-lineal moieties and clans together with patrilineal cult or ceremonial clans, while just north of Lake Eyre is the four-section system of the Southern Aranda. In this way, all the tribes of Australia could be classified into smaller or larger groups and then in most cases, differences between the in-dividual tribes could be indicated. It is very interesting to hear members of different tribes discussing the differ-ences in customs, myths, and even terms. This occurs at inter-tribal ceremonial meetings, and also on mission sta-tions and around our townships. But though the differences do exist, they are not insuperable barriers; adjustments in marriage-law, kinship rules, section, subsection and moiety systems are made, so that common life can go on.

The groups of tribes have been called nations by some writers, but in view of the linguistic differences which usu-ally exist between members of a group and of the lack of any common central organization or sentiment, it would seem inadvisable to use the term "nation" in this connexion. Perhaps *we* could call such a group a "community" of tribes though it is doubtful whether *the tribes* think of themselves as being united in any particular way. One of the best examples of such a community is that which in-cludes the tribes of north-eastern South Australia, called by Dr Howitt the Dieri nation. They have in common sev-eral kinds of totemism, matrilineal moieties, the kinship system and a novel method of adjusting grievances. With a few variations in marriage law and totemism, this "com-munity" could be thought of as including the tribes from

Birdsville and Innamincka right down to the Flinders Range and Port Augusta. The greatest bond between them is the possession of a common mythology centring around cult-heroes called *mura-mura*. Moreover, the custodianship of the mythology is a co-operative matter. No one tribe "owns" any of the greater myths in its entirety, but only a section of it. For example, one of these myths, which concerns the emu and red ochre, is about seven hundred miles in length; that is, it is associated with natural features and localities along that length of territory, and is "owned" by the tribes and local subdivisions of tribes over a distance of 700 miles. Thus on the one hand, the "ownership" of different sections of the myth serves to distinguish tribes, while on the other hand, as only one myth is concerned, each tribe is mutually dependent on all the others along this mythological path for the preservation of that myth. This is important, for the welfare of man and nature is bound up with the myth and the rites in which it is re-enacted.

Eastern Arnhem Land provides another striking example of a "community" in this sense—a community of social organization and culture, expressed in meetings for social and ceremonial purposes. The north-eastern part of this region consists of many distinct clans and sub-clans, each with its own "country" and portions of other "countries". Such a clan or sub-clan is also frequently distinguished by peculiarities of dialect, but may be linked to one or more other clans by the possession of the same dialect. They share, however, the same rules of marriage and descent, the same beliefs, mythology and ritual, and so are linked together through doctrine, intermarriage and mutual obligations, and in the performance of ritual. In spite of this common culture and life Dr Warner could not find a name by which the clans thought of themselves as a people, and in order to have a term of reference used the name of a central group, the Murngin, as mentioned above. Recent inquiry by Mr and Mrs R. M. Berndt, however, has revealed that, whatever was the case twenty years ago, these Aborigines nowadays possess a name for this total community or "confederacy" of clans and sub-clans: the Wulamba. In addition, on the west and south of the Wulamba several other tribes, such as the Rembaranga, Djinba, Dai and Ngalpun, possess the same social and ceremonial organization and doctrines and mythology, representatives of any or all taking their place naturally and smoothly in ritual. They may be regarded as belonging to one sub-cultural "community" of tribes. Likewise the tribes of western Arnhem Land, from the Liverpool River to the Alligator River, form another such "community", one distinguishing feature being the emphasis on descent and membership of groups through the mother, whereas in the east the emphasis is on descent through the father.

We cannot, however, lay down strict rules for differentiating groups of tribes, for some, which are linked together by common myths and rites, differ markedly in social organization, as is the case with the Aranda of Central Australia and the Aluridja "community" of western South Australia. Moreover, the subject is complicated by the spread of customs, rites and myths and the amount of association which the nature of the country allows. But a general knowledge of the languages, kinship and social groupings, totemism, rites, myths and inter-tribal relations does enable the student to group the tribes in larger though loose, aggregates. This is an important matter which should be borne in mind in the setting apart of reserves and the foundation of missions which are to serve more than one tribe. Where tribes are small, the grouping into "communities" provides a guiding principle in the organization of missionary and administrative activity.[9]

[9] Examples of "communities" of tribes may be seen in "The Social Organization of South Australian Tribes" and "Social Organization in the Kimberley Division, North-Western Australia" (both by A. P. Elkin) in *Oceania*, vol. ii, nos. 1 and 3 respectively. G. D. Wheeler in *The Tribe*, pp. 57–60, discusses

THE LOCAL GROUP

Important as the tribe is, the local subdivision of the tribe is even more important; indeed, it is fundamental. This subdivision is normally both territorial and genealogical. That is, a definite part of the tribal territory belongs to, or is associated with, a group of tribesfolk who are mutually related in some genealogical way. This group is ideally an enlarged family, consisting of a man and his living descendants in the male line. Sometimes, of course, through the death of a grandfather's brother or cousin, the actual genealogical link between some members of the group is forgotten or is somewhat tenuous. But even so, the persons who belong to it are reckoned as brothers, fathers, father's fathers, sons and son's sons, while the women who belong to it by birth are the sisters of these men. Such a group is a local patrilineal clan, as will be explained later. It is also exogamous, that is, its members must marry outside the local group. It is usually patrilocal which means that women of the group leave their own "country" and live in the local "countries" of the men to whom they are married. They may still be, and usually are, in their own tribal territory. The result is that any one local group consists of those who are born into it and those women who come into it by marriage. The former constitute a clan, but the total group does not; it is frequently referred to as a horde.

The local group owns the hunting and food-gathering rights of its country; members of other groups may only enter it and hunt over it after certain preliminaries have been attended to and permission has been granted. In some cases, such permission cannot be obtained and would not be sought. It is a matter of relationship, as will be ex-

the references in earlier literature. "Cult-totemism and Mythology in Northern South Australia", by A. P. Elkin, *Oceania*, vol. v, no. 1 deals with the local and inter-tribal aspects of great myths.

plained in Chapter III. Each local group has its head-
man, usually the oldest, provided that he be not too old
to take full interest in its affairs. The headmen of the various groups of a tribe constitute a council—informal in nature—who talk over matters of common interest and make
decisions, when several local groups are together. Their
authority depends on knowledge, position in the secret
life and personal respect. Young initiated men may be present at such meetings, but are not permitted to speak.

This form of local organization does not mean that the
clans spend all or even most of their time in their own
separate countries. Several clans, often from more than
one tribe, usually settle at missions and government Aboriginal settlements and on many cattle stations. Those in
charge of such places desire this, so as to influence the
Aborigines or to use their labour. Moreover, the Aborigines are quite willing to adopt a settled life for most of
the time—provided they can obtain rations and tobacco
and such other things for which they acquire a taste, and
provided that, for a generation at least, they can revisit
their own countries and go off to their ceremonies as sentiment and custom demand. Apart from these artificial and
new situations, however, in good coastal and river regions,
the Aborigines can, and do, spend a lot of time together
in large "base" camps, hunting and foraging in combined
groups without much concern for clan or tribal boundaries.
This is true in the Daly and Fitzmaurice rivers coastal
region on the west of Arnhem Land, where adjacent clans
and sub-tribes of one or more tribes form enlarged social
and food-gathering "hordes". These are not exogamous,
though the clan is. Further, clan members are related in
the paternal line, not only to one another but also to a
common totem and spirit centre. As we shall see, the latter,
though small, is their true "country" and "abiding place",
which no one would take from them. In north-eastern Arnhem Land, too, there are many patrilineal exogamous
clans, each with its own hunting country as well as its

spirit and mythological centre. But since parts of the region are rich in natural food-sources, the clans can meet together for ceremonies for quite long periods, even months. In addition, there is, as mentioned above, crisscrossing of ownership of areas in each other's countries, and also of dialects. Consequently, boundaries are not of great practical importance. Indeed, the dialect groupings are more significant, especially as they are correlated with the fundamental division of this Wulamba (or Murngin) "community" of clans into two large social and ceremonial groups or moieties (as explained in Chapter IV). A person's social affiliations and marriage possibilities, his mythological heritage, and his ceremonial duties, are broadly determined by his moiety. He is either Dua or Yiritja, to use the local terms.

In western Arnhem Land, between the Liverpool and the Alligator rivers, the situation is different again. Fifteen named tribes or linguistic groups occupied, and in some cases still occupy, their own territories, which average about 350 square miles each. This is something like the size of a clan country in north-eastern Arnhem Land. The division of such small tribal territories into clan food-gathering districts would hardly be practicable. Instead, families in the direct paternal line are linked to their own small piece of country, set apart by mythological events, and, associated with these, have their own line of personal names. Such lines of families, or lineages, are exogamous. All the more important social groups, clans, moieties and phratries, however, are matrilineal, that is, membership is determined by maternal descent. As it is important to marry outside of one's own social groups, there is much inter-tribal marriage, and for generations, at least, such marriage has often been matrilocal. Children are brought up living with their mother's tribe, wherever it may move or settle, and speaking its language. And yet, they belong to, or "own", that piece of patrilineal country in their father's tribal territory. Such complications make local food-gathering boundaries and local organization somewhat amorphous. Generally speaking, it is in the drier and arid regions where this organization is more clear-cut. In them the foraging groups must be comparatively small and be separated by miles, often for weeks at a time, otherwise the sources of food would soon fail. In very rugged terrains, too, where good valleys are separated by poor and dry tops, the local "countries" are clearly marked and the food-gathering groups perforce spend much time apart. Suitable grounds, accessible to many clans, and capable of sustaining a big gathering for weeks, then become set apart for meetings and ceremonies of a general nature. The Northern Kimberley Division is a good example of this.

The most important aspect of the local group, however, is spiritual in nature, and frequent reference will be made to it. From one point of view, the members who belong to the local group by birth, own their subdivision of the tribal territory. But it is truer to say that the country owns them and that they cannot remain away from it indefinitely and still live. The point is, the Aborigines hold the doctrine of pre-existence of spirits; they believe that the spirits of the members of the local group (or clan) pre-existed usually in definite sites in the country of the group until incarnation, and that after death they will return to those spirit-homes, there possibly to await reincarnation. It is this spiritual bond which explains the reluctance of most Aborigines to remain away for very long periods from their own "country"; they desire to revisit it from time to time to be near the home of their spirits as well as to see some of the places in it sanctified by mythological "history"; and finally they like to die in it so that their spirits will not be lost when they sever their connexion with the body. Many an old Aborigine would be better off some distance away at some mission station or government feeding depot, but no! "That not my country, this my country," he says, and he will not find peace until he settles in the latter and there awaits death. Nor is it only bush natives who feel this urge. Even civilized ones and half-castes, such as those in New South Wales experience it. They are tied to certain localities by beliefs regarding their own spirits or the culture-heroes of whom they learned at their initiation. In other words, the bond is a religious one. Therefore, since we respect the religious convictions of one another, so we should respect those of the Aborigines. The implications of these beliefs may be different in the case of the latter than with ourselves, but that should not prevent administrative and missionary bodies from paying due regard to them. The confidence of a people and power to influence them can be gained by respecting as worth while their sentiments and fundamental beliefs, whereas to ignore and disparage these and to ride rough-shod over them, even in ignorance, is to set up an impassable barrier which doles, never mind how attractive, cannot break down.

This discussion of the local subdivisions of the tribal territory which has led into the sphere of religious belief and native policy, is one illustration of a fact which will appear several times in the course of the following chapters; that the different aspects of Aboriginal life are almost inextricably intertwined, and to explain one of them fully demands almost a complete understanding of the whole culture.

Chapter III

THE FAMILY AND OTHER RELATIONS

The Home. As we have seen, the tribal territory is in a general sense the Aborigine's home. He is at home in it, whereas outside it lies the unknown. The mythological associations of his tribal territory are full of meaning to him, indeed, of life, while the language or dialects spoken, and the customs practised in it, are his. But what is true of the tribal land as a whole is much more true of the country of the local group. Those who belong to it, and own it, are usually a group related in the male line, together with their wives who come from other local countries. Each local group has its name derived from some natural feature in the country or from some totemic and historical association. But what really makes this local country "home" is the fact that the spirits of all who belong to it pre-existed in spirit-homes at known spots within it, and that, according to the usual belief, the spirits return to these places after existence in the body has come to an end. In this way a person is tied to his "country" for it is the home of his spirit. And because the spirits of all the members of a local group come from spirit-homes in their own part of the tribal territory, these folk are related by something deeper than genealogical descent. This in its turn finds its explanation in the mythological past, for these spirit-centres did not come into existence unrelated to a personal cause. They are associated with the great ancestors and culture-heroes who travelled through the tribal territory and horde country, and by various ritual and spiritual means left human spirits at divers places along their routes. It is this fact which ultimately binds together the members of the local group and also of the tribe and makes their country home.

The Family. From our point of view, however, the home is based upon, and centres round, the institution of the family, quite apart from tribal, local, historical and religious associations. The same is true of the Aborigines. The family, consisting of a man, his wife or wives and children, is the fundamental unit of society both in form and function. True, the ties between husband and wife are less permanent than we desire them to be in our own society; many women become successively the wives of two or more men in the course of their lives, and there are customs of temporary lending and exchange of wives which do not commend themselves to us. But these latter are subject to rules;[1] likewise, marriage is regulated by kinship and other laws, never mind how often the partners be changed. It is this fact which preserves the social and religious status of the children, for they mostly belong on the one hand to the local country and religious group of their father and father's father; and, on the other hand, to the social group (social totem or other division) of their mother. Moreover, these positions are seldom altered by the transfer of a child to its father's brother, own or tribal, or to its mother's sister.

The family is the bridge between the generations, the first mechanism by which a child learns its place in the social and economic scheme of life; moreover, in spite of some biased statements, the parents are truly fond of their children, the fathers no less than the mothers. I have frequently seen a father take his small child, even a girl, with him while doing odd jobs such as making weapons and implements. I once had an interpreter who brought his little daughter, aged about six, with him on a fortnight's

[1] Chapter V.

journey, and though she was frequently scared and often cried, he never lost patience with her.

The Australian family is a self-sufficient economic unit, in that the partners can between them obtain and make all that is required for daily life; and they often do so. At other times, two or more families of the local group or of different groups—related in certain ways—hunt and collect food together; on such occasions, the women form one party and the men another.

But from the point of view of this chapter the most important feature of the family is its bilateral character. The local group and totemic clans are unilateral; that is, descent and membership are reckoned through one line only, either through the father or the mother, in which cases, we speak of the descent as being patrilineal or matrilineal respectively. But the family traces its descent through two lines, those of the father and the mother and through the son and the daughter. This brings us to the study of kinship.

KINSHIP

Our Family System. In our own society we distinguish the family from other relations, but we must realize that we do so quite arbitrarily for certain purposes and that it is not easy to decide sometimes where the family stops or where our relations begin and end. The family consists of father, mother and children, and in some cases also of stepchildren and adopted children. But, when these children are married and become parents, are their spouses and children part of our family or not? Generally speaking neither our children nor their spouses and offspring are part of our families in the sense of belonging to our households, and yet for the purpose of inheritance of property and with regard to sentiment and affection, they do belong to it. The limits become even less defined when we think of collateral relatives, such as first and second cousins and their spouses and children. But, in spite of this, we are

[1] Wagaitj lad with fishing spear.

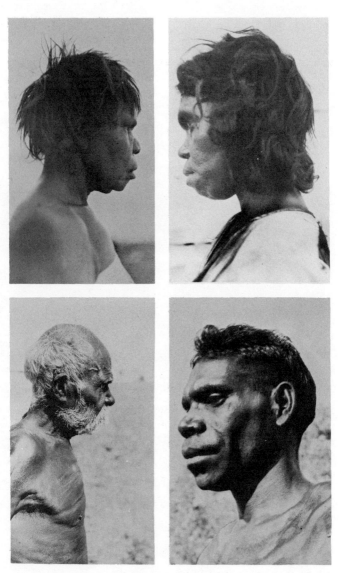

[2] Aboriginal types.

[3] *Top,* making fire by the twirling method. North-western Australia, 1927. *Bottom,* types of North-western Australian men.

[4] Arnhem-Lander.

related either genealogically or through marriage to a very great number of people. Of course, there are practical reasons for not bothering about our relations beyond first or second cousins, but theoretically there are no reasons for not tracing our relationships to every person in the community—apart from recent immigrants. In doing this, however, we would be hindered in two ways: by the lack of good all-embracing genealogical family records and by the lack of sufficient relationship terms to prevent confusion. We would probably have to speak of cousins from the 1st to the nth degree, of great uncles and so on. The point is that our kinship system is not meant to be all-embracing, but merely to describe the members of the family and a limited range of other persons most closely related to it. For this reason it has been called a family system of kinship. It consists of a limited number of terms which, as far as they go, indicate generation level, collateral position (indefinitely), sex (mostly) and marriage ties. To proceed by generations, there are (a) grandfather and grandmother; (b) father and mother, uncle and aunt, father-in-law and mother-in-law; (c) brother and sister, first cousin and sometimes, second cousin,[2] husband, wife, brother-in-law, sister-in-law; (d) son, daughter, nephew, niece, son-in-law, daughter-in-law; and (e) grandson and granddaughter. We also use the terms for great grandparents and great grandchildren, but usually we are satisfied with the above twenty-four terms. If we desire to refer to the relationship of persons outside the range of those terms, we have to use descriptive phrases, such as, my second cousin's son, or my mother's second cousin's grandson. Even so, we do not know whether these relationships are reckoned through male or female lines unless we add further details.

[2] By second cousins are here meant the children of two families one parent of each of which is a first cousin to the other. Thus A and B are second cousins if one of A's parents is a first cousin to one of B's parents.

The Aborigines' Classificatory System. The Aborigines, however, do reckon their relationships throughout the whole community and even beyond the borders of any one tribe. Indeed, every one with whom a person comes in contact is regarded as related to him, and the kind of relationship must be ascertained so that the two persons concerned will know what their mutual behaviour should be. In other words, relationship is the basis of behaviour; indeed, it is the anatomy and physiology of Aboriginal society and must be understood if the behaviour of the Aborigines as social beings is to be understood. This is not the case, except to a very limited degree, in our own community. There are certain more or less accepted patterns of behaviour which are usually to be observed between a limited number of our relations, and these differ from each other. The mother-child, father-child, grandfather-grandchild, brother-sister, uncle-nephew, mother-in-law—son-in-law are some of these relationships which do imply kinds of behaviour. They arise mostly out of custom only, though in some cases the sanction of the law operates, for example, in prohibiting certain marriages, ordering maintenance and directing bequests. In our case, however, such patterns of behaviour only concern the members of small groups of people centring around the family unit. In Aboriginal society, they operate throughout the whole community.

But how can the natives reckon their relations and so codify mutual behaviour? Do they use an infinite number of kinship terms, or do they describe in detail a person's relationship to every one else? They do neither. What they do in effect is to enlarge the family for the purpose of social behaviour until it embraces the whole tribe, and they do this not by increasing the number of relationship terms and speaking of third cousins, great-uncles, or anything of that sort, but by classifying various groups of the community under the normal relationship terms of mother, father, "uncle", "aunt", and so on, going no farther up and down than grandparent and grandchild, nor as a rule, collaterally (sideways) than second cousin. But once again: "How can they do this?" The question must be faced, for though it might be simple enough in a small tribe of one or two hundred persons, it seems to be quite another matter when the tribe is large or when members of other tribes are brought into the tribal scheme, for there is no limitation of locality, clan or tribe, in the range, use and influence of the kinship system and its terms.

The system is worked out according to certain principles which are observed by the Aborigines:

(i) A start is made from the family and close blood relations reckoned to the second generation up and down, and also collaterally to the second line on both the father's and mother's sides of any particular individual. I shall refer to this person, when necessary, as *EGO*, and will regard him as a male. We should remember that the Aborigines do distinguish "own" or blood relations from those related only by marriage or by "legal" fiction.

(ii) But in reckoning collateral relations, aunts, uncles and cousins, they employ a principle which distinguishes their kinship system from ours; they regard brothers as equivalent and sisters as equivalent, and apply terms according to this principle. Thus, mother's sister is classified with and called mother, and father's brother is classified with and called father. Likewise grandfather's brother is "grandfather" and so on. Moreover, certain consequential relationships follow from this; thus, since father's brother is my "father", his son is my "*brother*"; he is not my *cousin* as with us; and likewise mother's sister's children are not my *cousins*, but my "*brothers*" and "*sisters*"; or, a brother's children, in the case of a man, are not his nephews and nieces, but his "children", or if a woman be speaking, then her sister's children are "sons" and "daughters" to her.

(iii) In the third place, except for very special and rare purposes, the children of a brother and sister are distinguished in terminology, and different behaviour is observed towards them by EGO. Thus my children and *my brother's children* are sons and daughters to me, but the children of *my sister* are *nephews and nieces*; or, to look at the relationship from the point of view of these groups of children: my brother's children call me, and regard me as, "father" while my sister's children look upon me as "uncle", that is, mother's brother. This principle applies also to the brothers and sisters of my parents, grandparents or grandchildren. Thus, father's brother, according to principle (ii), is "father", but mother's brother is quite distinct, being called by a special term, say, "uncle"; likewise, mother's sister is mother, but father's sister is "aunt". Following from this are the facts that while my father's brother's children are my brothers and sisters, my mother's brother's children are my cross-cousins; and that my mother's sister's children are my brothers and sisters, whereas my father's sister's children are my cross-cousins. Further, my father's father's brother being father's father (principle ii), his son is "father" to me; but his sister's son is not my father's brother, but my father's cross-cousin, and I call him "uncle"; that is I classify him with my mother's brother, while his sister is grouped with my mother.

There are two important social facts associated with this third principle which make its operation clearer; in the first place, my father and his brothers and sisters, and also his father's brother's children, all belong to one "country", one local subdivision of the tribe, whereas my mother and her brother and also her father's brother's children belong to another "country". Now this difference of country or local group is reflected in the use of distinct terms for them, namely, "father" and "father's sister" for the first lot, and "mother" and "mother's brother" for the other group. The second fact is that in many Australian tribes two men frequently exchange sisters in marriage. This means, for example, that my mother's brother's wife is actually my father's sister, and further, that my mother's brother's children are in fact my father's sister's children. Hence, with very few exceptions, the one term is used for all cross-cousins, be they the children of mother's brother or of father's sister. In the former case they are matrilateral, and in the latter patrilateral, cross-cousins.[3]

The following table illustrates the principles under discussion by showing the normal arrangement of terms and relations in Australian kinship, reckoned from EGO, a male.

(iv) In the fourth place, affinal relations, that is, those related by marriage, are classed with blood relations, even though qualifying or distinct terms are usually applied to them. But even in the latter case, the persons concerned were before the marriage or betrothal, classed with EGO's own relations as cousins, uncles and aunts. This arises in the first instance from the fact that in most tribes, they are, or may be, close kin. If, as is possible in some tribes, a man marries his own mother's brother's daughter, or, as is more common, the daughter of his mother's mother's brother's daughter, then his wife and wife's brothers were already his cousins, his father-in-law was his own uncle (m.b.), or an "uncle" once removed, that is, his father's male cross-cousin, while his mother-in-law was his "aunt" (father's sister), or his mother's female cross-cousin. If, however, such cousin-marriages are prohibited, it usually follows that the normal marriage is with a person related in the same way, but more distantly; this amounts to mar-

[3] EGO's cross-cousin is his mother's brother's child or his father's sister's child. Mother's sister's child or father's brother's child are parallel cousins, and in the Aboriginal system are brothers and sisters.

By second cousins of the cross-cousin variety, I mean second cousins who are the children of cross-cousins. Thus, A is this sort of second cousin to me, if his mother or father is the cross-cousin of one of my parents; e.g., if his mother is my mother's cross-cousin, say, her mother's brother's daughter. The distinguishing feature of these cross-relationships is that the two persons of the one family through whom the relationship is established, should be brother and sister, and not of the same sex.

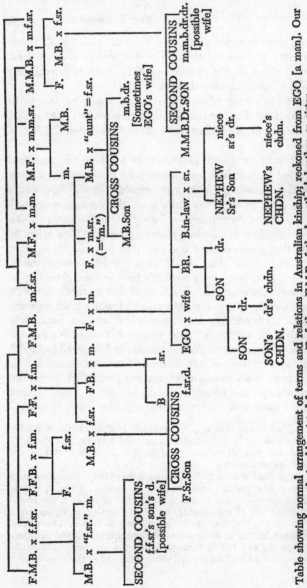

Table showing normal arrangement of terms and relations in Australian kinship; reckoned from EGO [a man]. Our terms are used, mostly in abbreviated form; e.g. F., father; F.M.B., father's mother's brother; sr, sister.

riage with a type of cousin of the forbidden woman, that is with the forbidden cousin's tribal or horde sister. The latter's relationship to EGO can be traced either actually or in theory.

On the basis of these general principles, the natives know or work out the relationship of any particular person to any one or every one else concerned. If nobody present knows the actual relationship of a particular visitor to a mutual relation, then such general matters are considered as the visitor's approximate age, his totemic affiliations or any local or social grouping to which he belongs; this is especially necessary if he comes from another tribe. If all else fail, he is regarded as the brother of the man introducing him. In such ways, the elders of the local group decide his relationship to one of themselves and therefore to everybody present. I have seen this happen in the case of my own guide. A great deal of ingenuity is displayed when the social organization of the visitor's tribe differs in important particulars from that of the local tribe. The one may have matrilineal moieties and the other eight sub-section groups divided between two patrilineal moieties,[4] but the visitor is given a social status in the home tribe, which can be shown to be theoretically justifiable and is practically workable. Such adjustments constitute further evidence of the intellectual ability of the natives to solve intricate problems associated with their own life.

Types of Kinship Systems in Australia. Just as there are differences in languages throughout Australia, even though these belong to the one linguistic family, so it is with the Aboriginal kinship systems; they are based on similar principles throughout, and yet there are interesting and important differences; the latter are associated with variations in marriage rules and in social behaviour. Four of these varieties are found in geographical order from south to north in the northern half of the coastal districts

[4] These tribal divisions will be discussed in the next chapter.

of Western Australia, while a variation in the direction of the fifth is found in the same region. This makes their study all the more interesting. Each type is named after one of the well-known tribes which possesses it. They are the Kariera, Karadjeri, Nyul-Nyul or Aranda, Aluridja and Ungarinyin. The rest of this chapter is devoted to a brief examination of the main features of each of these types, showing how the differences in the number and arrangement of terms in each are causally related to differences in social behaviour, particularly with regard to marriage. Those who feel that this might be a bit difficult and complex, would do well to read Chapters IV and V first. In the meantime the chief characteristics of each system may be summed up as follows: In the Kariera system cross-cousin marriage is allowed, descent is traced through two lines, and there are in terminology only two families in the grandparents' generation. In the Karadjeri system marriage with mother's brother's daughter is allowed, but marriage with father's sister's daughter is forbidden; as a result, descent is traced through three lines to three families in the grandparents' generation.[5]

In the Nyul-Nyul system marriage with a cross-cousin of either kind is prohibited but is usually allowed between certain types of second cousin, and descent is reckoned through four lines to four families in the grandparents' generation, as is usually the case amongst ourselves. The Aluridja system is marked by an irregularity in the use of terms as compared with the Nyul-Nyul. Thus, cross-cousins are called brother and sister, and father's and mother's cross-cousins are called respectively by the terms for the brothers and sisters of father and mother. Cross-cousin marriage is prohibited and descent is reckoned

[5] In actual life, a cross-cousin is not always married; and if a person's parents are not cross-cousins, there are four families in his grandparents' generation in fact, though in the Kariera and Karadjeri system, this is not reflected in the terminology. The natives, however, are quite aware of the fact.

through four lines, but because of the irregularity just mentioned, the kinds of second cousins who are eligible as spouses differ from those eligible in the Nyul-Nyul system.

The Ungarinyin system resembles the Nyul-Nyul in the prohibition of cross-cousin marriage and the tracing of descent through four lines, but the relationship terms are applied to local groups or clans of people irrespective of their relative ages; if a man is mother's brother to EGO, then all the men of the former's local group are classified with him as mother's brother, and all the women of that group as EGO's "mother". It seems strange to us to apply the same relationship term to a man, his father, father's father, son and son's son, but the Ungarinyin are not thinking of them as individuals so much as members of a local patrilineal group which is related to EGO in a particular way. It is his "uncle's" clan or "mother's uncle's" clan and so on. This makes a difference too, in the kind of second cousin who may be married; in fact, the emphasis is not placed on the kinship level of the spouse, but rather on the group to which she belongs.

There are other interesting variations in kinship systems and marriage laws in Australia, but so long as the general principles and main variations are understood, all other modifications can easily be grasped by those working with the Aborigines.

PART II. SOME DETAILS OF SYSTEMS OF RECKON-ING RELATIONSHIP IN AUSTRALIA

The Kariera Type. This is found in the Kariera tribe on the De Grey, in Western Australia, and in even more logical form in the Wailpi tribe of the Flinders Range, South Australia. This system is based on a rule of preferred marriage with either cross-cousin. Of course, every one does not marry his or her cross-cousin, but the number of terms in use and their arrangement are based on the legal fact that they could. As a result there are only four kinds of relations in EGO's generation, namely, brother and sister and male and female cross-cousin, for marriage is with the last, or with another woman classed with her. Likewise, in the parents' generation there are only four groups, namely, father, father's sister (who is mother-in-law), mother and mother's brother (who is father-in-law), while in the grandparents' generation there are only two terms because in that generation it is usual to apply the same kinship term to a man and his sister. Now, in this case, father's father is brother to mother's mother, and mother's father is brother to father's mother. That is, there are only two families in the grandparents' generation and incidentally, the wife's grandparents belong to the same two families; or to put it in another way, descent is traced through two lines only, through the father's father and the mother's father, or if reckoning in the female line, through father's mother and mother's mother. Such a system does not require many kinship terms; fourteen only are used. That is, EGO's relations, and they include every person in the tribe, are divided amongst fourteen classes, namely, the mother class, the cross-cousin class etc.

In the following table I am not using Kariera terms, but those of the Nyul-Nyul tribe farther north, for this will make it easier to see the differences between the types. In this and the other kinship diagrams, the terms are those applied by EGO, that is, oneself, to each of the relations represented, and both in the diagrams and the text, unless otherwise stated or implied, EGO is a male. Capitals denote males and lower case (ordinary type), females. The English terms are abbreviated, usually being denoted by the first letter of the word only; e.g., f., father; f.m., father's mother. To avoid confusion, sr = sister and son = son.

Looking at this table we see (i) that EGO or his brother marries the daughter of his *KAGA* (M.B.) and *yirmor* (f.sr) who therefore become his parents-in-law; (ii) that his father (IBAL) marries *berai*, the daughter of DJAM and *kalod*, the actual "uncle" and "aunt" of *IBAL*, and

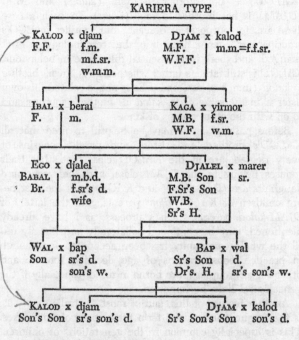

KARIERA TYPE

KALOD x djam   DJAM x kalod
F.F.   f.m.   M.F.   m.m.=f.f.sr.
     m.f.sr.   W.F.F.
     w.m.m.

IBAL x berai   KAGA x yirmor
F.   m.   M.B.   f.sr.
              W.F.   w.m.

EGO x djalel   DJALEL x marer
BABAL   m.b.d.   M.B. Son   sr.
Br.   f.sr's d.   F.Sr's Son
     wife   W.B.
              Sr's H.

WAL x bap   BAP x wal
Son   sr's d.   Sr's Son   d.
     son's w.   Dr's. H.   sr's son's w.

KALOD x djam   DJAM x kalod
Son's Son   sr's son's d.   Sr's Son's Son   son's d.

x joins husband and wife.   ⎰ joins parents and children.
⎕ joins brothers and sisters.

(iii) that EGO's children and grandchildren contract the same type of marriages. We also see that EGO traces his descent through two lines, namely, that of *IBAL-KALOD*, and *KAGA* (or *berai*)-*DJAM*. If, however, EGO's father *IBAL* did not marry a cross-cousin, then EGO's F.F. (*KALOD*) is not brother to m.m. (*kalod*) and M.F. (*DJAM*) is not brother to f.m. (*djam*). In such a case there are, for purposes of descent, four families in EGO's grandparents' generation, but the terminology is not changed, and there is no essential difference in behaviour. *KALOD* is still father's father whether he is "own" brother to *kalod* (m.m.) or not, and if he is not so related, his own sister is in the same class, *kalod*, as mother's mother; and so on with the other groups of kin.

Before passing on, it may be helpful to note that all *KALOD's* brothers and sisters, and parallel cousins of every degree, are in the *KALOD* class, and that their spouses belong to the *DJAM* class, and their sons and daughters are *IBAL-yirmor* and *KAGA-berai*, the first being children of *KALOD-djam* parents, and the latter, of *DJAM-kalod* parents. Such a process, as I have already mentioned, may be continued collaterally and lineally until the whole community has been accounted for, though in practice, considerations of age, locality, totemic and other social groupings, are borne in mind, especially if the genealogical links be forgotten.

Another feature of this, and of most Australian systems, is the frequent use of one term for persons of both sexes. This is especially common in the generations of children, grandparents and grandchildren, and sometimes also in one's own generation. Thus, son and daughter are both *WAL* (*wal*) and nephew and niece are both *BAP* (*bap*).[6]

Very often, however, when these young persons grow up, they are called by the terms of the parents' genera-

---

[6] Sometimes there are feminine forms of these terms to denote the daughter and sister's daughter. Thus in the Karadjeri tribe sr's son is *Djelanga*, and sr's d. is *djalbi*.

tion, son being called *IBAL* (F.) by EGO, and daughter *yirmor* (f.sr), sister's son *KAGA* (M.B.) and sister's daughter, *berai* (m.). In that way, the sex is distinguished in the terms used, but only when there is some social reason for doing so; in this case, when adulthood has been reached.

To us, of course, it seems strange that a man should call his son "father", and his nephew "uncle", but people like the Aborigines, with a classificatory kinship system, use such terms not so much to express status, as to indicate the mutual behaviour which is to be observed between the two individuals concerned. Thus there is the father-son behaviour which becomes denoted solely by the term for father, say, *IBAL*, or the "uncle"-"nephew" relationship and pattern of behaviour symbolized by the term for mother's brother, say *KAGA*. The same applies to the relationship of grandchild and grandparent. But we must remember that the native does not confuse the different biological and age positions of the two persons; when necessary he can make quite clear which person is being referred to. This must be emphasized, because white persons, being ignorant of the working of the kinship system, accuse natives of telling lies or at least of being hopelessly stupid when one of them says that a young child is his grandfather or uncle. From the point of view of social behaviour he is quite right; of course the boy would use the same terms with reference to the man, and both would live according to the "grandfather" or "uncle" patterns of behaviour. The same accusation is made when a native says that a certain woman is his mother, though it is known quite well that another woman is his mother. Indeed, the woman so designated might be the native man's sister's daughter. The white man, however, is doing the other an injustice. He is in ignorance jumping to a wrong conclusion. The native knows quite well the difference between the mother who bore him and the mother who is classified with her, being her sister, own or tribal; if he were asked he would use some qualifying terms (such as "own" or "little-bit") which would make this aspect of the matter clear.

In the table of terms given, only one term is used for male and female cross-cousins. This is the general practice in Australia, though in some tribes with "own" cross-cousin marriage, there are two terms, which then really mean spouse and brother-in-law, or sister-in-law. But the main point about the widespread use of one term for persons of both sexes is that from certain points of view, brothers and sisters are one or equivalent, especially in the case of "own" brother and sister. Their spirits have both been incarnated through the womb of one woman, and belong to the one spirit-home, or to spirit-homes in the one local division of the tribal territory, namely, that of their father who found them in a spiritual experience. Except for the members of the immediate family, the members of a local group are all "brothers" and "sisters" and, sex apart, are all of one relationship. There is always something of this attitude in one person's relationship to another local group, but it is taken to its logical conclusion in the fifth type of kinship, the Ungarinyin, to be described later. At present, it is sufficient to remember that for certain purposes the unity of a group is more significant than distinctions of sex. Thus, the cross-cousins are the persons of one's own generation level or age-grade, who belong to the country of a mother's brother, and are eligible as spouses.

The Karadjeri System. Passing just north of the Kariera and similar tribes we come to the Karadjeri tribe around Lagrange where we see a most interesting difference in the kinship system; this follows from a difference in the marriage rule. Cross-cousin marriage is allowed as in the Kariera system but only with one kind of cross-cousin, namely, with mother's brother's daughter. If we look at the kinship table we will see clearly how this rule, in both its permissive and prohibitive aspects, is reflected in its

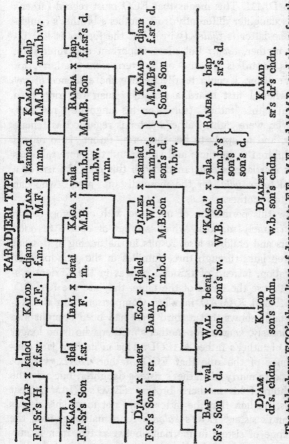

KARADJERI TYPE

The table shows EGO's three lines of descent to F.F., M.F. and M.M.B., and also a fourth line which provides the husbands for the sisters of EGO's own patrilineal line (son, B, F., and F.F.) and wives for the men of the patrilineal line of M.M.B. The females on the right are sisters of the males on the left of the table.

Top line (left to right):

MALIP x kalod
F.F.Sr's H. f.f.sr.

KALOD x djam
F.F. f.m.

DJAM x kamad
M.F. m.m.

KAMAD x malp
M.M.B. m.m.b.w.

Second line:

"KAGA"
F.F.Sr's Son

IBAL x ibal
F. f.sr.

KAGA x yala
M.B. m.m.b.d.
m.b.w.
w.m.

RAMBA x bap,
M.M.B. Son f.f.sr's d.

Third line:

DJAM x marer
F.Sr's Son sr.

EGO x djalel
BABAL w.
B. m.b.d.

DJALEL x kamad
W.B. m.m.br's
M.B.Son son's d.
w.b.w.

KAMAD x djam
M.M.Br's f.sr's d.
Son's Son

Fourth line:

BAP x wal
Sr's Son d.

WAL x berai
Son son's w.

"KAGA" x yala
W.B. Son m.m.br's
son's son's d.

RAMBA x bap
sr's d.

Bottom line:

DJAM
dr's chdn.

KALOD
son's chdn.

DJALEL
w.b. son's chdn.

KAMAD
sr's drs chdn.

terminology. Thus, mother's brother's daughter is *djalel* (wife), and her brother is DJALEL (brother-in-law), whereas father's sister's daughter is *djam* and her brother is also DJAM. This means that EGO must regard father's sister's daughter differently from mother's brother's daughter. The latter is *djalel* (wife), but the former is like father's mother, *djam*. But more important and interesting in this regard is the use of the term *ibal* (father), for father's sister. I could hardly believe the evidence of my ears when I first heard a Karadjeri man referring to a woman as his "father" (*tabalu* in his language); my ears, however, were right. Father's sister is regarded as female father, and to apply to her the term "father" is to regard her children as brothers and sisters and therefore taboo as far as marriage is concerned. With this goes the use of a special term, *yala*, for the more distant "aunt", who can be wife's mother.

Now this permission of marriage with one cross-cousin only (namely m.b.d.), which applies of course to one's parents and children also, results in the tracing of descent in three lines through three families in the grandparents' generation, instead of through two as in the Kariera system. To use the terms of the table, they are the *KALOD*, *DJAM*, and *KAMAD* families. Comparison with the Kariera table shows that a third term had been brought into use, namely, *kamad*, for mother's mother who is no longer sister of father's father *KALOD*. This in its turn is a consequence of the rule that EGO's father, *IBAL*, was not allowed to marry his father's sister's daughter, but only the daughter of his mother's brother (EGO's *DJAM*). That means, further, that the latter could not marry his sister's husband's sister (EGO's *kalod*). As a matter of fact, the exchange of sisters in marriage between two men is normally impossible under this system; if my mother's brother were married to my father's sister, I could not look upon his wife as a mother-in-law because she would also be my father's sister,[7] and therefore by the tribal rule I could not marry her daughter.

This brings us to the question: Why have some tribes prohibited marriage with father's sister's daughter? There are several reasons,[8] but the most important is the strict prohibition which is generally imposed in Australia on all social intercourse between a man and his mother-in-law, even though they may be closely related by genealogy. It may be that the prohibition was not always so intense, especially in places where marriage with father's sister's daughter was encouraged. But certainly, in recent years in north-western Australia, one of the most important considerations in arranging a marriage is the selection of the mother-in-law; she should be a woman from "little-bit-long-way"—that is a woman with whom EGO has had very little, and possibly nothing to do, and across whose track, or into whose locality, he is not likely to go in the future. Needless to say, she must stand in the right kinship relationship to him—a kind of "aunt". In this way the mother-in-law avoidance causes no social difficulty. Once this principle, which amounts to the selection of a suitable person to be avoided, and therefore to be mother-in-law, is adopted, we can understand why a man would prefer not to make his father's sister, mother-in-law. She belongs to his own and his father's local group, even though she marries, as she normally should do, into another group. Her spirit belongs where his does, and therefore no barriers to social intercourse should be set up between them. Marriage with her daughter is therefore prohibited.[9]

[7] The Kariera table shows this: m.b.d. is also f.sr's d. and *Ibal* and *Kaga* have exchanged sisters in marriage.

[8] A. P. Elkin, "Social Organization in the Kimberley Division", *Oceania*, vol. ii, no. 3, pp. 302–3.

[9] The Forrest River system is almost the same as the Karadjeri, though marriage with f.sr's d. does sometimes occur. The Murngin system is based on the same principles as the Karadjeri, but it extends the kinship terms laterally into seven distinct lines, so as to include the descent of the spouses of both EGO

Nyul-Nyul or Aranda System. There is, however, also a rule of restricted social intercourse between a man and his wife's father. Now the tendency with regard to such prohibitions in Australia has been, as I see it, to intensify them, but, at the same time to separate in geographical distance and genealogical relationship those between whom they operate. I have just shown how the mother-in-law avoidance seems to lie at the heart of the prohibition of marriage with father's sister's daughter. In the same way the taboo on wife's father is closely connected with the prohibition of marriage with the other cross-cousin (m.b.d.), for a man does not desire to avoid one so closely related to himself by the tie of blood as his own mother's brother; but he must do so if he marries the latter's daughter; obviously, the only way to prevent such a situation from occurring is to prohibit marriage with mother's brother's daughter, and this has been done. There are also other reasons for this prohibition, connected with the solidarity of local groups and with the general desire to bind individuals and groups together by the exchange of sisters in marriage.[10] But none of the reasons have anything to do with eugenics, they are purely social in character.

As a result of such urges, the Aranda or Nyul-Nyul system of kinship has come into being, which, with modifications is the most wide-spread of any in Australia. It is based on the prohibition of any sort of first-cousin marriage, but allows marriage between certain kinds of second cousins, namely, those between the children of persons who are themselves cross-cousins. Indeed, these marriages are the ideal; the usual example given is that of EGO to the

and his sister, and also his sister's daughter and sister's daughter's daughter. (W. L. Warner, *A Black Civilization,* pp. 57–9.) There is indeed a fourth line in the Karadjeri system which supplies the husbands for the women of EGO's local group (namely his f.f.sr, f.sr, own sr, and dr.). See Appendix to this chapter.

[10] A. P. Elkin, op. cit., pp. 302–9.

daughter's daughter of his mother's mother's brother.[11] This example, however, is not selected at random from the possible marriages. It expresses a significant fact, for in very many tribes with which I am acquainted from the Broome district, Western Australia, to New South Wales, and which have the Nyul-Nyul kinship system, the mother's mother's brother seems to be almost the most important relation a person possesses. He is mother's "uncle", and takes a leading part in arranging his niece's (sr's dr's) son's initiation and marriage. In fact, he is the marriage authority for EGO's matrilineal group of relations (EGO, sr., m., M.B.). It is his duty to find a wife or to see that a wife is found, for his "niece's" son, and one way to do that is to arrange for his daughter's daughter to marry the former.

But, strangely enough, his very position in EGO's mother's group of close relations has led to a disinclination to marriage with his daughter's daughter, and so, many tribes with the Nyul-Nyul kinship system forbid marriage with "own" second cousin, allowing it only with someone else, more distantly related, but classified with her and her parallel cousin.

An examination of the Nyul-Nyul kinship table, and a comparison of it with the Karadjeri table, will show the differences caused by the prohibition of all cross-cousin marriage. As neither parent may marry a cross-cousin of any kind, there are four families in EGO's grandparents' generation. Mother's father's family has been completely separated in terminology from father's mother's family and a new term has been introduced to denote the latter, namely, *kabali*.[12] This means that EGO's descent is now

[11] The other possible second-cousin wives are m.f.sr's dr's d.; f.f.sr's son's d. and f.m.b. son's d. Thus normally the wife's mother is cross-cousin to EGO's mother, or else her father is cross-cousin to EGO's father.

[12] This term was coming into use amongst the coastal Karadjeri at Lagrange during my visit there in 1928, but only for f.m. Her brother was *Djambad* (M.F.). It was, however, a sign of the growing dislike of marriage with m.b.d.

NYUL-NYUL OR ARANDA TYPE

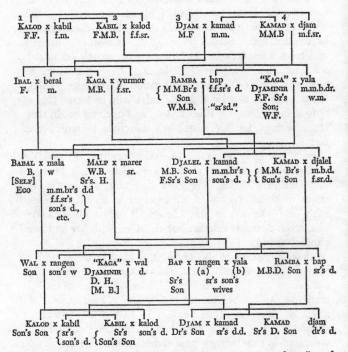

The terms are arranged as though brothers exchanged sisters in marriage and own "second-cousins" always married. In actual social life, this is all possible, but does not consistently happen.

The numbers at the top, 1, 2, 3, 4, represent the male lines of EGO or his son's son. For son, the lines are 1 (F.F.F.), 3 (F.M.F.), 2 (M.F.F.), 4 (M.M.F.).

Sister's son has two wives, (a) and (b). If the latter comes from a distant group and has no associations with EGO, he may marry her daughter.

traced through four lines instead of three or two as in the Karadjeri and Kariera systems respectively. The lines reckoning through males are: father's father (*KALOD*), father's mother's brother (*KABIL*), mother's father (*DJAM*) and mother's mother's brother (*KAMAD*).

The prohibition of marriage with both kinds of cross-cousin has also resulted in the differentiation of the "uncles" (m.brs) and "aunts" (f.srs) who can be parents-in-law, from those who cannot. Thus, own father's sister and mother's brother are *yurmor* and *KAGA* respectively, whereas wife's mother and father are *yala* and *KAGA DJAMINIR*. In EGO's own generation, too, there is a distinction of wife, *mala*, and wife's brother (or sister's husband, *MALP*), from cross-cousins, *djalel*.

There are several other interesting and important features about this Nyul-Nyul system, such as the use of a special term, *RAMBA*, for wife's mother's brother to distinguish him from an ordinary "father", the use of the same term for the husband of niece (sr's d.), and the use of two terms for sister's son's wife, one of which is the term for EGO's mother-in-law, *yala*, as though a man could marry his sister's son's daughter—and he can. These matters will be discussed later when dealing with customs puzzling to us.[13] There is also the use of a special term, *wainman*, to denote wife's mother's parents and the restricted social intercourse a person may have with those relations. It is a behaviour term, rather than a relationship term, and so is applied to two persons related as husband and wife. I think, too, it is here associated with the disinclination to marry the daughter's daughter of own mother's mother's brother. The latter finds a tribal "brother" who becomes EGO's wife's mother's father. Though such points as these may be tedious to us, they are very significant to the native, having to do with his family and social life.

The Aluridja System. There is no need to go into details

[13] Chapter V.

here about the two remaining principal types of Australian kinship systems, for in some ways they are varieties of the Nyul-Nyul type. They both prohibit cross-cousin marriage, allow certain kinds of second-cousin marriage, trace descent through four lines and designate four families in the grandparents' generation.

The fourth type is marked by a modification in the arrangement of terms as compared with the Nyul-Nyul system and, as a result, by the practice as the norm, of some marriages which would be at best irregular in that system. I call it the Aluridja system because it is most widespread amongst the group of tribes who inhabit the whole of the west of South Australia, and to whom I give the general name of Aluridja, but I first detected this type in the Bard tribe, the northern neighbours of the Nyul-Nyul, and have since noticed it in part of the central coast of New South Wales. Its characteristics are associated with, and indeed, arise from, the absence of a division of society into either two, four or eight groups, called respectively moieties, sections and subsections, which divisions, in one form or another, occur in about two-thirds of Australia. These groupings have their rules of descent, being either patrilineal, or matrilineal, and as they are also even in number, the result is that a person's relations are divided amongst them in an orderly way. This will be referred to again in the next chapter. It is sufficient to say here that EGO and his cross-cousins do not belong to the same half, or other tribal subdivision, and likewise mother and her cross-cousins, do not belong to the same social division. In other words, cross-cousins are never counted as brothers and sisters for the purpose of reckoning descent or arranging marriages.[14]

[14] If there are two groups or moieties, say A and B, which are patrilineal in descent, a man of A will find his father in A, but his mother and her brother in B, and his mother's brother's children also in B because they will follow their father. A's brothers and sisters, however, will belong to moiety A, like himself.

AN ALURIDJA TYPE—KOKATA, SOUTH AUSTRALIA

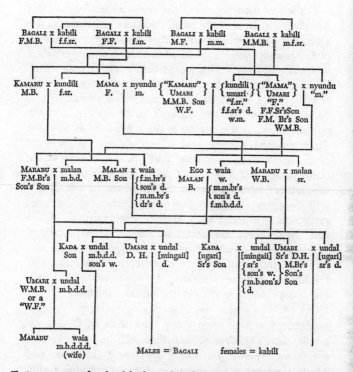

The terms are arranged as though brothers exchanged sisters in marriage, as they can do, and as though own "second cousins" always married as is permissible.

The table shows:

(a) The four lines of descent to F.F., F.M.B., M.F. and M.M.B.

(b) The paucity of terms especially in (i) grandparents' and children's generations—terms for males and females without distinguishing sisters from wives, and in (ii) own generation—cross-cousins = brother and sister.

(c) Type marriage is with m.m.b. son's d. instead of with m.m.b.d.d., as in the Nyul-Nyul system, and with f.m.b.d.d. instead of with f.m.b. son's d. This is the result of regarding mother's cross-cousins as brothers and sisters, KAMARU and Nyundu, and father's cross-cousins in the same way as MAMA and Kundili.

(d) Marriage is possible with m.b.d.d.d. provided that m.b.d.d. was not married to EGO's own son, which is possible for they are the right type of second cousin for marriage. Marriage with sr's son's d. does not seem to be possible and was never admitted; sr's son is classed with own son, because they are own cross-cousins. Marriage with sr's d.d. is theoretically possible, but I doubt whether it ever occurs.

(e) Special terms for wife's parents and W.M.B., indicating avoidance.

(f) Terms in brackets in children's generation are those used in northern South Australia.

But where there is none of the above social division, this does happen. In western South Australia cross-cousins are actually called brothers and sisters, and the cross-cousins of father and mother are named as though they were their brothers and sisters. This means that mother's male cross-cousin is called and classified with mother's brother instead of with father, as is more usual, and father's female cross-cousin is classified with father's sister instead of with mother. Now, as the custom is the same here as amongst the Nyul-Nyul, namely, that a man marries the daughter of an "uncle" (M.B.) and an "aunt" (f. sr), this use of the terms means that a man may marry the son's daughter of his mother's mother's brother instead of the latter's *daughter's* daughter. This was the only variation in the Bard system as compared with kinship and marriage in the Nyul-Nyul; there are more variations in the Northern Aluridja system, particularly in the terms applied to maternal relations; but it is in the Southern Aluridja, such as the Kokata, that the classifying of cross-cousins with brothers and sisters is carried to its logical conclusion on the father's side as well as the mother's side and in the younger generations as well as in those older than EGO. For example, sister's children are classified with his own sons and daughters. Another interesting feature of the developed Aluridja system is the use of only two terms for grandparents, corresponding to our grandfather and grandmother. In other words, the same terms are applied to father's parents as to mother's parents.

The Aluridja table shows the place of the terms in EGO's genealogy.

The Ungarinyin System. The fifth type is somewhat surprising at first sight. It is found in the Worora and Ungarinyin tribes just north of the Bard tribe across King Sound and north of the King Leopold Range and around Walcott Inlet and Port George IV. During my first hour or two at Walcott Inlet I asked a couple of natives a few kinship terms, but on looking over my notes in the evening, I was amazed to find that I had written down the one term, *KANDINGI*, for mother's brother, his father and his son, and the one term, *WAIINGI*, for wife's brother, wife's father and wife's father's father. On the basis of my knowledge of other kinship systems, I felt that there had been some misunderstanding, but the patient recording of the genealogies of the people around soon showed that I had been given the correct terms, and that I was dealing with an exceptional type of kinship system. As I have already said, it resembles the Nyul-Nyul system in prohibiting cross-cousin marriage and in tracing descent through four lines, but it also differs in several points:

(i) It applies the same term to people of succeeding generations, whereas no other types do this; in them the same term sometimes appears in alternate generations (being used reciprocally) but not as here; thus, in the Ungarinyin system, the term applied to a man is also applied to his father, father's father, son and son's son, while one term is applied to the sisters of all these men. In other words, the system is a vertical one, and with but one or two exceptions (e.g. own sister) is not concerned with relative ages. What it is concerned with is the relationship of local clans or groups to one another. Thus, if a man of one local clan or group be my "uncle", *KANDINGI*[15] (M.B.), then every man in it, irrespective of age, is my "uncle", and every woman is classified as my "mother", *ngadji*, being sister to *KANDINGI*. Likewise, if in another locality, one man is father-in-law, *WAIINGI*, to me, then every man is *WAIINGI*, and every woman, belonging to it by birth, is "wife", actual or eligible. This gives rise to one situation which seems very strange to us, namely, that

---

[15] The *-ng* in these Ungarinyin terms has the soft sound of *-ng* in singer.

wife's brother is called by the same term as wife's father, *WAIINGI*; this means that I may marry my wife's brother's daughter (a *maringi* or wife-woman), and this does happen.

The Ungarinyin do think of the various groups (local clans) within the tribe in this way; the country of one clan is my "uncle", of another is my "wife's mother's brother" and so on.

(ii) The second main difference from the Nyul-Nyul system is that the type marriage of the latter is not possible—for the daughter's daughter of mother's mother's brother is classified with mother, and cannot be a wife. Moreover, mother's mother's brother is not the important person in marriage matters that he is in the Nyul-Nyul type of organization. His place in this regard is taken by father's mother's brother, *WAIINGI*, who has to give a woman of his local clan, namely, his sister, daughter, son's daughter, or son's son's daughter, to EGO in marriage. One of these is a woman whom EGO could marry according to Nyul-Nyul law (f.m.b. son's d.), but the Ungarinyin do not think of it in that way, but rather from the point of view of the reciprocal duties of local groups.

(iii) There are other differences such as the impossibility of marriages with sister's son's daughter and sister's husband's sister, both of which occur in many tribes with the Nyul-Nyul system, but enough has been said to show how interesting the system is.

I have not referred to all the varieties of Australian kinship systems, but the foregoing should suffice to make us realize how necessary it is to understand the particular kinship system of a tribe before we can hope to understand its marriage law, and, as we shall see later, the general social behaviour of its members from childhood throughout life, in almost all of life's situations—in camping, hunting, fighting, visiting and in ceremonial life.

UNGARINYIN TABLE A

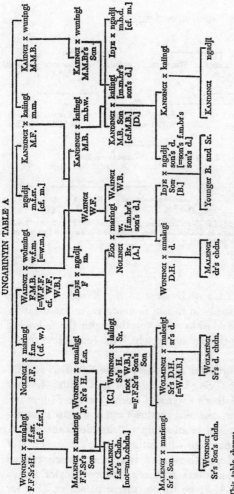

This table shows:

(a) The Vertical Nature of the System; e.g. M.F. = M.B. = M.B. Son's Son. The sisters of all these men are ngadji (=m) to EGO.
The only terms showing generation levels are (1) IDJE for F. and Son, NOLINGI for elder brothers and F.F., (2) laling = own sister.

(b) Type marriage is with f.m.b. son's d. So for Ego (A), also for (B), (C), and (D).

(c) Four lines of descent (or patrilineal clans) for EGO (F.F., F.M.B., M.F., M.M.B.); and two others which provide (1) spouses for F.M.B. and his line, and incidentally a wife for EGO; and (ii) spouses for f.f.sr., f.sr., sr. and. d. and for M.M.B. and his male line.

(d) Possibility of marriage with w.b.d., e.g. WUNINGI (F.F. Sr's H.) = F. Sr's H.

(e) No exchange of sisters in marriage.

(f) Sr's d. may marry W.M.B. (WOLMINGI).

UNGARINYIN TABLE B

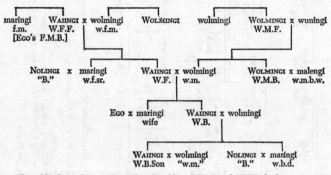

This table shows descent of EGO's wife; although W.F. and W.F.F. both marry women, who may be w.m. or w.f.m. to EGO, EGO's w.m. cannot be a br's d. of w.f.m., seeing that marriage with m.b.d. is prohibited.

APPENDIX

The Fourth Line of Descent in the Karadjeri System.
Reference was made to this in footnote 1. An examination of the Karadjeri kinship table together with the following notes will show the manner in which the fourth line comes into operation.

There is a fourth line of descent in the Karadjeri system. Its function is to bring the spouses of EGO, sister, father's sister, father's father's sister and mother's mother's brother, mother's brother, mother's brother's son and sister's daughter into a scheme of relationship which reflects the rule of prohibition of marriage with father's sister's daughter and the urge to find a mother-in-law who is not closely related to EGO. Thus mother's mother's brother marries into a group called *MALP*; he cannot marry *djam* (m.f.sr), for two men do not exchange sisters in marriage, and he does not marry a *kalod* woman for she is regarded as a "sister", and in the section system which prevails in the Karadjeri tribe, belongs to his section (see next chapter for the section grouping). Now, it is mother's mother's brother's marriage with a *Malp* woman which provides a wife for mother's brother and therefore a mother-in-law for EGO, while mother-in-law's brother (*RAMBA*) provided the wife (*kamad*) for mother's brother's son (*DJALEL*), and this woman's brother (*KAMAD*) is the father of *DJALEL's* son's wife, and so on.

Further, all of these males who provide wives for the male line of mother's father (i.e. for mother's brother, mother's brother's son and his son), must themselves have wives. Now, as I have said, mother's mother's brother (*KAMAD*) provides a wife for mother's brother by marrying into the *MALP* group, to whom therefore EGO is indirectly related through his wife, for this *Malp* woman is EGO's wife's mother's mother. And because marriage with mother's brother's daughter is allowed, each of the males referred to marries into the same *Malp* group or line. E.g. *RAMBA* (EGO's wife's mother's brother) marries actually or in terminology, his mother's brother's daughter (that is, EGO's mother's mother's brother's wife's brother's daughter) that is a daughter of a *MALP* man. She is a kind of *bap* (sister's daughter) or *berai* (mother). Likewise, *RAMBA's* son *KAMAD*, marrying his mother's brother's daughter, marries the son's daughter of *MALP*, who is usually called *djam*, but also *malp*; this *KAMAD's* son (another *RAMBA*) marries the son's son's daughter of *MALP*. Thus, the descent of the spouses of the mother's brother's line takes us into a fourth line, namely, the *MALP* line, the males of which are (to use the same set of terms) *MALP*, "*KAGA*", *MALP*, "*KAGA*" and so on. The only fresh term used is *MALP*, but the "*KAGA*" is qualified by some term such as *Djaminir* to show it is not own mother's brother.

There is no need for a fifth set of terms to denote the line into which these *MALP*-"*KAGA*" men marry, for their wives belong actually or in terminology to the line and families of EGO himself and his father's father, father, son and son's son. In other words, *MALP* (EGO's wife's mother's mother's brother) marries *kalod* (EGO's father's father's sister); *MALP's* son, "*KAGA*", marries *ibal* (EGO's father's sister); "*KAGA's*" son, *MALP*, (or indeed the older *MALP*) marries EGO's sister, and of course this *MALP's* son is EGO's own sister's son who married EGO's daughter.

Thus, if we think solely of EGO's descent, there are three lines of descent only, but if we take into consideration the female line of his wife and the male lines of the husbands of his sister and father's sister, we are taken to a fourth line.

This is all which the Karadjeri find necessary, and it enables them to pass into the Nyul-Nyul system with remarkably little dislocation of their own system, because they already have four lines of descent, though only three for EGO.

Chapter IV

SOCIAL GROUPS

PART I

EACH Australian tribe is subdivided into two or more social groups on the basis of locality, age, sex and uni-lateral relationship (moieties, clans, sections, subsections and semi-moieties):

(i) *The Local Group*. This has already been described.[1] It is generally patrilineal, patrilocal and exogamous; that is to say, the wife belongs to another group but lives in her husband's country and the children also belong there. But as we have seen, the members belong to the local group because their spirits belong to its country, and to definite "homes" along the path of some great culture-hero and ancestor in that country. In many tribes, each local group is also a distinct totemic clan; in such cases, the totem or totems belong to the country and its heroes, and therefore to all persons whose spirits belong there. In practice, this means that the descent of the totem or totems is patrilineal (through the father), though the deciding factor is the spiritual tie to the locality. In some tribes, however, the totemic differentiation of the local group is not so clear, and in any case the totemic aspect has seldom any social significance; it has mainly or solely to do with the sacred and ceremonial life.[2]

With regard to the kinship system, the local grouping divides a person's relations into "selected" groups, each of which can be thought of as a unity, and behaviour can be

[1] Chapter II.
[2] Chapter VI.

regulated accordingly. Thus, in my own local group or clan are my father, father's father, brother, son and son's son and all their brothers and sisters and brother's children, and probably also some parallel cousins, together with the wives of the married men. In another local group are my mother's brother, his father and children etc. Of course, there may not be as many members in a group as this list of relationship terms may suggest; sometimes there may only be a dozen or two. As a result of this local organization, a person regards one country as his mother's brother's country, another as his mother's mother's brother's country, and so on, even though other relations of both sexes belong there, and usually distinct kinship terms are applied, at least, to those of succeeding generations. For example, mother's brother and his son are distinguished by such terms as *Kaga* and *Djalel* respectively (Nyul-Nyul). But even so, the members of a local group or clan are regarded as "brothers" and "sisters" to each other, and as their mythological and spiritual ancestry is the same, we can see some reason for this point of view. The Ungarinyin of north-western Australia and also the Yaralde of Encounter Bay and the Lower Murray press this principle to its logical conclusion and for the most part apply one kinship term to all who belong by birth to any one local group. This attitude serves to strengthen and maintain the unity and cohesion of each group and incidentally of the whole tribe because each group is related to and dependent on the others; it is dependent on them for wives, uncles, mothers-in-law and other relations, and is bound to them by reciprocal duties. From this point of view, the tribe is not just an aggregate of individuals nor of inter-related individual families; rather it is a *family* of *countries* bound together by those sentiments which function between members of a family and its near relations. This is the key to the understanding of a tribal unity which is not based on political organization. It also shows how the kinship system can be extended throughout the whole community without becoming too diffuse to be of practical value.

(ii) *Age-grouping. Age and Authority.* Those who have associated with Aborigines know that great respect is shown to age, that is, to the elders—the men with grey hairs. One term usually applied to them signifies that their hair is going, or has gone, grey. They are however, distinguished from those who are too old to take an active and sensible part in daily life; the latter are referred to as "close-up dead". The treatment accorded to these varies, but they themselves like to remain in their own local country so that their spirits will be at "home" after death has come.

The male elders are those who exercise authority in the local groups, and at meetings of such groups. There is usually one head-man for each group who unofficially presides at meetings, settles quarrels and makes decisions bearing on the group's economic, social and ceremonial activities, though other elders also express their opinions. The position of elder and that of head-man are, however, not just a matter of age and grey hair; knowledge of tribal law and custom and the mythological sanction behind this, is also necessary. But as such intellectual equipment normally comes with age, following on initiation into the secret life, the term "elder" suffices to cover this position of authority and respect.

Age-grades. In the case of males there are roughly five stages in a person's life: childhood, during which there is much association with the mother; adolescence and initiation, during which the lad is passing through prescribed rituals and living "in seclusion" away from the corporate life of the group; early manhood and married life when he is learning more and more of tribal mythology and the sanctions or authority which it supplies for tribal law; "eldership" and a share in the control of social and ritual life; and finally old age. The stages are also marked by the imposition, especially during the years of initiation and early manhood, of taboos on certain valued articles of food, and their gradual relaxation during the years that follow. This custom has two effects; it disciplines the young fellow, teaching him self-control, and it preserves such good foods for the elders. But neither this nor any of the food-restriction customs of the Aborigines amount to "an old-age pension scheme" as some say who have never made careful inquiry into the incidence and function of food prohibitions. The people who benefit are not the "close-up dead", the pensioners, but those in the prime of life; they have, however, learnt self-control, and so share their food according to tribal rules.

The females, too, pass through stages, namely childhood; early married life which usually commences at puberty; later married life; and old age (close-up dead). They too have to observe restrictions on food, especially at times of pregnancy, but these are relaxed as one passes towards old age. Moreover, women of senior age are admitted occasionally to some portion of the secret knowledge of the tribe and to play a minor part in ritual; and in old age, kinship avoidance rules are relaxed.

Generation Lines. There is, however, a more definite age-grouping in many tribes. It is reflected in nearly all kinship systems in the use of distinct terms for the relations of succeeding generations, and in the frequent use of the same terms for relations of alternate generations. Thus, whereas I distinguish in terminology my brother from my father and son, in many tribes I call my father's father, *elder brother,* and my son's son, *younger brother,* and call my son by the term for *father.* Likewise, whereas I distinguish my cross-cousin from my uncle (mother's brother) and sister's son, I very often use the one term for mother's brother and sister's son.[3] In other words, members of alternate generations are grouped together as belonging to

[3] See the Karadjeri or Nyul-Nyul kinship tables in Chapter III.

one social group, or line. The significance of this is that marriage takes place between those grouped together, in accordance, of course, with kinship rules, whereas the two groups or lines should not inter-marry, because with very few exceptions in Australia a person may not marry into the generation of his parents or children.

There are sometimes reciprocal terms for these two groups; this is the case in the Broome district and also in all western South Australia. One pair of such terms is *Nganandarga* and *Tanamildjan*. I call *Nganandarga* the people of my own generation (brothers, sisters and cousins) and those of grandparents and grandchildren's generations, and *Tanamildjan*, my father, mother, uncle, aunt, parents-in-law, and also my children, nephews and nieces. It is from the former I get my wife, whether she is of my own age, or, as frequently happens, of the generation of my grandchildren, and it is for this reason that a native refers to the *Nganandarga* as the "right mob", that is, "right" from the point of view of marriage relationships. Incidentally, during secret chanting amongst the west-central tribes (the Pidjindjara and other Aluridja), the singers sit in two rings determined by this grouping. As I have said, these terms are reciprocal, which means that whereas my father and I are *Tanamildjan* to each other, and that whereas I regard my mother as *Tanamildjan*, my father or uncle or nephew etc. regard her as *Nganandarga*, that is, as belonging to their own generation line.

It is interesting to notice that this form of grouping functions both in western South Australia where there is no section system, and also around Broome where relations are grouped into four sections. As we shall see, it is really unnecessary when the latter is present; in any case, it does not depend on the presence of the latter, and indeed, it is inherent in most Australian kinship systems.

(iii) *Sex-grouping*. The biological fact of sex difference divides the Aborigines into two groups which for some purposes are mutually dependent, but otherwise are mutually exclusive. As members of a family they need each other, both for economic and biological purposes; although the Aborigines may not believe that sexual intercourse is the cause of conception, yet the father is necessary so that the pre-existent spirit of the child may be "found", and the mother is essential in order that it may be incarnated. With some exceptions their parts in the economic life are different; the woman gathers the roots, seeds and fruits and small animals, whereas the man does the hunting and fishing. He too makes the implements and weapons and does the fighting.

It is in the religious sphere, however, that we see the chief separation of the sexes. Initiation and the secret life are for the men alone; the women's part is subsidiary and "on the outside"; they show no interest in the inside ritual: "That's man business," they say. Likewise, men will *not* discuss the physiological functions which are peculiar to woman and motherhood; "that woman's business, you ask some woman," says the man. Moreover, in Central and north-central Australia, at least, the women have secret myths and ritual dances of their own, the knowledge and performance of which marks and strengthens their solidarity as a social group, and prevents them from being overcome by an inferiority complex. Needless to say, they will not reveal anything of their secret life to the men.

In Central and south-eastern Australia there is another way in which the natural grouping of the two sexes is marked, namely, by sex totems; all the men of the tribe are symbolized by one bird or bush and all the women by another. This totem is usually thought of as the mate, or the brother (or sister in the case of the women) of the group. Moreover, to hurt or kill one another's totem is regarded as an insult or injury and is resented. Quarrelling and fighting follow. Thus, the women as a group stand up to the men as a group. This is normally a ritual matter and in south-eastern Victoria is the setting of pre-arranged elopements and marriages.

(iv) *Social Totemic Clans.* The clan is a grouping of people related in one line only, through the father or through the mother, but not through both. In other words, a person belongs to his father's and father's father's clan by birth, if clan descent in the tribe be patrilineal, but if this be matrilineal, he belongs to the clan of his mother and mother's mother. All the members of a clan are related to one another because in theory at least, they share a common descent line.

The members of a local group or subdivision of a tribe (apart from the wives who belong elsewhere) normally form a clan, for membership of that group is unilateral, being reckoned in the male line. But as we have seen, this is fundamentally a matter of the existence of spirit-homes in the locality and the finding of the pre-existent spirits by the fathers. Of course, as *we* look at it, the descent is patrilineal, yet it is really a matter of locality: my spirit pre-existed in my country long before my father was born, and so I do not belong to it because I am his son. It is therefore helpful to distinguish this territorial form of clan from the social clan even though they may have some features in common, and may even coincide; this would happen if a social clan were both patrilineal and limited to one locality. On the other hand, if the social clans of a tribe be matrilineal, the members of each clan will belong to two or more local clans. In such a case, an individual has two loyalties, one to his local clan and another to the scattered group of people which constitutes his social clan.

There is, moreover, a distinguishing feature of the social clan, namely, that all its members profess a relationship not only to one another, but also to one (or more) natural species, which is their totem. They say that the totem is their flesh or meat; or conversely, if you ask a native of eastern Australia "what is his meat", he will give you the name of his clan totem—kangaroo, emu or such like. He will, moreover, usually say that it is his friend, or his guardian, and that he must not injure, kill or eat it, and further that he must not marry any one who has the same totem, or flesh, for that would be incest, like marrying one's sister or mother. In other words, these social totemic clans are exogamous. I believe, too, that the genuine *social* totemic clans in Australia are always matrilineal in descent, and that the view of the totem as the totemite's "meat" or flesh expresses the Aboriginal belief that "flesh and blood" are inherited through the mother alone and not through the father.

These matrilineal social totemic clans are, or were, found chiefly in south-western Queensland, western New South Wales and Victoria, eastern South Australia (except along the Lower Murray and around Adelaide), and in north-western Arnhem Land.

The territorial clans have some features in common with these matrilineal social clans, though if the latter exist in the same tribe, the only common feature is the bare principle of unilateral descent, for its character differs, being reckoned through the father and not through the mother. This is an important difference, not only because the patrilineal principle is an expression of the belief in local spirit-centres and the doctrine of pre-existence and the "finding" of the spirit child, whereas the matrilineal principle is physiological in character, but also because as far as the women are concerned, the territorial clan can never have as much significance as does the social clan; membership of the latter never varies and its meaning for the individual does not depend on knowledge or ritual; though the members of any one matrilineal clan belong, as they usually do, to different parts of the tribe, yet, male and female, they are all equally members of the clan—they are relations one of another and of one totem which they all respect. But with regard to the territorial clan matters are very different, especially for the females. Once a woman reaches puberty she goes to live with her husband's local clan and her children belong to the same clan; thus, she practically becomes an outsider to her own local clan. Moreover, in most cases, the female members of a territorial clan are never much more than outsiders as far as the real nature and function of that form of clan is concerned, for this has to do with the religious or cult-life of the tribe, membership of which is limited to the males and gained through initiation. Until this ritual admission has been made, even the males are only what might be called associate-members.

These local clans, which incidentally are totemic or at least have ceremonial functions connected with the increase of natural species, are therefore distinct from social clans, and the question is: "Are there any territorial clans which are not at the same time cult-clans?" This may have been so in parts of the coast of New South Wales and eastern Victoria and along the Lower Murray, but unfortunately it is almost or altogether too late to decide the matter. However, amongst the Kattang of Port Stephens and the Manning River, the totem of the territorial clan had none of the features of a social totem; it was not regarded as the totemite's flesh, nor did it act as his guardian spirit; and no taboo was observed with regard to killing or eating it. On the other hand, it was and is sometimes referred to as a man's "dreaming". This takes us into the spiritual, if not the cult-realm. Likewise, in parts of northern Australia, especially in the north-west and in Cape York Peninsula, the totemism associated with the territorial clans is fundamentally connected with the cult-life—the "dreaming", the culture-heroes and the increase-ceremonies.

The essential matrilineal nature of social clans is also seen in two other forms of social grouping which will be discussed more fully in Part II of this chapter, namely, the section and subsection systems. These two are fundamentally one, the second being formed by a subdivision of the four groups of the first. In both, descent is matrilineal, but indirectly so. That is, the section (or subsection) group of an individual is not the same as his mother's, but it depends on hers. In the Kamilaroi tribe, New South Wales, for example, the four sections are Ipai and Kambu, Kabi and Mari. The child of a woman of Ipai is always Kambu, and vice versa, and so with Kabi and Mari. Moreover, in many tribes these groupings are also totemic: each section includes not only a number of human beings but also one or more natural species towards which the former adopt some special attitude; they respect it and refrain from injuring or eating it, and it is even believed to watch over them, warning them of danger.

A section, however, is not, properly speaking, a clan, seeing that descent does not take place within it; it might be thought of as a semi-clan, and then two sections, if related reciprocally as parent and child, would constitute a clan. But any one section has some clan features: its members are related as "brothers" and "sisters" and where the section is totemic, they are bound together by a common relation to its totems; above all, they are matrilineal, expressing the belief that flesh and blood are inherited through the mother, the medium of incarnation, whereas, from this point of view, the father does not count—he is "thrown away".

The section system of dividing society into four social groups seldom exists in the same tribe with social totemic clans. It may be that possessing so many of their features, it supersedes them. Still, they used to co-exist with the latter in parts of central New South Wales, but the various ways in which they were related to the totemic clans in neighbouring tribes suggests that the section system was comparatively recent in the region.[4] In Western Australia,

[4] In part of the Wiradjeri tribe no totemic clan appeared in two sections; whereas in another part of that tribe and amongst two of its neighbours, each totemic clan (and totem) was found in the two sections related as mother and child. (See Part II of this chapter); also A. P. Elkin, *Studies in Australian Totemism. Oceania* Monographs, no. 2, pp. 112–14.

[5] Females, young and middle-aged.

[6] Paddling a dug-out canoe. Sail rolled up. North Coast.

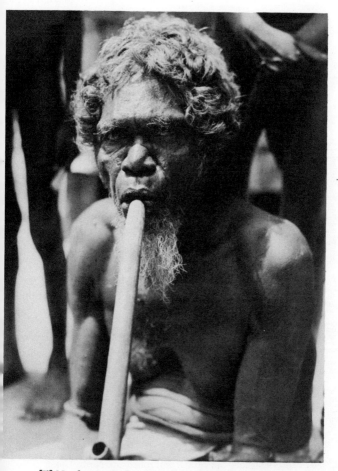

[7] North-east Arnhem-Lander with Malay-type pipe.

[8] A family, Bathurst Island.

sections exist along with local cult-clans, but have no significance as far as these are concerned.

To sum up, territorial clans should be distinguished from
social totemic clans, and the latter are probably always
matrilineal. It is doubtful whether the totems of patrilineal
territorial clans were ever really social in function; apart
from a few doubtful cases, they belong to the cult-life.

(v) *Moieties.* Moiety means half, and over quite a large
area of Australia, each tribe is divided into two halves or
moieties. This division, known as the dual organization, is
a definite social and ceremonial grouping. Moreover, it is
usually extended to embrace all things in heaven and earth
so that it is also totemic in nature, bringing man and nature into a common scheme which is animistic or even
"personal" in character. More specifically, each moiety has
in some regions an animal or bird for its totem and name,
such as eagle-hawk and crow, white cockatoo and black
cockatoo, plains kangaroo and the hill kangaroo. This is
the case in western New South Wales and Victoria, south-
west of Western Australia and Northern Kimberley. Each
moiety consists of a group of people related either patri-
lineally or matrilineally, and so has something of the nature of a clan. Moieties are also for the most part exogamous though not absolutely, because one type of second
cousin, with whom marriage is allowed in many tribes as
an alternate spouse, must belong to a person's own moiety.
This person is mother's mother's brother's son's daughter.[5]
The chief proviso is that the two persons should not belong to the one social totemic clan and therefore be of the
one flesh. They would probably never belong to the one
local group (territorial clan) for they are related as a man
and son's daughter of the mother's "uncle", that is, she
belongs to the local group of the man's mother's mother's
brother. This just means, surprising though it may seem,

[5] This subject is explained further when discussing the subsections and alternate marriages in Part II of this chapter.

that the primary function of the dual organization is *not* to control marriage. In actual practice, however, where there are patrilineal moieties in a tribe with only patrilineal territorial clans, the moieties are exogamous, but only because the local groups are so. In any case, the kinship system and local organization are quite capable of regulating marriage without moieties, social matrilineal clans, sections or subsections, as is the case in western South Australia, and several similar regions of Australia.

But though this is true, where a tribe has adopted the moiety system, a definite grouping of relations is ultimately made, which, of course, varies according to the principle of descent; if it be patrilineal, my own moiety includes my father and my children, while my mother and sister's children belong to the other moiety. But if it be matrilineal, I belong to my mother's moiety and my father belongs to the other one. In any case, the dual division separates brothers and sisters on the one hand from cross-cousins, and necessitates the use of distinct terms for these two groups of relations. As we have seen in Chapter III, where such a division is absent, this distinction is not necessarily made.[6]

The relationship of the moiety organization to kinship and marriage is incidental to its main function which is

[6] In Part II of this chapter we shall have to distinguish moieties (a) from descent lines of sections and subsections; these do form halves of the tribe, but they are not definite social groupings, and (b) from generation levels. Sometimes, as in part of Eastern Kimberley and south-west of Western Australia, there are definite names (as distinct from reciprocal terms) for the intermarrying groups which incidentally belong to alternate generations. But this does not make them moieties, even though they function sometimes as distinct groups, because the members of such a half of the tribe are not related as father-child or mother-child. They are brothers, sisters, husbands, wives, cousins, and also grandparents and grandchildren to each other. It would be using the term moiety rather loosely to apply it to such a division.

almost wholly ceremonial. In many tribes, the members of one moiety camp apart from the members of the other moiety, on opposite sides of a creek, for example, or on high ground and low ground respectively. But such a disposition of families is seldom seen except at the time of some ceremony, for at other times only a few families camp together and then they are usually members of the one local group.[7]

Ball games are, or were, played in Victoria and the Gulf of Carpentaria country by moieties, and where the full facts are known these games are shown to form part of a ceremonial programme—for example, of initiation. Indeed, it is in the ceremonial life that the moiety organization is of importance—in initiation, totemic and burial rituals. The members of each moiety have particular duties to perform, prohibitions to observe, and privileges to enjoy, and this is true whether the moieties be patrilineal or matrilineal; if there be any difference, the characteristics are most marked in the case of matrilineal moieties, but this may be only apparent, the result of the greater knowledge we have of them. Moreover, the opposition which is symbolized by the ball games, is sometimes expressed in these rituals; thus in north-eastern South Australia, the members of one moiety have the privilege of "killing" or initiating a youth of the other moiety as a means of settling a grievance or "debt". It is thus correct to speak of an opposition of the moieties of the dual organization in Australia.

It is interesting to notice that the moieties are, generally speaking, matrilineal in eastern Australia, south of the Gulf of Carpentaria and east of Lakes Eyre and Gairdner, and that they formerly existed over most of that region, sometimes with, and sometimes without, the section system. Where there was no section system and even some-

[7] When I visited Kunmunya Mission at Port George IV in 1928, the native camps were arranged according to moieties. There was a large number present, attracted by the mission.

times where there was such, each matrilineal moiety consisted of a number of matrilineal social totemic clans. Matrilineal moieties were also found in western Arnhem Land and in a small region around Perth, Western Australia, but none existed in the eastern region along the coast of New South Wales, eastern and south-eastern Victoria, nor in the Lower Murray-Adelaide district.

Patrilineal moieties exist in the Northern Kimberley, in much of the east of the Northern Territory (combined with subsections), in most of Cape York Peninsula south of the Batavia River, and strangely enough in former days in a small isolated region in south-central Victoria and possibly also in a small region around Albany in Western Australia.

(vi) *Sections, Subsections and Semi-moieties.* Reference has been made to the division of some tribes into four or eight social groups with their own rules of marriage and descent. These groups have been called marriage classes, but as the term class bears a significance of social distinctions which finds no place in the thought and life of the Aborigines, it is better to use the neutral words section and subsection, as has been the practice in scientific writings for many years now. Moreover, as we shall see, the function of these groupings is not so much to regulate marriage, as to group types of relations in certain useful ways, more particularly so as to separate persons related on the one hand as cross-cousins and on the other, as parent and child. This will be made clearer in Part II of the chapter.

The study of sections, subsections and semi-moieties may seem to savour somewhat of mathematics, but that is only because of their even number and the rules of marriage and descent which are associated with them. This allows symbols to be used in place of the named groupings. But, to the Aborigines, these groupings are of great importance and interest in their social life; indeed, except when discussing them with individuals of an inquiring turn of mind or with anthropologists (and sometimes even then), the natives always think of definite persons, their totems, and the mutual behaviour which is prescribed for the speakers and the groups under consideration. If then we are to understand the Aborigines, we must understand the meaning and function of the sections, subsections and semi-moieties.

PART II SECTIONS

Over a large area of Western Australia from Derby and the lower Fitzroy down the coast to the Gascoyne River and thence south-east to Laverton; in the southern part of the Aranda tribe (on the Macumba River, north of Lake Eyre); over most of Queensland (except the far north and far west) and in north-eastern and central New South Wales, a person's relations are divided into four named groups or sections. Many people know the names used by the Kamilaroi and neighbouring tribes of New South Wales (Ipai, Kambu, Mari and Kabi), while in Western Australia the commonest names are Panaka, Burong, Karimba and Paldjeri. There are often, too, feminine forms of these names. Associated with these groups are rules of marriage and descent, which can be represented as follows:

For the Kamilaroi tribe:

$$\begin{array}{c} \nwarrow \text{Kambu} = \text{Mari} \nearrow \\ \swarrow \text{Ipai} = \text{Kabi} \searrow \end{array}$$

and for the Karadjeri and Nyul-Nyul tribes:

$$\begin{array}{c} \nwarrow \text{Panaka} = \text{Burong} \nearrow \\ \swarrow \text{Karimba} = \text{Paldjeri} \searrow \end{array}$$

The sign = connects intermarrying sections and the arrow sign connects the sections of mother and child.

Using the Nyul-Nyul names, the diagram represents the following facts; a man of Panaka section marries a woman of Burong section and her child belongs to Paldjeri section; further, a Paldjeri man marries a Karimba woman and her child is Panaka. Or to start with a Burong man; his wife is Panaka and her children are Karimba; his son marries a Paldjeri woman whose children belong to Burong.

This rule, if followed, results in a certain grouping of relations. If I am a Panaka man, my wife is Burong, my son is Paldjeri and my son's wife is Karimba and my son's son is back in my section, Panaka. Further, as I am Panaka, and Panaka's mother is found in section Karimba, therefore my mother is Karimba and of course, my father is Paldjeri. My father's sister is likewise Paldjeri and my mother's brother is Karimba. The latter's wife is Paldjeri and his children are Burong; incidentally, my father's sister's children are also Burong, seeing that she is Paldjeri. Now these two lots of Burong people are my cross-cousins. This means that my cross-cousins and my wife, (I being Panaka) are both found in the one section, Burong. My sister is, of course, in my own section, Panaka; her husband is therefore in Burong, and her children (my nephews and nieces) are in Karimba. Again, my mother is Karimba; her mother is Panaka and therefore my mother's mother's brother is Panaka; now his wife is Burong and his daughter is therefore in Paldjeri; from this we see that my mother's mother's brother's daughter's daughter is in Burong where my wife is also found.

These and other relations can be tabulated in the following table. It is usual for the purpose of generalization and discussion to substitute the letters A, B, C and D for the section names; I have, therefore, added them under the Nyul-Nyul section names to help readers later on in this chapter or when consulting other works on the Aborigines.

Now, the daughter of mother's mother's brother's daughter is one of the kinds of second cousin, who can be married according to the Aranda and Nyul-Nyul rules. But as Panaka's cross-cousin is also in Burong, it follows that whether the rule of marriage be own cross-cousin or

EGO; B; sr;
m.m.b.son's d.
(and son);
m.f.sr's son's d.   PANAKA=BURONG
(and son);   (A)   (B)
f.m.b.d.d. (and
son);

f.f.sr's dr's d.
(and son);
F.F.; m.m.;
M.M.B.;
W.M.F.;
Son's son and d.

m.; M.B.; W.F.;
f.m.b.d. (and
son)   KARIMBA=PALDJERI
f.f.sr's d. (and   (C)   (D)
son)
son's w.; Dr's
Hd.
sr's chdn.

w; W.B.; Sr's Hd;
cross-cousins;
m.m.b.d.d. (and
son);
m.f.sr's d.d. (and
son);
f.m.b.son's d. (and
son;

f.f.sr's son's d. (and
son);
f.m.; m.m.b.w.;
w.m.m.
dr's chdn;
sr's son's chdn.

F.; f.sr; w.m.;
m.m.b.d. (and
son);
m.f.sr's d. (and
son);
chdn.
Sr's Dr's H.; sr's
son's w.

second cousin,[8] the spouse is found in the same section. If, then, cross-cousin marriage be prohibited, I, a Panaka man, must not think of all Burong young women as possible wives to me; I must distinguish between certain types of Burong relations, even of my own age. In other words, the section system is not sufficient in itself, or combined with a consideration of age, to regulate marriage, unless cross-cousin marriage is permitted. In the vast majority of tribes, however, with sections, cross-cousin marriage is forbidden. Thus, the essential factor in determining marriage mates is kinship relationship, even if there be sections. What the latter do is to summarize relations into four groups, in one of which a possible spouse is normally found; but in the same group various other types of relations are also included.

[8] That is, one of the four second cousins allowed by the Aranda and similar systems. See previous chapter.

Sections, Generation Lines and Cross-cousins. A much more important function performed by the sections is the grouping of relations according to alternate generation lines and cross-cousin relationships. Thus, the brothers and sisters, son's children and father's father of a Panaka man are in his own section, while his cross-cousins, wife, sister's husband, mother's mother's brother's wife, sister's son's children are Burong. On the other hand, such relations as mother and her brother and wife's father and sister's children belong to Karimba, and father, children, and wife's mother belong to Paldjeri.

These and other members of each section can be derived from the diagram of marriage and descent in the way I have shown above.

Thus, in the case of a Panaka man, the members of his own, his grandfather's and grandchildren's generations belong to Panaka and Burong sections, while the members of his parents' and children's generations are Karimba and Paldjeri. In other words, each intermarrying pair of sections represents a generation line as this is conceived by the Aborigines. To use the terms referred to when dealing with age grouping, Panaka-Burong people are *nganandarga* to one another, but *tanamildjan* to Karimba-Paldjeri.

But the section system also divides each of these generation lines into cross-cousin groups; thus, Panaka's cross-cousins are found in Burong and vice versa, and the same is true of Karimba and Paldjeri.[9]

[9] These two functions of the section system suggest how it could have been evolved, namely, by separating on the one hand brothers and sisters from cross-cousins, and husband and wife in another, say B; cross-cousin and wife in another, say B; mother and mother's brother in a third, say C, which belongs to a generation one above, and a fourth, D, which contains mother's cross-cousins, who in some tribes

Sections and Maternal Descent. One very interesting point emerges from a study of the section system, namely, that in the minds of the natives its principle of descent is always based on the mother-child relationship. Not only do they speak of it in that way, namely, from Burong woman, Paldjeri child, but in any case of alternate or irregular marriage, the father is "thrown away"; that is, he is not considered. The child's section is the one related to its mother's section, as child to mother; or as it is often put: the child goes into the section to which it would belong, if the mother had married according to the normal rule. Thus, in the Broome district a man of Panaka section normally marries a woman of Burong section and his children are Paldjeri; but if he marries one of the second cousins who belong like himself to Panaka, his children go into Karimba, not, however, because they are his children, but because they are the children of a woman of Panaka.

The same principle is shown in the way the natives of north-western Australia adjust the sections of different tribes, especially when the sections may have the same names, but are differently arranged. They drop the person's own section and place him in the other tribe according to the section of his mother. For example, around Broome and Lagrange the arrangement of the sections is

$$\left(\begin{array}{c} \nearrow \ \text{Panaka} = \text{Burong} \ \nwarrow \\ \searrow \ \text{Karimba} = \text{Paldjeri} \ \swarrow \end{array} \right)$$

whereas in the De Grey district it is

$$\begin{array}{c} \nearrow \ \text{Paldjeri} = \text{Burong} \ \nwarrow \\ \searrow \ \text{Karimba} = \text{Panaka} \ \swarrow \end{array}$$

are father and father's sister; in such tribes the latter is wife's mother and therefore wife's father is in C; indeed, he is a mother's brother. A principle of marriage and descent is inherent in the grouping, and this, combined with the Aborigines' custom of linking alternate generations together, would give the grouping of relations as we know it.

If a Karimba man of a Broome tribe goes to the De Grey, he is no longer Karimba, and in the method of adjustment, neither his nor his father's section is considered. He receives status according to the section of his mother. She actually was a Panaka woman in his own tribe at Broome. He is now regarded as the son of a Panaka woman in the De Grey. This makes him Burong, and to that section he belongs as long as he remains on the De Grey.

Thus, in addition to expressing the principle of generation lines and the important distinction between cross-cousins and brothers, the section system expresses the native belief that social affiliation or grouping is derived from the mother, and not from the father.

Sections and Natural Species. This brings us to another important aspect and function of the section system: it usually expresses the Aborigines' general totemistic view of life, namely, that man and natural species share a common life and are mutually interdependent—a belief which is symbolized by the bearing of the names of one or more natural species by groups of human beings. Now, this is very often true of the sections, especially in eastern Australia and in some tribes in Western Australia; that is, the members of any one section bear the names of one or more of the totemic species which belong to that section, and take up some ritual attitude towards such species. This will be discussed again in the chapter on Totemism; it is sufficient to notice here that section totemism is a variety of social totemism; the latter is matrilineal in descent and symbolizes that special relationship of flesh and blood which exists between a mother and her child, and which we have already seen is a feature of the section system.

Sections and Moieties. In most of Queensland and about half of New South Wales, the sections are associated with matrilineal moieties, mother-child pair of sections being in one moiety, and the other pair being in the second moiety. Thus, in the Kamilaroi tribe, the Ipai-Kambu sections are in the Eaglehawk moiety and the Kabi-Mari pair are in the Crow moiety. This makes no difference to the functioning of the sections, nor is it necessary that sections were developed by subdivision of the moieties. In any case, they are spreading in parts of Western Australia and New South Wales (namely, the Laverton-Warburton Ranges region and the north coast of New South Wales) where there was no moiety system prevailing.

SUBSECTIONS

What has been said of the section system is true in principle for the subsection system, according to which a person's relations are divided amongst eight groups instead of four. This is clearly a subdivision of the section system, on the basis of the distinction between cross-cousins and the children of cross-cousins. As we have already seen a man of A (Panaka) finds in B (Burong) not only his cross-cousins, but also his mother's mother's brother's daughter's daughter (and of course her brother);—his father's father's sister's son's daughter also belongs to the same section. Now, if cross-cousin marriage be prohibited, the section system, as we have already observed, is not of much use as a guide to marriage. But if the section B were divided into say, B^1 and B^2, and my cross-cousins grouped in B^2, leaving the second cousins whom I could marry in B^1, then the system would be of more use for the purpose of marriage regulation. And, this is what, in effect, has happened to each section. The result is the system of eight named social groups which seems to have arisen in Eastern Kimberley and spread in a south-eastern direction and also west and north-east and east. It is still spreading in Arnhem Land and during the past few years has spread west to Fitzroy Crossing, and we have known for many years that it spread through several parts of the Aranda tribe, but did not reach its southern portion.

I give in the following diagram the Eastern Kimberley subsection names:

$$
\left(\begin{array}{l}
\nearrow \\
\swarrow
\end{array}\left(\begin{array}{l}
\nearrow \\
\subset
\end{array}\right.\right.
\begin{array}{llll}
A^1 & \text{Djangala} & = \text{Djungura} & B^1 \\
A^2 & \text{Djuru} & = \text{Djoan} & B^2 \\
C^1 & \text{Djoalyi} & = \text{Djakara} & D^1 \\
C^2 & \text{Djoangari} & = \text{Djambadjina} & D^2
\end{array}
\left.\left.\begin{array}{l}
\nwarrow \\
\searrow
\end{array}\right)\right)
\begin{array}{l}
\nwarrow \\
\swarrow
\end{array}
$$

The arrows unite subsections of mother and child. The letters alongside the names[10] are used for the purpose of generalization and express the principle that the system is formed by the subdivision of each of the four groups of the section system. If I belong to A^1, my cross-cousin belongs to B^2, but the daughter of my mother's cross-cousin belongs to B^1, and normally in tribes with the subsection system, I may marry her or a woman classed with her. Conversely, the cross-cousin of A^2 is in B^1, and his correct wife is in B^2, and so on with all the groups. The diagram of marriage and descent of the subsections enables us to determine the subsection of all the relations of any individual, provided, of course, that we know his subsection. Conversely, each subsection normally contains a limited number of classes of relations, reckoning from any one person. Thus, the father of A^1 is in D^2, his mother in C^2, his sister's son in C^1, and so on; that is, if each person marries the type of second cousin implied in the Aranda system (mother's mother's brother's daughter's daughter, etc.).

We must remember that this is not a matter of algebra or academic calculations. The Aborigines give the inquirer the table as I have recorded it here, and while they are doing so, they are thinking of definite individuals—husbands, wives, sons and daughters, mothers-in-law, and so on. Djangala man marries Djungura and has children Djambadjina; Djuru man marries Djoan woman and their children are Djakara. In this way they can work through

---

[10] The Dj at the beginning of each of the names represents the sound of the English j. There are feminine forms of these names and even in some tribes, forms to be used for children.

the complete subsection pattern. But in addition, the careful recording of genealogies reveals this ideal pattern even though there may be departures from it. It is learnt by the child in the natural way as the years pass by. As range of contacts increases, he learns that this person who is his "uncle" is also Djoangari, and that person, his cross-cousin, is Djoan and so on; at the same time he learns the kind of behaviour he should adopt towards his various Djoangari, Djoan and other subsection groups of relations. Speaking generally, there are eight patterns of behaviour, that is, one for each subsection group, sometimes with modifications for the two sexes. This makes the system a very useful method of summarizing the twenty classes of relations that an individual possesses—a number which would be increased by about eight if the sexes were always denoted by different terms. It also makes the system a very useful guide to social behaviour.

This is especially true in inter-tribal meetings. It is much easier for one group to learn the other's subsection system than to bother about all its kinship terms, and so mutual behaviour during the gatherings is largely controlled by the subsection grouping, but only, of course, because fundamentally this is a grouping of kinship relations. Thus, as far as a man of A^1 is concerned, B^1 is the wife group, D^2 the children or father's group, C^2 the mother's group, A^2 the mother's mother's brother's group and B^2 the cross-cousin group. Of course, there are other relations in each of these groups, but except in the case of close relations, and certainly as far as strangers are concerned, the above socially significant relationships in each subsection suffice to indicate the mutual behaviour to be adopted. There is little doubt that the practical usefulness of the system at meetings of an inter-tribal character is the cause of its spread, even into tribes whose kinship system and marriage rule are not easily adjusted to it. I have referred in the first chapter to such a case, namely, from north-eastern Arnhem Land, and a similar adjustment in the descent lines

is being made by a Daly River tribe. This system does not
adequately group relations in tribes with cross-cousin marriage, for in these the same terms are used for cross-cousins
and the children of mother's female cross-cousin and of
father's male cross-cousin; and therefore, when the subsection system is introduced, separating these two groups
of relations, the one term would appear in two subsections. In such tribes, however, the Aborigines rearrange
the subsections so that a man of A^1 finds in B^1 his cross-
cousins as well as his marriageable second cousins. He may
also marry into B^2 which includes his sister's son's daughter,
a marriage widely associated with the subsection system.

Likewise, people with a subsection system are quite capable of adjusting the subsections to the sections of their
neighbours, equating their A^1 and A^2 to the A of the latter
and so on. This usually leads to the spread of the subsection terms. Thus, in 1928, the Punaba tribe at Fitzroy
Crossing had the same four sections as the Broome tribes,
which they equated to the subsections of the Lunga, their
north-eastern neighbours, as follows:

Panaka	= Djambadjina Djakara		Burong	= Djoangari Djoalyi
Karimba	= Djoan Djungura		Paldjeri	= Djuru Djangala

Now, however, they have adopted the subsection system.
Incidentally, this has not caused any difficulty here because the Punaba kinship system and rule of marriage
were of the Nyul-Nyul type, an important feature of which
is the distinction of cross-cousins from second cousins. This
means in practice that each of the four sections is divided
into two divisions: $Panaka^1$ and $Panaka^2$ and so on.

Descent of the Subsections. The descent of the subsections, like that of the sections, is indirect matrilineal; in
other words, the child's subsection is not the same as its
mother's, but it does depend on hers. A child of a woman
of subsection Djungura (or B^1) is always Djambadjina

(D^2) whether the father belongs to the group from which her husband should normally come or not. For example, there are definite matrilineal cycles of descent; omitting the sons, and using the letters for simplicity, the daughter of B^1 is D^2, her daughter is B^2 whose daughter is D^1, and the daughter of D^1 belongs to B^1, thus completing the cycle of descent through the mothers and daughters. The other cycle is A^1–C^1–A^2–C^2–A^1.

Subsections and Totemism. Like the section system, the subsection system is frequently combined with totemism, and indeed where it has been spreading recently, it has done so partly as a system of social totemism; that is, each subsection contains not only a number of human beings, but also one or more natural species, towards which the former adopt a special attitude of respect. This symbolizes the fact that the members of a subsection are "one relation" —all of "one skin", as the natives say. In the south-east part of the subsection area, the subsections are combined with cult totemism; this raises a complex problem to which reference will be made in the chapter on Totemism.

Alternate and Irregular Marriages. The division of the tribe into eight or into four groups, together with the rule that the members of any one group can only marry into one other group, and that one definitely named, must seem to us to be a strange attempt on the part of society to control human affections: for the prohibition on marriage covers not only the members of one's own family, not only persons of one's parents' or children's generation, but also persons who, as far as distance of relationship is concerned, are no closer than those who can be married. Thus, to take the subsection system, the norm is that a man of A^1 should marry a woman of B^1 and not of any other subsection. This woman of B^1 is to be a second cousin (own or tribal) of the mother's mother's brother's daughter's daughter type. But A^2 includes second cousins of almost the same type and certainly of the same degree, for example, a granddaughter of the same mother's mother's brother, only in this case it is the latter's *son's* daughter instead of his daughter's daughter; likewise, though subsection B^2 is the group of the forbidden cross-cousin, it contains probably quite distant parallel cousins of the cross-cousin (EGO's mother's mother's sister's son's daughter and so on) who are not first cousins. In view of these facts, we might well ask, is not the permission of marriage with one of these groups of second cousin, and its prohibition with the others, very arbitrary? And further, can human nature be so confined to channels in this matter of sex relations? The answers are: first, it is an arbitrary arrangement; the purpose of the subsection system and also of the section system seems to be concerned more with the descent of groups through the mother than with the control of marriage; and second, that the system does not regulate human affections, and apparently is not expected to do so. In all tribes of which I have definite information, alternate marriages are allowed, and indeed, provided for. Thus, in some section tribes, a man may marry into his own section as well as into the ideal section; and in some subsection tribes, a man of A^1, for example, may marry into B^2 or B^1, in others into A^2 or B^1, and in others into any of these three groups.

When I first came across marriage between persons of the one section, I was somewhat astounded, but I soon realized that the formal and mathematical nature of the section system had caused me to overlook the actual relations in a man's own section. The alternate marriage allowed was, as I have already said, with a second cousin of the mother's mother's brother's son's daughter type, and where there are subsections, this amounts to marriage between A^1 and A^2. In the Nyul-Nyul tribe the men put this very simply by saying that a person could marry his Kamad (mother's mother's brother's son's daughter).

All this indicates that the Aborigines are human beings and that their various systems of social organization were made for man and not man for these systems. Their society recognizes this fact, allows for alternate marriages and provides rules of descent which relate solely to the mothers so far as social grouping is concerned.[11]

Moiety means half, and a moiety organization means that for certain purposes the community is divided into two parts, membership of which is regulated by a principle of descent. It may be thought that the discussion of semi-moieties with which this section is concerned, should follow on a study of the moiety system, but this is not so; the semi- or half-moieties to be discussed here are not primarily a subdivision of moieties but a combination of pairs of subsections. There are eight subsections in a tribe; if we group them into the right four pairs, we have four semi-moieties. The question is which pairs? A^1-B^1, A^2-B^2, etc. are intermarrying pairs; one is not descended from the other and members of an Australian moiety are related by unilateral descent (i.e. in one line, male or female). A^1-A^2, B^1-B^2, C^1-C^2 and D^1-D^2 only give us four sections and once again the two subsections of any one of these pairs are not linked by descent; that is, they are not related as parent and child. Likewise, no two subsections of either matrilineal cycle give us the required semi-moieties, because though, for example, D^2 is the child of a woman of B^1, the opposite is not true; the child of D^2 is outside the D^2-B^1 grouping. A study of the subsection table will show that A^1-D^2 is a semi-moiety, because, if the marriage norm be followed, A^1 is the father of a person of D^2, and D^2 is the father of a person of D^1; likewise, A^2-D^1, C^1-B^1 and C^2-B^2 are semi-moieties. But of which moiety is each of these pairs half? A^1-D^2 is half of A-D moiety; the other half is A^2-D^1. Likewise, C^1-B^1 and

[11] With regard to the ceremonial life, the descent is fundamentally patrilineal and local, and marriage into an alternate subsection may sometimes affect the child's position in the cult-life.

C^2-B^2 are halves of the one moiety. That is, each patrilineal "half" of the tribe is itself divided into two patrilineal
"halves".

So much for the theory and what looks like algebra. By
going to the tribes along the southern shores of the Gulf
of Carpentaria we would find this form of organization
functioning and named. In some other tribes extending
down into Central Australia, the semi-moieties are not
named, but are functioning.

Why should this further complexity be added to the native social organization? The explanation is found in the
local organization and in the religious aspect of Aboriginal
life, both of which are intimately linked. As we have seen,
the local groups are patrilineal, and therefore with a subsection system, the father-child couple of subsections (e.g.
A^1-D^2) would normally be found in the one local group.
Moreover, this group is bound to a definite locality because
its spirit-homes are associated with the mythological paths
of totemic heroes and ancestors whose cult is their responsibility; further, knowledge of this cult is handed down
through the local group and as far as possible from father
to son, or if there be any irregularity, from father's father
to son's son. Thus, the father-son couple of subsections or
semi-moiety constitutes a definite cult-group. In such case,
the one cult totem, or "dreaming" as it is usually called, is
shared by both father and son, that is by the two subsections of the semi-moiety, and there may be several cult
totems for each semi-moiety, because there are several local groups belonging to it.

When referring to subsection totemism as it is found in
Eastern Kimberley and Arnhem Land, we saw that each
subsection had its own totem or totems, and that therefore
father and son had different subsection totems; moreover, a
person's subsection totems depended indirectly on the subsection of his mother. Obviously, this subsection totemism
is a different institution from the semi-moiety totemism of
the Gulf of Carpentaria and Central Australia. It is asso-

ciated with a form of *social* grouping, but the latter is derived from the cult-life of the tribe, which is usually related to the local patrilineal groups within the tribe.

Both forms of totemism may co-exist in one tribe, as does occur in Eastern Kimberley, and possibly further acquaintance would show that this is the case elsewhere; though when the subsection system spreads into tribes with very strong localized and patrilineal cult-life, it is possible that its totemic aspect is forgotten or ignored, for it is of comparatively little importance. The subsections are still of social use at inter-tribal gatherings and for summarizing kin, but as far as totemism is concerned, they do not stand on their own, but are made to fit into the religious and local organization of the tribe by being grouped into four patrilineal semi-moieties, each with its own group of cult totems.

Very often, too, the two semi-moieties which together form a moiety (i.e. A^1-D^2 and A^2-D^1; C^1-B^1 and C^2-B^2) are grouped together into a moiety, named or not, which has influence in such a social matter as marriage, and is of especial importance in the religious and ceremonial life. A person pays respect to all the totems of his moiety even though some of them do not belong to his own half of the moiety, and in ceremonies the moieties act as units.

Apart from the interest which these semi-moieties have as a form of social order, they illustrate the general principle, that it is difficult to understand any one aspect of the social life of the Aborigines without a knowledge of the rest. All are interdependent.

Chapter V

KINSHIP AND MARRIAGE CUSTOMS
PUZZLING TO US

The Need to Understand These Customs

ANY people whose history, tradition and beliefs are different from our own, is almost sure to have customs that seem strange and puzzling to us. We may even feel that these customs are not so good as ours, that they are degrading and should be abolished, but before we pass such opinions or act on them, we must first understand what those customs are, the traditions and beliefs on which they are based, the meaning which they possess for the individuals who practise them, and the social function which they perform. But while such an understanding undoubtedly makes another people's customs less puzzling to us, it does not necessarily commend them all, and we may still feel constrained to use our influence or authority to have some of them abolished or modified. Here again an understanding of those customs is essential so that we may know what we are doing when working for their abolition or modification. Even practices and rules which seem to us objectionable may have served quite useful purposes in the life of a people, and, moreover, they are often intertwined with many other institutions. We have already noticed how, in Australia, the local organization is bound up with the doctrine of pre-existence of spirits, kinship-grouping, mythological history, totemism and the economic life. If then we undermine the belief in the doctrine of pre-existence, or in the validity of the myths, we shall most likely cause a collapse of the local organization itself; certainly we shall take away the meaning of life from the individual, for no longer will he be sure that he has existed from the "eternal dream-time" or that after death he will return to his spirit home. This uncertainty undermines his zest and desire for life, and he becomes resigned not only to his own passing, but also to the passing of his people. The only hope for saving such a person lies in his being gripped by some other theory of the soul and human existence, which would make life here and now worth while. Of course, to destroy or desecrate his spirit-home—though it be but a waterhole or a heap of stones—leads to a similar disastrous result; this could only be avoided by the individual embracing another view of life, in particular, one which makes the individual independent of any localized spirit-home. It may be puzzling to us that interference with mere material sites, though sacred to the Aborigines, should lead to such disastrous results; but once we understand their doctrine of pre-existence and its close relation to the local organization and mythology, we see that this is quite inevitable, unless the fundamental beliefs can be changed; that, however, is very difficult indeed.

We must also recognize that if changes of belief and custom are to be made amongst the Aborigines without disaster, they must be made through the elders, and not just by external authority. As we have seen in the preceding chapters, many important changes have been made in social organization and custom, and also in the ceremonial life; but they have been made after consideration by the elders, who are the custodians of law and tradition, and in time mythological (that is, "historical") sanction or authority has grown up to account for that change.

I have referred to these very important aspects of culture-contact and culture-change, because some of the puzzling customs to be discussed now, are just the type which we often feel should be modified or even prohibited. These customs are associated with the kinship system, marriage, the relation of the sexes and the position of women.

THE CLASSIFICATORY KINSHIP SYSTEM

The Aborigines' method of grouping relations into classes, and applying to each of these classes a relationship term, such as father, mother and sister, is puzzling to most white persons and leads to misunderstandings; I hope, however, that Chapter III has shown that the system is useful and logical, that it does not conceal any ignorance of actual genealogical relationship, and that it does codify behaviour.

This last point enables us to understand a custom which sometimes puzzles and even annoys us. We give a present or make a well-earned payment to an Aborigine, and very shortly after we find that he has little or none of it left—whether it consist of food, clothes, tobacco or other objects. We are apt to think and say that the old men or possibly the Aborigines as a whole are unjust, or are lazy and impose on the one who does happen to work. Possibly, too, we are confirmed in our opinion when we ask the native why he gave the objects away and he answers simply, "I must do that." But we are apt to mistake the implication of this "must"; it does not represent the pressure of the other natives, but of social obligation as expressed in the kinship system. A person must make gifts to his relations; if a number be present, there is usually an order of precedence; for example, natives of one tribe say that they must give to father first, to mother's brother second, to wife's parents third, while a slightly different order may be given by members of other tribes. Except, however, at times of group meetings, there is no question of order of precedence, but, at all times, there is the obligation of making gifts—an obligation arising from the principle of reciprocity which runs through all native life. The individual concerned has received gifts in the past from those with whom he now shares his pay, the results of the chase or of his industry, and he will be a recipient in the future. Moreover, he may be under an obligation arising out of marriage, betrothal or initiation: gifts are made to the wife's parents and often too, to the wife's mother's brother from the time of betrothal; it is a kind of "payment" for the wife, and likewise gifts must be made to those who have assisted at one's initiation; as a matter of fact, the latter is frequently a question of return-gifts because the elders, as I have seen, make gifts to the newly initiated youths.

We must bear in mind too, that in the case of employment in the white man's service, the native may not have been able for some considerable time to fulfil his social obligations; he has not been able to hunt and send food to his mother, or wife's mother; he has not been able to make spears, boomerangs or any other objects to give to his relations in return for what they have done for, or given to, him. But when he receives his pay from his white employer, he can fulfil these obligations, and what is more, he can do so in a way which they appreciate and of which he is proud. He has given them some of the white man's desirable goods. Instead, then, of objecting to this distribution of our payments, we should realize that we are enabling our native employee to perform his kinship duties in a way appreciated by himself and the recipients. What happens to his pay is his business and concerns himself and his relatives; it is not our affair. The paternal attitude which we adopt in this matter of payment of Aborigines is sometimes overdone. We only allow him a small proportion of his earnings and bank the rest, because we feel that his tribal relations will get it all from him; let us see, however, that we do not make it impossible for him to fulfil his social obligations, for in such a case, we are in reality defrauding certain of his kin of their rights. Incidentally, we are also undermining the native social structure, and endeavouring, whether intentionally or not, to turn the Aborigine into an individualist. The wisdom of the latter endeavour is, at least, open to question. Of its difficulty there is no doubt. In any case we must prevent the native from being defrauded of his money by white persons, including his employers, his official protectors, shop-keepers and hawkers.

KINSHIP AND LAW

The obligations of kinship govern a person's behaviour from his earliest years to his death, and affect life in all its aspects: in conversation, visiting and camping; at the crises of life, namely, child-birth, initiation, marriage, sickness and death; and in quarrels and fights. Membership of a common moiety, section, social clan or local group intensifies or modifies these duties, but does not overrule them. They are, moreover, both positive and negative in nature, prescribing what must be done and also what must not be done; moreover, for the breaking of such rules there are usually definite punishments, some of which are "supernatural" in character. For example, the law says that a man must not co-habit with his sister, mother or wife's mother; the punishment is death, though if the actual relationship be not a close one, banishment from the corporate life of the tribe, or else some severe physical punishment may suffice. These matters are decided by the elders, or more particularly by certain relations such as the "uncle" and "father-in-law", but a couple caught committing an act of serious incest would be speared on sight, because the person seeing them would be so shamed.

Some cases arise, however, which are very puzzling to us and might lead us to take wrong actions. The most interesting of these that I came across concerned a murder in Northern Kimberley.[1] An old man had died and left two widows, the younger one of whom was "willed" to a certain man, aged about thirty-five or forty. This was known by the tribe. She, however, reciprocated the attentions of a younger tribal brother of the inheriting husband, and went away with him three times. The husband, being incensed, prevailed on another tribal brother, a warrior,

---

[1] I have already referred to this in the small booklet *Understanding the Australian Aborigine,* now out of print.

to assist him kill the "co-respondent". The latter was apparently decoyed out by a third man, on the pretext of hunting, to a prearranged place where the warrior hurled two spears into his back and the aggrieved husband rushed up and finished him off. The two of them buried the body.

The question is, who was guilty of the murder? Or if all three were, what were the degrees of guilt? We might quite naturally say that the warrior who cast the two spears actually caused the death, though we should be inclined to attribute equal guilt to the husband, seeing he was the person most interested and that he rushed up to see that the victim was really dead; while if we could prove that the third man had led the victim into a trap, he, too, would be deeply implicated. From the Aboriginal point of view, however, the case was much more complicated. The warrior who no doubt caused the death was the least guilty of the three. He had been persuaded to do the deed not just to satisfy the anger of the aggrieved husband, but also as an act of revenge for the death of the old man whose young widow was the cause of the trouble. This death had been attributed to three men including the young murdered man; the latter, of course, could be supposed to have a motive for bringing about the old man's death seeing that he wanted the young woman. In fact, all three had quarrelled with the old man about his two wives. It was stated that these three men had sent some of the old fellow's tobacco to a group in a tribe to the north, for magical use. Incidentally, this northern group was closely related to the murdered young man.

The warrior explained that not only did the husband strongly urge him to do his duty in this matter of revenge, but also reminded him that the young fellow was not liked because of the way he sneaked about, and especially that he was interfering with his (the husband's) wife. The husband argued further, so the warrior informed me, that he could not himself initiate the revenge as he had not himself drawn blood in a fight, and that therefore he, as a

warrior, must do so. The husband then sent the latter his
spear and it was one of the two spears thrown.

After the murder, the husband disappeared for some
time. The warrior went to several of his relations, com-
mencing with his mother's brother and announced that he
had killed the young fellow. They in turn reprimanded him
and meted out physical punishment to him. Before long,
the news spread to a settled centre and a local Justice of
the Peace, who was well disposed towards the natives,
arrested the murderer. He was looking very abject. I knew
him well and also the other three men most concerned.

Now, according to native law and opinion, this man was
receiving all the punishment which he deserved. The husband when caught would be severely dealt with, because
he had gone too far; the proper punishment for the co-
respondent (and the wife too) was a severe beating, and
perhaps also, a fight with the husband. Further, though
the husband and warrior would have been justified in making a row over the old man's death, no one wanted a murder over it, so that neither the husband nor the warrior
could use this as an argument to justify the murder,
though it did add fuel to the fire.

But, strangely enough, the most guilty person, and the
one worthy of death in native law, was the third man who
had gone out hunting with the young victim and left him
in a place where the other two would have the opportunity
to kill him. He did not actually see the murder, but he did
know what was afoot. His great guilt lay in the fact that
knowing this, he did not warn and, if necessary, protect
the young man. Why? Not because of a general principle
of protecting people from danger, but because the two
were related as brothers-in-law, and, in this area, persons
so related must protect each other throughout life.[2] But,

---

[2] This arises chiefly from the custom that the novice's guide
and guardian through initiation is a brother-in-law—a guardian-
ship which becomes mutual and life-long. They must not quar-

in this case, this sacred bond of kinship had been broken, and the only adequate penalty was death.

As a matter of fact, a revenge expedition from the country of the murdered man's relations arrived soon afterwards to spear this traitorous relation, but on my representations, very grudgingly refrained. They returned home and, contrary to the general belief, have not attempted to exact vengeance. The case in our courts against the warrior was wisely dismissed, and the three men concerned in the murder were sent to different Government settlements both as a punishment and to be out of harm's way. They went back later to their tribal country.

KINSHIP AVOIDANCE

One of the most puzzling native customs, at least to the new-comer, is the rule of avoiding various relations. Most people know that son-in-law and mother-in-law avoid each other, never seeing or speaking to one another, but probably only a few are aware that prohibitions and restrictions of various kinds and degrees of intensity operate between quite a number of relationship groups. Perhaps we could give psychological and social reasons for the taboo on mother-in-law and through her on certain of her close relations; we might follow the logic of extending this taboo to people grouped with her in the classificatory system; but we are apt to be surprised when we learn that there are also restrictions on social intercourse between own blood kin, such as brothers and sisters, uncles and nephews.[3]

---

rel and, moreover, should endeavour to shield one another from unjustifiable attacks.

[3] The restriction between mother's brother and sister's son, where it prevails, is not so much a matter of blood relationship as of possible marriage relationship. In some tribes the former may be a possible father-in-law of the latter, while in other tribes (which allow marriage with sister's son's daughter) the position is reversed. Thus, uncle or nephew being the husband of mother-in-law, is himself to some extent avoided.

We often see things without understanding their significance, or indeed, without realizing that they have any significance at all. For example, many a white man has seen a group of Aboriginal families having a meal, without seeing any plan in the grouping; they have probably obtained the food at the station or mission kitchen and gone off to eat it near by. But, unless their old rules have been forgotten, the various small family groups sit about in a manner dictated by kinship rules; one is a few yards from the others, facing away from them and saying nothing to them; two families are sitting near and talking to each other, but facing in different directions; while another family may be facing one of these two. Likewise, a group of men, sitting in the shade talking and working, do not dispose themselves as we would, so that each one could see every one else; on the contrary, they sit facing in all directions, in some cases back-to-back; there may even be a complete division into two lesser groups either according to the age or generation lines already referred to in Chapter IV, or in accordance with a restriction on intercourse between men mutually related as sister's daughter's husband and wife's mother's brother (i.e. "niece's" husband and "niece's uncle"). This arrangement of the men may seem to us haphazard or absurd, but it is not so, for it is governed by kinship rules of avoidance and familiarity. White persons who constantly see such situations as these, seldom ask any questions about them, but I remember a lighthouse-keeper who was very puzzled by the social happenings amongst the natives who used to visit his native employee; some would come along and enter the latter's hut; others would sit at the back of it and carry on a conversation with the man and his wife inside, while others would sit down some yards away and speak from there; but strange as this may seem to us, the conduct of all the visitors was regulated by kinship rules.

Speaking generally: (i) an individual is free to approach and talk to some relations, but not to others; he may joke with some, but on no account with others; he may refer to the names and totems of some but not of others; (ii) the restrictions vary in degree according to the type of relationship; thus, the avoidance of a mother-in-law is the greatest of all; (iii) they apply to classes of persons and not merely to actual blood and marriage relations; women who could be mother-in-law, or rather, the sister and parallel cousins of the actual mother-in-law, are avoided, though sometimes the prohibition becomes less severe, the more distant the particular relationship; (iv) the solidarity of the local group and the tendency to regard brothers and sisters in such a group as equivalent, tends to strengthen and extend the restrictions. But (v) the avoidances are not an expression of enmity; they are associated with mutual duties and gifts.[4]

There are two types of kinship avoidance, namely, between relatives by marriage and relatives by blood, and these can be further subdivided into avoidance observed between members of different sexes and those of the same sex. A full understanding of these avoidances would demand a knowledge of the motives and purposes served by them; it is doubtful, however, whether we shall ever really obtain this; still, suggestions can be made which will at least enable us to see some sensible reasons for the avoidance rules.

RELATIONS BY MARRIAGE

The severest taboo is that which is observed all over Australia between a man and his wife's mother. From the time of, and if possible previous to, the betrothal of the former to the latter's daughter, son-in-law and mother-in-

---

[4] In addition to these general kinship avoidances and restrictions, there are others which arise temporarily out of death and initiation, and in other ways. E.g. in some tribes the operator who performed the circumcision rite, must not see the newly initiated man for a considerable period which must be terminated by prescribed customs and ritual.

law must neither see nor speak to one another; this, at least, prevents the possibility of any competition between a girl and her mother for the affection of the same man—a danger which might be very real where so often the wife is much younger than the husband and the husband and mother-in-law are of the same age; indeed, the former is sometimes older than the latter. I have already suggested in Chapter III that this prohibition of intercourse was probably a cause of the prohibition of marriage with father's sister's daughter.

In many tribes this avoidance rule is extended to wife's mother's mother, probably because this woman and mother-in-law are in a sense equivalent, inheriting their flesh and blood through the one line of women. Sometimes, too, she belongs to the same generation level as the son-in-law, for example, in marriages of the sister's son's daughter type, and apparently the tradition has grown up that it is not wise to have any intercourse with a woman through whom the mother-in-law was incarnated. A special term is often applied to her, more particularly if marriage with the daughter of own mother's mother's brother's daughter (that is, with own second cousin) be regarded with disfavour.

Further: in many tribes the wife's mother's brother is brought within the range of the same taboo, no doubt because he belongs to the same local clan and country as the mother-in-law and therefore has the same "spiritual" history as she, and also because he was incarnated through the womb of the same mother as herself. He is therefore equivalent to her, a male mother-in-law—one of the tabooed group. It is worth noticing that his mother, who is also mother-in-law's mother, belongs to the same local group by marriage, and so, apart from her close blood relationship to the mother-in-law, is also associated with her by the rule of residence.[5]

[5] The members of the local group by birth and spiritual pre-existence form a local or territorial clan. If the local group is

This avoidance of wife's "uncle" is not a mere form. He is usually called by a term signifying tabooed, and often it is the term which is used for mother-in-law. In some tribes, especially in the north-west where the local groups are clearly defined territorial totemic clans, the whole male membership of the tribe is divided by this avoidance relationship. No man will go near or talk face to face with his *ramba, wolmingi, dalu,* or whatever be the term, with the result that this avoidance is often the first thing observed on entering a native camp, even at a mission. The men gossip or work in two groups separated by this relationship. A man swerves aside from the track to avoid meeting his *ramba* face to face, as I have seen happen with my own carrier. On one occasion I was recording genealogies with a group of men, when another group of about fifty, all painted up for a ceremony, appeared a hundred yards away; desiring to take a photograph of them, I asked those around me to call them over; the answer was simple and clear: they cannot come "because *ramba* belong us". Similarly, three men who were talking to me one day said that some men around the creek near by were waiting to give me some bull-roarers. In reply to my suggestion that these should join us, I was told that they could not do so, "because *ramba* belong us". Thus, on account of the wife's husband—wife's "uncle" taboo, I had to go for the bull-roarers just as previously I had to leave my own group and go to the painted group so as to take the photograph. The avoidance is not so complete as in the case of mother-in-law and son-in-law for the *ramba* men do see, and may sometimes speak to, one another from a distance. Membership of the one sex group and of the secret life of the tribe is the explanation of this modification.

---

thought of as including the wives who, of course, belong to other territorial clans, it is generally called a horde; some prefer to call it a band or hunting band. The natives themselves often use the word camp for it; e.g. *ngura.*

Three other classes of men are brought into the range of avoidances between relations by marriage; these are father-in-law, mother-in-law's father and wife's brother. The first two are the husbands of the most tabooed women, and so would have to share the avoidance which primarily concerned their wives; in order to avoid his wife's mother, a man must avoid his father-in-law's camp and that frequently amounts to avoiding the father-in-law himself. But there is, no doubt, more in the avoidance than this. Father-in-law belongs to, and may be the head-man of, the local horde which includes the wife's mother, and he himself "found" the wife's pre-existent spirit and later was one of those who arranged that she should be given to her husband. He is therefore in a position of creditor to his son-in-law, while the latter is in a position of "inferiority" and of indebtedness to his father-in-law. This is expressed in the attitude of reserve and partial avoidance which is adopted between them, and in the making of gifts of food and artifacts to the father-in-law; such gifts are sent through the debtor's wife.

The mother-in-law's father is in much the same position; he "found" and provided the mother-in-law and therefore ultimately gave the wife. The natives in many tribes actually express the position in this way. Normally, this person is mother's mother's brother (or in the Ungarinyin type of kinship system, father's mother's brother); and as I have already stated in Chapter III, he is the leading person amongst a man's relations, that is, from the point of view of matrimony. Respect is therefore paid to him, gifts made to him, and a rule of restricted social intercourse must be observed. Incidentally, he is the husband of wife's mother's mother and an elder of the local horde which includes this woman, and to which the mother-in-law, by reason of her birth, belongs. This fact is frequently expressed by the use of the one term (e.g. *wainman* in the Nyul-Nyul tribe) for both parents of wife's mother.

Brothers-in-law usually adopt a somewhat formal attitude towards one another, sitting a little distance apart and talking quietly—certainly not quarrelling. They are, in many tribes, very guarded in the use of each other's names. Moreover, except in a few tribes, they may marry each other's sisters, own or tribal, and they are also bound by ties of initiation, an older brother-in-law being the guardian of the younger during the ceremonies; this ritual bond lasts throughout life. One sign of it is the special language (or code of words) which they use in conversation with one another, and which is also an indication of the ceremonial reserve which they must mutually adopt.

BLOOD RELATIONS

Ignoring the fact for the moment that relations by marriage are sometimes quite close blood relations, we have to note that some of the latter have to be avoided irrespective of marriages.

A very wide-spread avoidance rule applies to brothers and sisters, own and tribal. Once childhood has been passed, they must not converse freely; when they are talking, they must face in different directions. If a man enter his sister's camp to talk to her husband, his brother-in-law, he sits with his back to her. If he asks for a drink she will put it down near him, but not hand it to him. He will not mention her name, nor in some cases, her totem—not even to the anthropologist. The reason for this prohibition may lie in its function as a means of preventing incest within the family. At any rate, there is an association between some of these avoidance rules and the prohibition of marriage. This seems clear in the extension of the brother-sister taboo to cross-cousins in many tribes, perhaps all, in which cross-section marriage is prohibited. In tribes without any moiety or section organization, the cross-cousins are usually called brothers and sisters,[6] and so all thought of marriage is ruled out. But even though social grouping

[6] Western South Australia, Port Stephens District (New South Wales), and the Kurnai (south-eastern Victoria).

causes them to be called by special kinship terms, distinct from brother and sister, and also from wife, they are still regarded as "all the same" brother and sister, and the same rules of behaviour apply. One of the most interesting examples of this is found in the Karadjeri and Murngin tribes,[7] in which father's sister is called father, with the result that her children are included in the range of the sentiment which attaches to father and children; they are like brothers and sisters, with the result that there can be no thought of marriage between a man and his father's sister's daughter, even though the actual term used towards her is not the one for sister. But, as we have seen, this sentiment is associated with the tribal prohibition of patrilateral cross-cousin marriage.

I have seen a case of partial avoidance and restricted intercourse between two brothers, but this seems to be rare. More common is the observance of such a rule between a man and his sister's children. This may seem strange, seeing that a man and his mother's brothers are bound by the closest blood ties that can link two men, except possibly that of two brothers. But it should be remembered that in tribes with cross-cousin marriage, own mother's brother is a possible or an actual wife's father and therefore a "creditor" to his daughter's husband; moreover, in most tribes, outside the Northern Kimberley, which prohibit cross-cousin marriage, the father-in-law is a tribal brother of own mother's brother; in other words, he belongs to the "uncle" class and has a part to play in arranging the betrothal or marriage of his sister's son as well as in the latter's initiation. In the tribes of northwestern Australia, the obligation thus incurred by the nephew may be ultimately removed by the betrothal of the daughter of the latter to his "uncle". This means that the nephew is a possible father-in-law to his mother's brother, and that a father-in-law—son-in-law pattern of behaviour is involved.

[7] Chapter III.

Apart from the special relations referred to in these two groups, there is seldom any avoidance rule to be observed in Aboriginal society. Gifts, of course, have to be made and other mutual duties to be performed in all cases, whether there are avoidances or not, and perhaps it should be emphasized again that the avoidances are not an expression of hostility or opposition; the persons observing them are all related closely or distantly by genealogy; moreover, they exchange gifts and also arrange for reciprocal marriages between their respective groups. Finally, we may generalize by saying that the avoidances are practised by those actually related by marriage and by those who *must not* be related by marriage (such as sisters and certain cousins); in the former case, they operate between members of succeeding and alternate generations, and in the latter, usually, between those of the same generation.

There are some variations here and there in Australia in the depth and incidence of these avoidance rules, but the general principles are those just described.

Taboo on Names

In addition to an avoidance of the names of certain relations, there is a general disinclination in Australia to the use of the personal name. I have recorded a whole genealogy with the correct references to the spirit-home, local country, moiety and totems of over twenty individuals, and with what purported to be their personal names, only to realize that in every case I had been given a nickname. This objection to the use of the personal name, however, must not be confused with the kinship avoidance of names. It belongs mainly to the realm of the secret life, for names are usually taken from sacred mythological and totemic associations, and therefore must not be bandied about. They represent the real self which belongs to the spiritual and sacred sphere, not to the world of everyday affairs. For the latter, kinship terms, subsection or section names, or nicknames suffice.

There is also in some parts a fear lest magical use could be made of the personal name to the hurt of its owner, and so it is never mentioned except in a whisper and then only in the presence of men of one's own group. For our part, we do not need a knowledge of such names and should not press for them.

PUZZLING MARRIAGE CUSTOMS

There are several customs connected with Aboriginal marriage, which seem to imply that woman is only regarded as a chattel—as a means of settling or balancing obligations between individuals or groups, and a method of expressing certain prescribed desires or intentions. We have already noticed that there is another side to this picture, but these facts must be faced and their significance understood. We should also remember that some of these customs have either been practised by Europeans or by peoples of early historical times, for whose contribution to civilization we have great respect.

METHODS OF OBTAINING A WIFE

There are several methods or prescribed ways in which a wife is obtained. The commonest is that of betrothal which is arranged through the parents, mother's brothers, mother's mother's brothers and wife's brother with the consent of the elders of the local groups concerned. Infant betrothal is the normal thing; indeed, a woman's daughter is promised to a man or the latter's son or nephew before she is born. This means that affection and attraction are not considered, but are made subservient to the reciprocal obligations of individuals, families or larger groups. For example, in some regions, a group which is held responsible for the death of a member of another group, may escape the extreme measure of being attacked by a revenge expedition, by giving one of its women in marriage to a member of the injured group. Likewise, a man who has performed the operation of circumcision on a member of another group, must, in some regions, provide a wife for the latter.

In many tribes, too, a married man is duty-bound to arrange for his sister's daughter to be given in marriage to his wife's mother's brother; this exchange of nieces between two men of succeeding generation levels leaves little room for an expression of opinion or feeling on the part of the females concerned—in fact none whatever as far as the younger niece is concerned; if she did have any say, she would probably always refuse to marry her "uncle's" wife's "uncle". Likewise, marriage with sister's son's daughter, which is practised widely in north-western Australia, allows no reference to the girl's likes or dislikes, nor is much consideration given to the women concerned in the very general custom of the exchange of sisters in marriage. In these two marriages, the main object seems to be the balancing of the obligations incurred. My mother's brother takes a part in arranging my marriage; I must therefore find a young wife for him, namely, my daughter, so that he marries his sister's son's daughter. Or again, if I marry a certain man's sister, I must in return give him my sister in exchange. Of course, such balancing of marriages, of women and their subsequent children is also a matter of interest and importance to local groups and social clans.

Both the sororate and junior levirate likewise ignore in principle the wishes of the women, and sometimes too, of the men. According to the first custom, a man who marries the eldest daughter has the right, if he desires, to marry her sisters. He may, however, waive this right in favour of a brother. According to the second, a man's wives are inherited by his younger brother who, however, may waive his right in favour of other brothers.

Although the arrangement of such marriages seems to contain no thought of women as individual personalities, yet the women abide by the scheme and are often happy; neither the method nor result is very different from the former European institution of arranging marriages for political, national, family or economic motives without consideration of the bride.

Such marriages inevitably lead to a great many "divorces"; and it is usual to find that each woman has been in her day, the wife of more than one man. The reason is not so much that her betrothed husband was cruel, but that her affection or fancy was drawn elsewhere and she had eloped with her lover or been "pulled" (captured) by him. There are occasional cases of genuine marriage by capture, such as occur during a successful revenge expedition, but usually such capture is a ritual matter and has been prearranged. In the Kurnai tribe of Victoria, for example, it occurred during a fight between the men and women, which itself had been deliberately started by injuring a sex totem, so that the capture of a bride, consenting though resisting, could be made. In some northwestern tribes, there is a special term which means, according to the natives, "pulling a woman". She is already married or betrothed, but is usually willing to be pulled in spite of setting up a well-designed resistance necessitating a hit on the head with a club. These cases of elopement or pulling are usually followed by a fight between the husband and the co-respondent or capturer, but even though the former wins, he often lets the woman go as he realizes the inevitable, and in any case, the new husband must compensate him with gifts, perhaps, with another wife. Such episodes are especially apt to occur in the case of a girl married to an old man, for on the death of the latter, if she has not already eloped successfully, she has to go to his younger brother or some man according to a plan prearranged by the deceased husband and the elders.

If we now remember the marriage rules inherent in the kinship system with their theoretical limitation of spouses in most tribes to a small group of persons of a special type of second cousin, and combine it with the betrothal customs just mentioned, we realize how narrow is the choice allowed even to men in marriage, while to women there is really none. But such a system has to bend, and in bending, be careful not to snap. The Australian systems have succeeded in this in three ways: first, by allowing, as we have seen,[8] alternate marriages which really enlarge the range of choice two or three times; second, by making an institution of marriage of old men with young girls,[9] and third by legalizing elopement and capture.

Marriage of Old Men and Young Girls. Particular exception is taken to this custom on the part of whites, though it is not unknown in our own society; we are, however, fairly consistent, for general approval is seldom or never given to it. Where it still occurs amongst the Aborigines, or would occur were it not for the missions, the old men argue that it is an institution of value to the girls and young men. The girls must be married at puberty, but the boys should not be married until they have been initiated and disciplined. The early marriage of the girls to the old men means that the former are protected, whereas if this form of marriage be stopped, loose living results between these girls and the youths. It is easy to reply that this is only rationalization, and that the old men really want all the girls for themselves. But we must realize that the motive is not simply sexual; it is social and economic. In the first place it does, as we have seen, make possible an equitable balancing of marriage obligations; and in the second place, it ensures an efficient provider of food in the

[8] Chapter IV, pp. 109–11.

[9] Reference back to the Nyul-Nyul and Ungarinyin tables will show the way in which this custom of marriage of old men to young girls is reflected in the terms. In the former, the term for daughter's husband is *KAGA* (m.b.), showing that EGO's mother's brother may marry his sister's son's daughter. This same type of marriage is reflected in the use of the term for wife for EGO's own sister's son's daughter. In both systems the term for wife's mother's brother is the same as that for sister's daughter's husband; this reflects the exchange of nieces in marriage.

old age of the man and his old wife if he has one. The latter, too, has her point of view; she is apt to answer if questioned: "poor old man must have young wife to get honey and water for him."

The changing of this custom is part of the whole question of altering the status of woman in Aboriginal society —a very slow process in any society; but the institution of elopement and capture suggests that this custom, at least, can be changed, especially if adequate provision is made for the very old age of the men and women. Gifts must be made to the promised old-men husbands not only by the men in whose favour they relinquish their rights of marriage, but probably also in the first instance by the mission or administrative authority concerned. This latter payment should be in consideration of the postponement of the girl's marriage from puberty until say eighteen years of age. This is not a case of purchase in the ordinary shopping sense, but of the substitution of gifts of material objects for a female (wife or food-gatherer), who will be married in due course to a person of her own generation level—perhaps a man with whom she would have eloped.[10]

Changes in the other betrothal customs can only be made slowly, as a different view of female personality is developed, though if marriage of girls be postponed until late adolescence, and attachments be made between young folk, a system of satisfying promised husbands could be planned, even without resort to the duel.

USES OF WIVES—OBJECTIONABLE TO US

There are some other customs, connected with marriage, which, though not unknown in the past in Europe, are considered by us to be objectionable, such as the tem-

---

[10] The custom of old men marrying young girls is changing in those parts of northern Australia occupied by whites. Many young men are now seen with young wives though seldom with any children. Polygyny is also being dropped. Such changes are apparently the direct or indirect result of white influence.

[9] *Top*, making a spear-point by pressure-flaking. String made of fibre of baobab root. Northern Kimberley. *Bottom*, Camp-life, Musgrave Ranges. North-western South Australia.

[10] Man dragging a spear between his toes.

[11] *Top*, chanting about the mythological heroes. Secret engraved boards symbolize their activities. Lagrange District, North-western Australia. *Bottom*, two lads excluded from the camp during the period of initiation, Central Australia.

[12] *Top,* sacred site for increase of totemic species. South-west Queensland. *Bottom,* actors in Molongo ritual. Central Australia, 1930.

porary exchange of wives and wife lending. These customs are, however, subject to rules, and must be studied in connexion with the other institutions of the tribe. Here are some examples:

(i) Just before a revenge expedition sets out on its dangerous enterprise, its members temporarily exchange wives, thus expressing their unity and friendship to one another.

(ii) When an attacking party is about to attack the home party, the latter if it does not want to fight, sends a number of its women over to the former. If these are willing to settle the matter in dispute without fighting, they have sexual intercourse with the women; if not, they send them back untouched.

(iii) In some parts (e.g. north-eastern South Australia), the temporary exchange of wives between the two parties to a quarrel is a regular part of the method of settling it, if each has an admitted debt or charge against the other.

(iv) The final making of peace between two groups may always include the temporary exchange of wives, and on such occasions, all the usual tribal marriage laws (except those concerned with incest within the family) may be and are usually broken. This apparently marks the renewed friendship in a special manner; all groupings are transcended.

(v) Very often at times of great excitement during ceremonies, the men go aside to prearranged places and there have sexual intercourse with the women, and once again, the usual rules governing the intercourse of the sexes are ignored. Sexual excitation is a feature of some rites, and it may be thought that sexual intercourse will add to the effectiveness of the rites,[11] or it may be just another occasion for expressing the common unity which those participating in the rites feel. In any case, it is for

[11] Marriage and other rituals, such as the crowning of a king, are associated elsewhere.

them just part of the traditional pattern, and they do not look for reasons.

(vi) The above five occasions are communal in nature; but there is another similar in some ways, which differs in being a mark of friendship or hospitality and in being practised between individuals. This is the lending of a wife to a visitor. In such cases, kinship rules governing marriage apply, and "incest rules", interpreted tribally, are not broken. This is more than a mark of hospitality in some tribes (e.g. north-east of South Australia); it is an institution. In addition to having a wife or wives, a man also has one or more secondary wives—a relationship which is socially acknowledged by a ritual action. Such secondary wives are the primary wives of tribal brothers of the man concerned, but if the latter visits any of the former—his secondary wife is given up to him during his visit. A secondary wife usually accompanies a man when he is officially going the rounds of groups to summon them to a ceremonial gathering; and if the summons be received in the affirmative, some of the local group may have intercourse with her.

This institution of secondary wives is the *pirauru* (or *piranguru*) relationship which has been made famous in anthropological literature. Some regarded it as a relic of group marriage, arguing that a group of men had a group of women in common, while others argued that it did not undermine, or prove the non-existence of marriage as we understand it. Thinking that it might be as well to get the opinion of the natives themselves on this controversial matter, I mentioned the term *pirauru* to my informants in different tribes; the translation of the word, by one of the ablest and most reliable of them, surprised me a little, but settled the argument; "*pirauru*, oh! you mean 'benjamin' (fancy-man)," said he, with a smile. In other words, the *pirauru* is a "lover" outside the regular marriage relationship, but it happens to be an institution, and ensures that a man will have a sexual mate in several places. Now, though this may not be such an organized institution in every tribe, the principle of lending a wife to visitors is widespread, and, in some tribes, men realize that white men desire to be accommodated by the custom, and they offer them their women. But there is another side to it; those who accept the loan of such sexual mates put themselves under a debt to their husbands and people— they enter into a *pirauru* relationship with its obligations as well as privileges, and if they fail to make gifts in return, trouble will sooner or later be made. A great many clashes between white men and natives are caused in this way; the latter demand certain gifts as their right; the white man resents and shows his resentment in a forceful way to the husband and other relations of his native *pirauru* woman. Spear-throwing and, maybe, shooting ensue, to be followed up by a police patrol, a trial and imprisonment of some native or other. But surely, a white man who goes black should undertake the obligations as well as the privileges of this step!

PROSTITUTION OF NATIVE WOMEN

Wife-lending is associated with the readiness of natives to prostitute their womenfolk in order to get material goods from white or yellow men. Obviously, one cure for this is to make such a practice economically needless by giving the men an interest and share in new pursuits so that they need not be tempted by the offers of visiting men. Further steps must, of course, be taken, and those quite apart from inflicting severe penalties on non-Aborigines who consort with native women. The status of the latter must gradually be raised in their own eyes and in the opinion of their menfolk. Possibly too, when both men and women realize that sexual intercourse is the cause of conception, or allow themselves to accept the full significance of this fact, there might be less readiness to "trade" and be "traded". At present the physical act is a source of pleasure or a means of expressing or renewing friendship, warding off hostilities, or putting others under an obligation. But this is almost solely the man's point of view; it is not concerned with the offspring and implies that woman is but an object to be used in certain socially established ways. The fact that woman may often not object[12] does not justify the custom. But those who would modify or prohibit them must do so through the elders and help them find other means of expressing friendship, symbolizing a readiness to negotiate for peace and such like. It should be noticed that the motives in at least four of the five corporate uses of women are not primarily sexual, and that therefore, it should be possible to find some means of expressing friendship and unity of purpose and life other than the sexual use of women. One such means is used by many tribes, namely the bull-roarer—or *tjuringa* (*churinga*); this sacred symbol of life is lent to show and cement friendship, and in the rites associated with its lending and return, common emotions are stirred and all feel strengthened. Its use might be extended, and other substitutes for the symbolical use of women might also be found.[13]

[12] They sometimes live in terror of the use which is made of them at some ceremonial times.

[13] See Chapter VII, pp. 185–86.

Chapter VI

TOTEMISM: MAN, NATURE AND THE PAST

THE Australian Aborigines possess an unsought fame which has arisen from some elements of their culture, such as the boomerang, circumcision, the classificatory kinship system and totemism. I have arranged these four claims to fame in order of worth, rather than in the popular order. It is not usually realized that the boomerang, more particularly the returning variety of this weapon, was not known to the natives over wide areas of the continent, for example, in the far north-west, in north-eastern Arnhem Land, and the western half of South Australia. Likewise, circumcision, while raising interesting historical problems, was not practised in the eastern third of Australia nor in the far south-west; it is a comparatively recent custom which has spread from the north-west. But in spite of these limitations, the Australians are usually known as a primitive people possessing a remarkable weapon, the boomerang, and practising a rite, circumcision, which was associated with some of the great nations of antiquity.

With regard to the kinship systems, however, their fame is limited to the circle of students of social anthropology. Very few outside of that circle are aware of the existence of these systems, let alone understand them, but the anthropological literature of many countries is rich with studies of their form and function. On the other hand, both students and the merely interested associate the Aborigines with totemism. Probably Australian totemism has been more discussed in anthropological writings than any other feature of the culture, but the general reader has little, if any, understanding of it. The self-constituted authority who has a smattering of knowledge about the Aborigines usually asserts that their marriages are based on totemic laws. I trust, however, that enough has been said already to show that marriage in Aboriginal society is regulated primarily by the kinship system and secondarily by one or more of the social groupings which are found in each tribe and which may or may not have a totemic aspect.

Totemism is more than a mechanism for regulating marriage. It is a view of nature and life, of the universe and man, which colours and influences the Aborigines' social groupings and mythologies, inspires their rituals and links them to the past. It unites them with nature's activities and species in a bond of mutual life-giving, and imparts confidence amidst the vicissitudes of life. The Aborigine is, from our point of view, a parasite on nature; he neither tills, fertilizes nor sows, but only reaps. His life, therefore, depends on nature's maintaining her normal course, but experience has proven that nature of herself is not always consistent. Droughts, floods and diseases come and go. If man is to live, he must prevent or shorten the period of such disastrous occurrences. In other words, he must rouse himself into action and not be parasitic. Our reaction to this need has been to cultivate and irrigate the land—a reaction common to many primitive and prehistoric peoples, although in their case, they have felt that cultivation needed supplementing; they have, therefore, tried to bring into operation unseen life-giving powers of a magical or religious nature or both. By the performance of rites and the adoption of circumspect behaviour, they have assured themselves that their efforts would be rewarded—that rain and fine weather would come, each in its due season, and that crops would be abundant.

The Aborigine, on his part, brings nature into his social and ritual life, adopts an attitude of respect towards it, frequently performs ceremonies designed for its welfare and his own, and looks for its assistance not only as the source of food and water, but also as a protection from danger and a guide to the future. In other words, nature is thought of in an animistic, and indeed, personal way. This, however, is not a generalized view of nature as a whole, though such an aspect is not altogether absent. Just as normally, any one of us thinks not of mankind as a whole, but rather of this man, or of this or that group, so it is with the Aborigines' view of nature. They depend upon it, share a common life, and enter into mutual relations, with it. But this is not a relationship between black mankind or all the tribe, and nature as a whole or in the abstract. It is a relationship between an individual or group of men on the one hand and a natural species or several species, that is, a part or parts, of nature on the other. In other words, there is a segmentary aspect to this relationship and bond which exists between man and nature, and it is this very feature which distinguishes totemism from a generalized nature-religion.

This feature is expressed in the usual definition of totemism as a relationship between an individual or group of individuals on the one hand and a natural object or species on the other—a relationship which is denoted by the bearing of the name of the latter, the totem, by the individual or group. Some such definition is useful provided we realize that it states rather than answers a question: namely, what is the nature of the relationship which exists between the totem and the human group[1] associated with it? Does the totem do anything for the totemites, such as assisting or guarding them? Do they contribute anything to its welfare, such as performing ritual for its increase, guarding it from destruction or, at least, from

---

[1] For certain purposes in this discussion it is convenient to regard one person as constituting a group.

disrespectful use? Do they themselves refrain from injuring, destroying or eating it, and if so why? Is this because the relationship is a social and "physiological" one, such as exists between members of a blood-clan, or because it is religious and ceremonial? Does the totem merely exist to give a name to a group, and so provide a symbol of the common relationship of its members one to another, and incidentally serve as a method of classifying and denoting members of the tribe? And does the totem perform its functions of assisting, warning and acting as a name in waking life only, in the dream life only or in both? Then there is a second series of questions which concerns the human group rather than its totem. Thus, what is its constitution? Is it a local group, a patrilineal or matrilineal clan, a moiety or some other subdivision of the tribe? Is membership of it determined by descent through the father or mother, or in some other way? Is it a social group only or a cult or religious group? And finally, there is the important question, what is the bearing and influence of totemism on the general economic, administrative and social life of the tribe?

Such a list of questions must be borne in mind whenever we are confronted with any totemic phenomenon. At least, it makes us realize firstly, that the subject is a very complex one, the understanding of which demands that we enter deeply into all aspects of native life; and secondly, that totemism does not stand just for one phenomenon of Aboriginal life. It is now regarded as a term used to cover a number of diverse phenomena of social, religious and magical significance. Therefore, it is necessary in every case of totemism to study the nature and function of the natural and human groups, and of the relationship which binds them together.

To do this we classify totemic phenomena from two points of view, namely, form and function. By form I mean the manner in which the totems are distributed amongst the members of a tribe and the way in which the totemic groups are constituted; such forms, for example, are moiety totemism, clan totemism and sex totemism. By function, I mean the part played by the particular form of totemism in the life of the tribe; thus, it may help to regulate marriage, to preserve moral and social sanctions, or to provide a psychological adjustment to the conditions of life. In addition, each form of totemism has some meaning or significance for the individual totemite, and this must not be overlooked when studying its general social function; he regards the totem as his assistant, guardian, mate, or the symbol of his social or cult group, and he frequently regulates his thoughts and his behaviour in accordance with his convictions in this regard.

FORMS OF TOTEMISM

The various forms of totemism are:

(i) *Individual totemism* in which the totemic relationship is between one person on the one side and a species of nature on the other. In one variety of individual totemism, in at least one area, only one member of the animal species seems to be involved.

(ii) *Sex totemism,* which divides the whole tribe into two groups on the basis of sex and the possession by each of its own totem.

(iii) *Moiety totemism,* which also divides the tribe into two groups, but in this case on a principle of relationship and descent; this may be either patrilineal or matrilineal.

(iv) *Section and subsection totemism.* In this each of the four or eight groups of kin into which the tribe is respectively divided, is associated with its own totem or totems. The descent of these groups and totems is indirectly matrilineal as has been explained in the discussion of sections and subsections.

(v) *Clan totemism.* In its normal form a totemic clan consists of a group of kin directly related by patrilineal or matrilineal descent, the members of which share in common one or more totems. Sometimes, too, the local patrilineal patrilocal group (territorial clan) is also a totemic clan.

(vi) *Local totemism.* In this, membership of the totemic group, and the possession of its totem or totems, depends on the principle of locality and not on that of descent. Membership of the territorial clan just mentioned is, as we saw in Chapter IV, primarily a matter of the spiritual tie to the locality and not one of descent. Moreover, in some cases at least, the totems belong to the group because, like the totemites, they belong to the country. Mythology generally shows how the totems came to be associated with the locality.

Most people have heard of the totemism of the Arunta (Aranda) tribe of Central Australia, which was made famous by the writings of Spencer and Gillen. According to their accounts, the most striking feature was that although a person belonged to the local group or territorial clan of his father, he did not necessarily belong to the local *totemic* group of his father's ancestors in the male line; this was all the more striking because the "country" of the two groups was the same. The explanation lay in the different methods of determining membership: in the first case this was patrilineal, at least, in the degree and manner which characterizes territorial clans; but with regard to the totemic group, membership was determined in a fortuitous manner: a person belonged to the local totemic group associated with the locality or country in which his mother realized that a spirit child had entered her womb. Normally, as a result of patrilocal marriage, this was in her husband's country and therefore their children belonged to the totemic group associated with his country. But this need not happen, for conception might be realized when on walk-about in another country, and Spencer and Gillen reported many instances of this. Thus, on the one hand, a father and his children could belong to different totemic groups, while on the other hand, several persons of different local or territorial clans could belong to the one local totemic group, and conduct the totemic activities of a locality which was not their own by descent. It should be noticed in passing that the type of totemism associated with these local groups is purely ceremonial in character, and that the various countries derive their totemic associations from the travels and activities of totemic heroes within their borders, as they passed through the tribal territory.

Now, everywhere in Australia, membership of such ceremonial groups, while being fundamentally local in character, is either definitely patrilineal or tends to be so. A man likes his son and son's son to belong to his own local "lodge", and even in the Aranda groups studied by Spencer and Gillen, this tendency is clear: a person cannot become the head-man of a local totemic group or "lodge", unless he was conceived in the country of his father or father's father: that is to say, the position of totemic head-man is patrilineal in succession and a man cannot become head-man of the totemic country and group where he was conceived if this is not his father's country. He will be given a share in the totemic responsibilities and privileges of that country, but unless the local group be extinct, he will not rise further.

Of course, the principle of determining a person's totemic local group by the place of conception is the logical conclusion of the belief in the pre-existence of spirits in localized spirit-homes; it simply means that after incarnation, the person should continue the same totemic associations which were his while in the pre-existent condition. But in spite of this, the Aranda leaned towards patrilineal descent. Indeed, according to a recent research worker, the Northern Aranda had established this as a principle, while another field-worker has shown that this is true of most of the tribes of north-central Australia.

It is possible that Spencer and Gillen did not distinguish clearly two kinds of totemism, namely, one which is associated with membership of a local group—the group of the father's line, and is ceremonial in function; and another, the purpose of which is to associate a person's conception with a particular natural species or totemic country; for this reason I have called the latter conception totemism. It will be referred to again later on; sufficient is it to say here that it may or may not have any ceremonial implications: in the former case, as in the Aranda tribe, it gives a person an interest in the ceremonial life of the local group in whose country he was conceived.[2]

The same tendency to override a fortuitous principle of local totemic group membership is manifested in the tribes of western South Australia. Here a person's totemic group is the one associated with the locality and totemic path where he was born. In other words, the difference as compared with the Central Australian tribes, is that membership is determined by place of birth instead of by place of conception. But though a man is admitted to a part in the totemic life of the country where he was born,

---

[2] I think that this is the solution of the problem raised by Spencer and Gillen's evidence in the light of more recent work in South, Central, North and North-West Australia. We have learnt much more of the complexity of totemic phenomena than was ever dreamed of by those two workers, and I am convinced that they not only mixed different varieties of totemism, but failed to notice the presence of some. This applies to their investigations from Lake Eyre to the Gulf and Darwin. It was as a result of this conviction, that specially trained workers have been sent out in recent years to examine these very points—to disentangle what was mixed and to fill in the gaps. But I do not wish to detract from the great value of Spencer and Gillen's work as published in *The Native Tribes of Central Australia* and *The Northern Tribes of Central Australia*, nor do I mean that their value is only a thing of the past—the value attached to pioneering work. I think that the first of the two (republished in two volumes under the title *The Arunta*), at least, should be read by all who want to deepen their understanding of Aboriginal life. They should, however, bear in mind that its sections dealing with social organization and kinship are not satisfactory, and that the authors had not understood the totemism of the tribe in all its complexity.

if it is not his father's father's he cannot lead in its ceremonial singing or be its ceremonial head-man. He may,
however, in such a case become a leader in the totemic
group of his father's country, even though he was born
away from it. Strangely enough, it is amongst part of the
Aranda tribe, namely, its extreme southern division which
lives along the Macumba River in South Australia, that
this is clearly expressed as a principle; indeed, the totem
gained by birth is called by the native term for *father*,
expressing the idea that a person's local totem should be
that of his father's line. No doubt, before white occupation had dislocated the economic and ceremonial life of
the tribes, this was nearly always the case, for a person
was born in his father's country, but now that this happens
less often, resort is had to the device of admitting the son
to membership of his father's local totemic group. In more
northern parts of Central Australia, as in north-western
Australia, if there be any doubt concerning a person's
local totemic group, he is assigned to the group associated with his father's country.

(vii) *Multiple totemism.* In this form of totemism, a
number of natural objects or species, as well as men and
women, are grouped under the name of one or more principal totems. This can be a feature of moiety, section,
clan or local totemism. It is really a method of classifying
natural phenomena.

To sum up: The forms of totemism are individual, sex,
moiety, section and subsection, clan, local and multiple.
This variety of forms gives some idea of the complexity of
totemism—a complexity which is increased by the co-
existence in very many tribes of several forms; it is quite
common to find three or four in the one tribe; that is, each
person has three or four totems or rather, belongs to as
many totemic groups. But this is only the beginning of
the complexity, for as we shall see, on the one hand, one
form may have more than one function and on the other
hand, several forms perform a similar function. It is,

therefore, necessary to study totemic phenomena from the point of view of the function which they perform in social and religious life. Some reference has already been made to this in Chapter IV in connexion with social groupings.

THE FUNCTIONS OF TOTEMISM

Passing then from a study of the forms and organization of totemic phenomena to a study of their function and meaning, we may classify such phenomena under the following headings: social, cult, conception, dream, classificatory and assistant.

Social Totemism. Possibly the most important point to be made clear is the distinction between social and cult totemism. Had earlier investigators realized this distinction, less confusion would have resulted. The former is concerned with human relationships and marriage, whereas the latter has little if any concern with these matters; it has to do with mythology, ritual and the sacred side of tribal life.

Further, social totemism is nearly always, perhaps always, matrilineal in descent, while cult totemism is local and patrilineal. The former is very frequently expressed in matrilineal clans. The members of such a clan belong to it because their mothers do or did, and ultimately they have all been incarnated through the womb of a common ancestress. Now, it is this common flesh and blood relationship which is expressed by the term for social totem, namely, "flesh" or "meat". To ask a native what is his "flesh", is to receive the name of his matrilineal social totem, say, kangaroo or emu. It is his flesh, or rather the symbol of the common flesh shared by the members of the clan, who, therefore, speak of themselves as relations. As a result, they will not injure, kill or eat their social totem, their flesh, nor will they marry any person who has the same social totem, never mind how distant is his genealogical relationship or how far away is his country, for he is one flesh. Such a marriage would break the fun-

damental incest laws which forbid marriage with mother
or sister, because all who belong to one social clan are
mothers and children or brothers and sisters.

This relationship is also very frequently shown in another way, namely, by an action on the part of the totemic
partner; the animal or plant in actual life or in a vision or
dream acts as a mate or friend of the persons whose
totem it is; it warns them of danger, gives them courage
or strength and imparts to them information regarding
absent clansfolk. The very presence of the totem does this,
or rather it sets the person meditating, and the condition
in which, or the place where, he happens to be, has a
lot to do with the interpretation put upon the action or
presence of the social totem.

Matrilineal moiety totemism has in part a similar significance; all its members are relations, and the moiety
totem (eagle-hawk, crow, black cockatoo, white cockatoo, etc.) symbolizes the sharing of a common life based
on descent through the mothers, though in a more extended sense than in the case of the social clan. In some
cases, the members of a matrilineal moiety speak of
themselves as one flesh, and will not eat the moiety totem
unless driven to do so by hunger; in such a case, they express their sorrow for having eaten their friend or flesh.
Such moieties are usually exogamous provided that *clan*
exogamy and the kinship rules are observed, for the primary function of moieties, as previously stated, is not to
regulate marriage.

Section (and subsection) totemism is either wholly or
chiefly social in function. The sections group relations in
certain ways for social purposes, separating generation
lines and cross-cousins. Moreover the members of any one
group are, for certain purposes, regarded as relations, or
all of one kind; this is even more true of subsections. But
so close to nature do the Aborigines live and so all pervad-
ing is the totemic attitude to life, that these groupings,
comparatively recent as they must be, are mostly (and

possibly were generally) thought of in a totemic manner; that is, the members of any one section are not only related to one another, but also to one or more natural species, their totems. Subsections are frequently referred to as "skins" in northern Australia; this corresponds to the use of the term "flesh" for the totem of the social clan; indeed, in one part of eastern Australia, "skin" is used instead of "flesh" for the latter. Moreover, the section and subsection totemic groups are indirectly matrilineal in descent and in most of the tribes with sections in eastern Australia, an individual adopts a ritual attitude towards his own totem, or even all the totems of his section. He neither kills nor eats it, and indeed, expresses sorrow when he sees it killed. The section totem, too, in some tribes, acts as the totemite's mate or guardian. Thus, the section and subsection forms of totemism are similar in function and meaning to the totemism of the social clans. Like the latter also, the sections and subsections are ideally exogamous; often, however, this is not so in practice, though marriage between members of the same totemic group would not occur, for there are usually several totems in each section or subsection.

Sex Totemism. Sex totemism is also a variety of social totemism. As we have already seen in our examination of social groups it stands for the solidarity of each sex, a solidarity which is expressed in ritual quarrels and marriage preliminaries and is symbolized by each sex possessing a bird or plant totem. But this is not just a matter of having a name or emblem, for the men and their totem on the one hand, and the women and their totem on the other hand, are said to share a common life. Some tribes believed that the men and women were each descended from their totems, and in this way all the men of the tribe were brothers and all the women were sisters, while the totem (bat and night owl, bat and wood-pecker, emu-wren and superb warbler) was the mate or brother (or sister) of its totemic group, and indeed might itself be a transformed man or woman.

Thus, sex totemism is social in nature because it functions as a social grouping and also because it symbolizes and expresses social and kinship relationships in much the same way as does social clan totemism.

Cult Totemism. Over the greater part of Australia, perhaps formerly over all of it, there has existed a variety of totemism which may best be described as a secret religious or cult organization. In each tribe there are a number of cult societies or cult groups or lodges, each of which consists of a number of fully initiated male members whose affiliations were designated by right of birth. Each group exists to take care of and hand on a prescribed portion of the sacred totemic mythology and ritual of the tribe and often, also, to be the custodian of sacred totemic sites and to perform ceremonies for the increase of the species which is its totem. The portion of mythology and ritual and the sacred sites entrusted to such a cult group are determined by mythological history. It is basically the mythology which records the travels and actions of the tribal heroes in its subdivision of the tribal territory. The country of each local group is crossed by paths or tracks, usually unmarked, along which there are a number of special sites where a hero performed some action which is recorded in myth; it may have been only an ordinary everyday act, or it may have been the institution or performance of a rite. A site with its heap of stones, standing stone, waterhole or some other natural feature, may mark the spot where he rested or went out of sight temporarily. Another may mark the final stopping place where his body was transformed into stone and his spirit was freed to watch everything which should happen afterwards or, possibly, it may be the "home" where his spirit awaits reincarnation. In some cases too, such a hero is believed to have left the pre-existent children in the spirit-centres, in the same way as by his rites and actions and the virtue inherent in him, he caused certain places to be the life-centres or spirit-centres of natural species.

This conception of the mythological path is especially important in most of South Australia and the Northern Territory, including Arnhem Land, and wherever we penetrate sufficiently far into the secret life, we find it exercising a constant influence in the cult-life. For example, in the Bard and Karadjeri tribes, north and south of Broome respectively, when the bull-roarers and sacred wooden objects are left in the sacred storehouse or when brought out to be displayed, they must always be placed with the ends pointing along the track or direction travelled by the culture-hero represented by them. But in South and Central Australia, as we have seen, birth or conception on the mythological path determines an individual's secondary if not primary "lodge" affiliations, and moreover, it is the path which really makes or constitutes a person's "country", the "ancestral estate" as it has been well described. The special emphasis on the "paths" in South and Central Australia and adjacent areas of Western Australia also is probably a reflection of geographical and economic facts, namely, the dry nature of the country and the scarcity of readily accessible water in the past, as in the present. Permanent rock-holes and shallow soaks are few and often far between, with the result that, except immediately after rain, the natives are not free to roam far to the right or left of the shortest routes between the sources of water. Under such conditions it is not surprising that the natives are often vague concerning the boundaries of the countries of local groups, just as they sometimes are with regard to tribal boundaries. A kind of no-man's-land exists in which no one is particularly interested. It has no permanent economic value and is of little, if any mythological significance.

The existence of these paths explains one fact which sometimes puzzles students of Aboriginal cult-life. They notice that though the natives say they know quite well

the direction and the exact location of a certain sacred
site, they very seldom approach it by the shortest route;
indeed, they frequently set out as though going somewhere else altogether, or they seem unable to find their
way to the place. The explanation is that the sacred place
must only be approached by the same path as that taken
by the hero connected with it; this may lead for some
time away from it, and some informants may have to
search round until they find signs of the track before they
can move with certainty.

These paths are inter-group and inter-tribal in character, that is to say, they pass through the countries and
territories of local clans and of tribes and in doing so serve
to bind these groups and tribes together. Certainly, all
those whose countries, irrespective of tribe, are situated
along the path of one hero or a group of heroes, have a
secret bond of friendship and a mutual claim to hospitality and protection. This enables members of a cult-
group which is responsible for the myths and rites associated with the hero of the path, to travel safely along
that hero's path even when it leads into other tribal territories, provided their purpose is peaceful and associated
at least indirectly with the cult. A notable instance of
this is the expedition for red ochre from north-eastern
South Australia down to the deposits at Parachilna, a distance of three or four hundred miles; but all the way,
the travellers could follow the path of the mythological
emu and dogs whose blood ultimately caused the red
ochre deposit.

The inter-group aspect of the path has another important effect, namely, it makes the various local groups and
tribes mutually dependent for their cult-life. To obtain
the whole story of many of the great myths and to see all
the rites connected with it, we must pass from group to
group and tribe to tribe—in other words, from lodge to
lodge. Each one is the custodian of a particular chapter of
the myth and of the particular rites and sites associated

with that chapter. But as continuity with the past, a full knowledge of social and ritual sanctions, and a complete assurance for the present and future can only be maintained and gained by a knowledge of the myth as a whole and the performance of all the rites, it is essential that each "lodge" should do its part. Thus the groups and tribes are linked together by the cult-life.

This is particularly clear to us if we think of the rites which have to be performed for the increase of natural species—such as yams, fish, marsupials, rain and other things on which life itself depends, and for the care of the sites associated with the life or spirits of these species. Each local cult-group is responsible for one, sometimes for a few, of these rites and sites, but as it requires for its sustenance the regular increase of other species, the rites and sites for which it does not possess, it is dependent on the ceremonial knowledge, sites and activities of other local cult-groups for its own life. As this is mutual, we see that the cult-life is a vast system of ritual co-operation binding together local groups and also tribes.

The inter-dependence of groups is also brought about in another way, namely, by the fact that very often the paths of two or more heroes or bands of heroes pass through the country of the one territorial clan; these paths sometimes cross one another, in space, though not necessarily in time, and the points of intersection are frequently known. This fact has two consequences: in the first place members of a local group have an interest in the paths and myths of all the heroes who passed through their country, though they themselves are usually concerned primarily with only one, namely, the hero of special importance in their country; in the second place, according to the places in which their spirits were found, or in which they were conceived or born, different members of the one local group may be attached to different mythological paths and heroes, and consequently their primary affiliations are to different "lodges", even though they may all

assist each other in their respective cult-duties. This sometimes explains why members of one local group have
different totems, and at the same time each man has several or all the totems. It is a matter of the historical associations of the locality of his father's clan.

The Cult Totem. The question, however, might well be
asked: "What has all this business of cult societies and
'lodges' to do with totemism?" The answer is simply that
cult totemism is based on a belief in the mutual inter-
dependence of man and nature, on the need one has of
the other, and on the urge to bring the latter into the historical and ceremonial life of the former. The heroes whose
paths we have been discussing are often referred to in
totemic guise, that is, as animals or birds, though often
too as human beings. Sometimes they are men and
women bearing totemic names, possibly endowed with
the power of assuming some of the characteristics and attributes of their totems when the occasion demands it,
and sometimes they are animals or birds who always remain such, though they talk and think as human beings.
Moreover, to ascertain a man's cult totem or lodge the
best way is to ask him what is his "dreaming" or else,
what is his "big ceremony". The answer may be merely
the name of an animal, plant or natural object, that is, a
totem, but it may also be a myth, long or short, narrating
the doings and travels of a great hero or heroes in the
mythical age, "the eternal dream-time",[3] a time which is
past and yet, in a sense present. In other words, the Aborigine gives a summary of the mythology of which he and
the members of his cult-group are the custodians and
which they represent and re-enact in rites. If he only gives
one word, the name of the totem, as his answer, this is
but the key to, or the name of, the myth of the local
lodge.

Cult Ceremonies. These cult lodges are responsible for

[3] This is discussed further in Chapter VIII.

two kinds of ceremonies. The first are solely historical and instructive in nature and function. They re-enact the doings of the hero or heroes concerned, and in so doing act out the myth. The actors, representing animals, birds, or human beings, "dress up", adorning themselves with the paint and design peculiar to the rite, and wearing or carrying symbols which express some fact about, or incident in the life of the hero. Songs are chanted during the preparations for the rites, as well as during their performance. These are the poetical versions of the myths. At the conclusion of each act which usually lasts only five or ten minutes or so, the old men explain it and the decorations and symbols to any newly initiated men present or to any whose memories need refreshing. In this way tribal history is handed down, and the patterns of life which the myths enshrine are instilled into the minds of the younger men present, for men must do to-day what the great heroes did in the dream-time.

There are many interesting features in these rites, such as the part played by the moieties, whenever present; the manner in which requests are made to the totemites or members of the particular cult-group to perform one of the rites; the way the performers are embraced at the end of an act as an intimation to stop and as an expression of thankfulness, and the pitch of excitement often reached by the singers, some of whom jump up to do a peculiar shuffling kind of dance and at times, draw blood from themselves. The importance of the rites, however, lies not in these and similar customs, but in two important functions which they perform. In the first place, they preserve and inculcate the historical traditions and social sanctions (or authority) of the tribe and thereby strengthen the social sentiments; in the second place, they enable the members of the assembled group or groups to express and feel their unity and common life—a life which in the ritual wells up from the past and becomes available for the future.

Such means of maintaining the social sanctions and ideals, and of strengthening the common life is essential for the Aborigines if not for all mankind. If the cohesion of the Aboriginal community is to be maintained, the cult-life must not be destroyed. The ceremonies might, however, be modified, or, indeed, replaced by others capable of performing the same essential functions.

There is no need to discuss here the second type of cult ceremony. Concerned with the increase of natural species, and like the ceremonies of the first type, it has an historical basis, being associated with the travels and deeds of the totemic heroes; moreover, the increase ceremony is usually performed at sites sanctified by those heroes, whose bodies were possibly transformed there, or where they themselves performed increase rituals. In rare cases, however, the special site does not seem to be necessary, and the performance of the historical ceremony is believed to be sufficient to ensure the increase of the species. Normally, the rite for any one object is performed by the members of the cult lodge which has the particular species for its totem, though they have assistants, usually their sisters' sons or male cross-cousins. Such rites possess many interesting features, some of which will be mentioned in the discussion of Aboriginal philosophy. It is sufficient to state that the effect of these rites is once again to enable the groups concerned to realize their unity and common life. By the correct performance in the proper centres assurance is gained that nature will proceed on her wonted way and man will be able to get food and so live. The converse of the picture is that if the natives do not perform, or are prevented by us from performing these increase rites, they cannot, and do not, have that assurance. Their life is based on a ritual co-operation with nature and if they fail to do their part, there is no certainty that nature will be able to perform hers; indeed, it is almost certain that she will not be able to do so.

Membership of cult-groups was discussed when dealing

with the patrilineal and local clans. But it should be pointed out that one person can be a member of two or three. Thus in South and Central Australia, quite apart from the interest in a lodge which he has through being conceived or born outside of his father's country, or on another path, each person is admitted to a knowledge of the myths and rites of his mother's brother's (or mother's brother's son's) cult-group; henceforth he must assist in the performance of the rites connected with the latter; indeed, the sisters' sons are often referred to as the "bosses" of it, probably because they must see that the mother's brothers perform the rites in the prescribed manner. There is usually a special term denoting that a person is a sister's son type of member of a lodge. Thus, amongst the Dieri, it is *maduka* as compared with *pintara*, the term for the primary patrilineal members. It should be noted that while the latter, the cult totem of the father's line, is handed on to a person's son, the former cannot be passed on. A person's son gets his *maduka* from his own mother's brother. This membership of two cult-totemic groups is widespread: and although Spencer and Gillen did not recognize the *maduka* amongst the Aranda, it is present there and also farther north; indeed, we should always be on the watch for it. It is based on two strong urges; one type arises from the very close physiological and social bond which exists between a man and his sister's son, and the second consists of balancing the male and female lines in matters of descent and inheritance. A man belongs to the local cult-group of his father; but his mother's line cannot be ignored, and so he is admitted to the cult-group of the mother's brother.

The Cult Totem and Marriage. It should be emphasized that this totem has nothing whatever to do with marriage, and if it appears to be implicated it is only because the totems are distributed amongst the local exogamous groups of the tribe.

Cult Totems and Taboo on the Totem. A taboo on the

cult totem is quite widely observed. In some tribes it is never eaten by the totemites except ritually once a year at the first gathering of the species; in other tribes, it cannot be eaten until after a period of abstinence, and a ritual eating. In some cases, there seems to be no taboo at all. But in general, there is a tendency or rule to regard the cult totem as too sacred a symbol to be used in a profane way; indeed, in symbolizing membership of a cult society it is often also the symbol of a patrilineal and spiritual relationship to a mythological ancestor; in this regard, the cult totem resembles the social totem, only the latter symbolizes a matrilineal physiological relationship.

Cult Totems and Social Totems. We must also notice that cult totems and social totems frequently co-exist in one tribe. The tribes of north-eastern South Australia are the most striking examples of this: a man has his patrilineal local cult totem and a share in his mother's brother's cult totem; he also belongs to his mother's social totem (his flesh), and one may add, to her moiety; in addition, he has a sex totem. But these tribes are not alone in this regard. We know that many tribes of the Northern Territory and Eastern Kimberley have subsection social totems as well as cult totems, while some of them also have distinct social clan totems.[4]

Cult Totemism and the Women. The women have cult totems just as their brothers and fathers have, but they are only admitted to "associate" membership of the cult societies and to "outside" parts in ritual.

Conception Totemism. Reference has already been made to conception totemism in the examination of local totemism; in the latter case it is really a method of determining affiliation to localized totemic cult societies. In some tribes,

---

[4] The very unsatisfactory nature of the information regarding the descent of totems in north-central Australia suggested that Spencer and Gillen had not distinguished patrilineal cult totemism, mother's brother (assistant) cult totemism and social totemism. Later investigations have shown that this was so.

as we shall see, it functions as a dream totem. From our point of view, conception can only be realized by the mother, nor would the Aborigines deny this, and in Central Australia they use this fact in determining cult totems. But the father may also play a part in conception—a spiritual role and not the physiological part that we know to be a fact. As already seen, in very many parts of Australia, the father finds in a vision of the day or night, the pre-existent child which ascertains from him who its mother is to be, and then enters her womb. The mother may dream of the spirit-child later. But the father knows ahead that a spirit is to be incarnated through his wife. In some parts, the spirit-child is "found" or dreamed of in association with some natural species; this is usually one of the totems of the father's own country or section or subsection—the vision being "controlled". In any case, this natural species becomes the child's conception totem—the tie between his spirit and the natural world; and although normally, it is also a cult totem or a section totem, there are instances which suggest that it is distinct. In one case, Eastern Kimberley, this totem is said to be the one animal or bird in or with which the spirit was found, and therefore no taboo is observed towards the species as a whole.[5]

Throughout a vast northern region, the "finding" happens when the man, spearing some creature or pulling a plant, sees not this object but a spirit-child. He may dream of it later. This animal or plant, through which the pre-existent spirit makes its way to incarnation, is called its "protector". It is the conception totem. In a large south-western region this totem is the animal or plant species, of

[5] Much more investigation is needed with regard to this problem of conception totemism. It is possible that the finding and dreaming of a totem in association with the pre-existent child is always a means of determining the cult, social or dream totem where there are several possibilities; this certainly does happen. In some areas, however, there is no conception totem; there is a spirit-home and a culture-hero—a provider of spirit children, who puts them there.

which a woman was eating just before experiencing the first indications of pregnancy.

Dream Totemism. By dream totemism is meant the belief that a person is represented in dreams (especially the dreams of others) by a natural species or object, so that even the dream life has an intimate relationship with nature. In most of the great cult-totemic regions of Australia, the cult totem also acts as the dream totem; indeed, it is called the "dreaming", but not so much in reference to this function, as to its significance as a link with the "eternal dream-time". Amongst the tribes of the Great Victoria Desert, however, the cult totem is not the dream totem; instead the conception totem performs the functions of the latter. This totem is associated with the first sickness of pregnancy. If a woman becomes sick after having eaten some article of food and later on dreams of a spirit-child, she knows that a spirit-child has entered her womb with, or in the form of, the natural species thus eaten. This species, which is the symbol and indeed, the sacrament, of its incarnation, becomes the child's dream totem. In the Forrest River one of the parents dreams of the child's dream totem and then informs it, while amongst the Worora and probably the Ungarinyin also, a person's dream totem is his mother's brother's local cult totem.[6] I have also found the dream totem amongst the remaining Aborigines of the north coast of New South Wales, and I have no doubt that it was and is very widespread.

Classificatory Totemism. Classificatory totemism is perhaps the most interesting variety of totemism; in form it is multiple totemism, and the latter may be a feature of moiety, clan, section or local totemism. Broadly speaking this means that each moiety, clan, section or local group totem includes not only men and women but also certain

[6] This suggests that a person has a share in his mother's brother's totemic cult as well. Amongst the Southern Aranda, a man's dream totem is his mother's brother's cult totem and he also shares in the rites associated with the latter.

natural species and objects. In the case of clan and local (cult) totems, these are often referred to as subsidiary totems, and in any case, a person looks upon the various species and objects grouped with or under his totem, as in some sense his own totems, and if he takes up any sort of ritual attitude to the primary totem, he acts towards the rest in much the same way. In other words, there is felt to be some kind of relationship between man and all natural species and objects; all things in heaven and earth —including man—are classified into moieties, clans, cult-groups or sections. Totemism is then a method of classifying natural phenomena, and it does so by bringing them into man's social and cult-groups on the basis of the Aborigine's conviction that the life of nature and man is one. To us, it may seem strange to be told that lightning is crow and so are thunder, rain, clouds, hail and winter, that the moon and stars are black cockatoo, that fish, eels and seals are *karato* (a non-poisonous snake). But the major totems represent social clans and by grouping in these all the other natural phenomena which come into his life in any way, he has a workable method of classification and one which does not add any further complications to ritual and social behaviour. We cannot always see the principle by which the classification was made, but no doubt there are, or were, associations in the Aboriginal mind and culture which would have no significance for us. Such animistic and social classification of natural phenomena, however, does at least show that Aboriginal man is at home in nature, and also that he makes nature at home within his own social organization.

Assistant Totemism. In most parts of Australia, the medicine-man stands in a special relation to one natural species, usually an animal or reptile which acts as his assistant, going forth either to work his will for good or ill on the patient or victim, or to gather information from a distance. This variety of totemism, which is individual in form, is most strongly developed in eastern Australia, but the possession of similar "familiars" is also a characteristic of the medicine-men of north-western Australia.[7] Such totems and "familiars" are both within and without the individual. They are like a second self or spirit, and yet they are also externalized in the species, and may be exhibited in a tamed member of it. The lace lizard and certain snakes are the commonest varieties of assistant totems.

This totem is usually given by medicine-men and generally only to persons who are destined, or desire, to be magical practitioners. A dying medicine-man may leave his totem to someone else—in so doing, he bequeaths part of himself. In south-eastern Australia, at least, assistant totemism is akin to social totemism; the totemite does not eat his totem; indeed, an injury to the latter will entail injury to him; and, for its part, the totem assists and guards the individual. It should also be noticed that the social totem and the dream totem are often believed to guard and warn the totemite and even to help him recover from illness. But the element of positive assistance in the performance of one's work or calling is not present; this seems to be limited to the profession of medicine-men and the workers of magic, and so requires a subdivision for itself, namely, assistant totemism.

[7] Spirit snakes are the commonest form of "familiar" or assistant totem; they are often, especially in north-western Australia, associated with or derived from the mythical rainbow serpent. In such cases they cannot be seen under natural conditions.

Chapter VII

THE SECRET LIFE AND INITIATION

CULTURE CONTACT AND THE SECRET LIFE

TOTEMISM in Australia may be thought of as a link between the social life of everyday and the secret life of myth and ritual, and in our study of it we have passed from the one to the other. There is, however, only one door which admits to the inner shrine and to a knowledge of the mysteries, namely, initiation; and every male member of the tribe must pass through it, enduring the discipline and pain as well as receiving enlightenment. You and I, too, whether students at home or field-workers, must, in spirit, do the same, for then and only then shall we gain some conception of what life means to the Aborigines, and some idea of the hidden springs of their conduct, faith and hope, and of the depth of their thought.

There are many white folk who are said to be great authorities on the Aborigines. I have frequently been told to consult them, but ever and anon I came out by the same door by which I went in. They had some idea of the subsections or sections, of the mother-in-law taboo and a few obvious customs such as circumcision, but they had no real knowledge of the inner life of the natives. It may seem surprising to be told that a settler, missionary, policeman or settlement manager can spend years and years amongst such an apparently primitive type of people as the Aborigines, and yet know very little of importance about them, but it is a fact, and no one knows it better than the Aborigines themselves. But such is their loyalty to their secrets, that they never drop a hint to the white "authority" of the great world of thought, ritual and sanction of which he is unaware. They feel either that he would not understand it or that he would despise it, and so the "past-masters", the old custodians of secret knowledge sit in the camp, sphinx-like, watching with eagle eye the effect of white contact on the young men, and deciding how much, if any, of the knowledge of their fathers can be safely entrusted to them, and just when the imparting of the secrets can be effectively made. If the young men are too much attracted to the white man's ways, if they are inclined to despise the old ways, and above all if they show a looseness of living which denotes lack of stability in character, the old men either teach them nothing, or else traditional false versions of some myths as a means of testing their sincerity and loyalty. But only too often, after contact with the white man, the time is never propitious for the imparting of "truth", and so the secrets pass away with the old men; and though the latter die in sorrow knowing that the old rites and myths will pass into oblivion, that the sacred places will no longer be cared for, and that the tribe is doomed to extinction, yet they die triumphantly, having been loyal to their trust.

Surely we must admire the nobility and depth of character manifested by such men!—though I am afraid that few of us ever attribute such virtue to them. They are just regarded as the old fellows, for whom it is too late to do anything, and about whom it is not worth bothering. But ultimately, the only satisfactory and authentic way into the secret life is the one guarded by these old men. The young men do not know it. Moreover, the attempt, not yet quite abandoned, of trying to keep the adolescents away from the old men and the rest of the tribe, leads either to a dichotomy between the young and their elders or to a conflict of loyalties in the mind of the former. Of course, I am referring to regions where the tribal life is still functioning in some degree. Nothing is more disastrous than the cultivation of an attitude of superiority on the part of the rising generation towards the old ways, for these were the ways of their own people for countless generations; and foundations which consist partly of a disrespect for, and shame of, one's own culture and people are a sandy and unreliable basis for the building up of a new religion and culture.

This attitude is especially deplorable seeing that it is adopted by those who have not been admitted to a full knowledge of the spiritual and secret life of their fathers. It also makes the discerning tremble, for we now know what the old custodians of the secret life realized, that the day of disillusionment must come for nearly all Aborigines. They sooner or later learn that they can get little more from our culture than a few of its tools—tomahawks to motor-cars—and an inferior position as hewers of wood and drawers of water, if no one else wants the job. Admission into white society is denied them, and they very seldom seem able to get a real grip of the Christian religion, largely because of the way in which it is usually presented to them—that is, as a revelation quite unconnected with their own past life of belief, ritual and conduct. As a result, we are finding that in the course of two or three generations, the Aborigines, full-blood and half-caste, realizing this, endeavour to return to the secret life of their fathers and once again adopt its beliefs and rites, though somewhat modified, and from our point of view, purified and rendered less harsh. They try to equate Biblical characters to the heroes of the old myths, and say that the old teaching contained what is valuable in the new. This is a great opportunity for civilizing and missionary agents provided that they have a sound understanding of Aboriginal culture, philosophy and belief, and a good knowledge of the secret life. Unfortunately, however, not only does the white man lack this, but so too does the Aborigine, just because the old men of the previous generation were so careful of their trust. They would not bestow their knowledge on those who were philandering with the new ways and beliefs, and so the disillusioned men have but the husk upon which to fall back. But how helpful it would be if we could say to them: "Here is the essence of the teaching of your fathers—a teaching which was their light and guide for generations and which even now can be a strength and stay to you, provided that you modify and build on it so that it may help you to adapt yourselves to, and live under, modern conditions!" Herein lies a motive for studying the secret life wherever we can, so that we may hold it in trust for the sophisticated and, later, disillusioned Aborigines. Just as most Christians take a long time to pass through the Old Testament type of life to that required by the New Testament, so it is with the Aborigines. They, too, must pass through the Old Testament state before attaining to our view of life, but it must be *their own* old testament of myth and sanction, for this alone has intimate relationship with their social and economic life. Now, the graded secret life is the means by which this progress is made.

MISSIONARY PROBLEMS

I referred above to the possibility of a conflict of loyalties in the mind of the individual. This can hardly help arising amongst many of the young men and girls who are associated with missions in the isolated parts of the continent. The parents, still nomads or partly so, are often willing to leave their children at missions until they reach adolescence, but they would then like them to take their place in society. The girls have been promised in marriage, and unless the promises be kept or adjustments made, a general disturbance of social equilibrium must occur. They may like the mission life and the missionaries, but if they have not been completely isolated since infancy, they know what is expected of them according to tribal custom and are drawn towards fulfilling those expectations. But this is nothing compared to the conflict that is set up in the minds of the youths. Having reached adolescence, they should commence their progress through the various stages of initiation which will make them good men and full members of the tribe, inwardly as well as outwardly, and which will enable them to take their place in those rituals which are essential to the life and well-being of the community. The lads themselves, as a result of hints given them by the elders, desire to move along the path of mystic progress and become true men; and the more obstacles that are put in the way by the conditions of employment, or by the authority and arguments of the missionary, the more are they drawn to follow the path already trodden by the wise old men. The result is a conflict of loyalties and desires. The young fellows respect the missionary or employer because of his superior position, often too, by reason of his kindness, and also on account of the opportunities for material gain which association with him provides. But their allegiance is given to their fathers and the old men, and their real interest is in that world of secret life and action which stretches far back into the days of the great heroes, and forward beyond death itself.

We often fail to realize how little meaning our way of life possesses for the Aborigines, even for those who are to all intents and purposes civilized. I can think of regions where they have been in touch with us for sixty years and where for six months of the year, the dry season of the north, they play a very valuable part in our country life, principally on the stations; during that time they dress in our way, shave and wash, appreciate our food and seem quite presentable. At the end of the time, they receive the small share of their pay which they are allowed to handle, buy a few objects (often at an exorbitant price) mostly of a kind which we regard as ridiculous for grown men, and then with their families go bush, casting off their clothes and all else that belongs to our culture. They paint themselves, camp, hunt, perform corroborees and take part in secret ceremonies; and all this in spite sometimes of the fact that their social life has been most degraded and demoralized by association with whites during the past fifty years or so. We, of course, may think that their conduct in returning to this bush life every year is somewhat unintelligible and shows a lack of appreciation of the higher stage of living to which they adapt themselves for six months a year. But we must remember two things: in the first place, the only part of our life with which these seasonal native employees become familiar is its economic and material aspects, and they do not thereby gain the impression that our way of life is of more value to them than is their own; it has some interest for them, mainly because it enables them apparently to satisfy us and also to obtain a few material objects which they find either useful or fascinating. In the second place, our economic life is not *their* life— it is only an external means or a tool enabling them to do something which is obviously expedient, but it is not connected with their life of ritual and belief; on the other hand, the time in the bush with its paint and hunting and ceremonies *is* their life, and has meaning for them. What they do there is for themselves, and in the ritual they keep in touch with the heroes and ancestors of old, realize their common life, and derive hope for the future.

Such a fact as this helps us to understand why the young fellows are drawn towards initiation and the secret life in spite of the counter attractions and influences of missionary and other civilizing agents. It means, however, that they are drawn in two ways which seem to be incompatible. What then is the result? There are two alternatives: the missionary or civilizing agent may be successful in putting an end to initiation and other secret rites, or in getting such a grip over the rising generation that the old men make the initiation a mere form and not an entry into the full secret life of the tribe. But this implies a breakdown of tribal authority and a loss of the knowledge of, let alone the respect for those ideals, sentiments and sanctions which are essential to tribal cohesion; and in Australia, such a condition is the accompaniment, and a cause, of tribal extinction. The other alternative is, for a period at least, the failure of the missionary or other civilizing agent. The old men and the glamour of the secret life win. The missionary may be quite unaware of this, for he is apt to rely on outward conformity to his demands and teaching, and if he is not conversant with the language and secrets of the tribe he cannot do otherwise. But slowly and surely, step by step, the young fellow advances along the secret path, and in heart is getting farther and farther away from the white man's doctrines and view of life. See him this morning outwardly playing his part on the station or in mission compound or church. But see him again this afternoon completely wrapped up in the performance of a secret rite and the exposition of a sacred myth by the elders—perhaps only a mile or so away from the mission or station, but an age away in mind. Yes, see him there and you will know where he finds meaning for life, sanction for conduct and hope for the future. And unless the tribal life breaks down, he will sooner or later spend a great deal of his time traversing the paths and localities sanctified by the wanderings and exploits of the great heroes of old, and performing the rites on which the life of the tribe and of nature depends.

THE LIFE APART

What then is this secret life of the Aborigines? It is the life apart—a life of ritual and mythology, of sacred rites and objects. It is the life in which man really finds his place in society and in nature, and in which he is brought in touch with the invisible things of the world of the past, present and future. Every now and then we find the tribe, or groups from more than one tribe, going apart from the workaday world. A special camp is arranged where the women remain unless some of them are called upon to play a subsidiary part in a ceremony. Then the men go on a mile or so to a secret site or to sites where they spend hours, or maybe days and weeks and even months, singing and performing rites, and in some cases even eating or sleeping there. When they return later to the world of secular affairs they are refreshed in mind and spirit. They now face the vicissitudes of everyday life with a new courage and a strength gained from the common participation in the rites, with a fresh appreciation of their social and moral ideals and patterns of life, and an assurance that having performed the rites well and truly, all will be well with themselves and with that part of nature with which their lives are so intimately linked.

There are three kinds of rites, namely, initiation, historical and increase. As we have already seen (Chapter VI), the last two are totemic and historical in character and perform psychological and social functions which seem to be essential for the well-being of the tribe. But before a person can take part in these, he must be initiated.

RITUAL OPERATIONS ON THE BODY

Initiation rites differ in details in various parts of Australia. Thus, circumcision was an especially prominent feature in Central and north-western Australia, tooth-avulsion in New South Wales, depilation south of the Murray, cicatrization in South Australia and eastern Queensland, and the tying of arm-ligatures in parts of Western Australia. This does not necessarily mean, however, that only one of these bodily operations was performed in each of these areas, but that the others, if present, were of less ceremonial importance. Thus, in many tribes of New South Wales, the knocking out of a tooth was an essential preliminary to the revelation of the secrets, whereas in some north-western Australian tribes it is only a preliminary to the more sacred rite of circumcision, and in other tribes it has no ceremonial significance whatever. In most of Victoria, the plucking of the hairs from the face and body and in some of the tribes of the central-western coast district of Western Australia, the tying of arm-ligatures were, respectively, the only ordeals of pain to which the novices were submitted. The arm-ligatures which were very tight and left on for some days, were really a preparation for the letting of blood from an arm vein, a duty incumbent on every adult man in the course of sacred ceremonies—a custom found in most tribes, though the first binding of the arm may not always be made a prominent feature in initiation. Likewise, the making of cicatrices on the body was the main, and indeed, the only bodily operation in parts of northern Queensland; but in some Northern Territory tribes it was only a means of beautification, for circumcision and subincision were the outstanding ritual operations; on the other hand, the pattern of cicatrization cut on the initiate's back in South and much of Western Australia was a pass sign of his initiation into the highest degree, whereas circumcision was not of such significance.

Likewise, there are what can be called regional differences in other initiation ceremonies. I have, however, mentioned the physical operations because many white folk imagine that the operation is initiation and that, having been present at a circumcision or tooth-knocking rite they really understand Aboriginal secrets. The bodily operations, however, are not the important and essential element in initiation. They are, in some cases, performed at the ordinary camp corroboree ground, and are sometimes very mild in nature. They can, moreover, be omitted if circumstances render such a step necessary, without endangering the real purpose and effect of initiation. We know that this is true of the rituals of our own and also ancient secret societies. In such cases the bodily operations are performed in symbolical fashion only, but the doctrine, meaning and social function of the rites are not thereby impaired. And so it is and can be with Aboriginal rites. Many groups have dropped subincision, either because of the pain involved, or more usually, because it interfered with a quick resumption of duties on the cattle station. White influence has also been brought to bear directly in this matter. Others have dropped such severe ordeals as the pulling off of finger nails before the highest revelations are made.

The older men are naturally somewhat resentful of the softer manners of the younger men, seeing what they themselves had to endure, and express the opinion that they have handed on the secrets at too cheap a price. However, they have taken care to test in other ways the worthiness of those men to whom they have entrusted any knowledge of the mysteries.

The bodily operations, like the other rites in initiation, have their own meanings, though it is often difficult or impossible to ascertain what these are, and the natives can seldom help, except to the extent of providing a myth which justifies them historically. Circumcision, cicatrices and the absence of an upper incisor tooth can and do serve as an outward sign of having reached a certain degree of initiation, though none of these signs are considered necessary by some tribes. The tying of arm-ligatures is but a preparation for the duty of blood-letting, and subincision prepares the genital organ for a similar purpose; blood is drawn from it for ritual use, to express emotions in a prescribed ritual manner both in initiation and totemic ceremonies.[1] The distribution of the rites suggests that circumcision and possibly also subincision entered Australia at the north-western corner and spread thence east and south-

---

[1] Subincision is not practised as a means of preventing conception: (i) It does not do so. In almost all tribes where it is or was practised, every male is subincised before marriage, and yet children are born. (ii) Whether the male genital organ be partly or wholly subincised (i.e. cut open to the urethra from underneath), the position in which sexual intercourse occurs, ensures that all or most of the male seminal fluid enters the female organ. And (iii) the Aborigines do not think of it in this way, for in all the area where subincision is practised, sexual intercourse is not believed to be the cause of conception. The finding of the spirit-child by the father or mother or both, and its entry into the womb is the essential cause. Intercourse may be also necessary, but there is some doubt, and also complete denial of this.

east. It was, no doubt, believed to have some magical efficacy, but as I have already implied, its real significance lies not in the first operation of subincision which takes place—sometimes without ceremony—during the course of initiation, but in the subsequent ritual cuttings; by these, the incision is extended or blood is drawn by piercing the subincised part. Such blood may be used for anointing or painting the candidate, or it may be merely allowed to run on the thighs of each man concerned. In the former case, it symbolizes the new life into which the young men have entered, and indeed, it imparts such life to them and binds them to the elders. In the latter case it expresses the emotions aroused by the thought of the youths facing their ritual trials or by the contemplation of the deeds of the heroes. In some secret rituals, too, the actors are anointed on the shoulders and chest with subincision blood.[2]

Arm-blood is sacred, and is used for sticking ornamental material (bird's down and ochre) on the body in preparation for a ceremony, for anointing the candidates, and for sacramental drinking by the candidates and the elders. It gives strength to the young fellows so that they will be able to bear the sight of the sacred symbols and rites which are to be revealed.[3] It also binds them by a lifebond to the sacred community of initiated men.

[2] This drawing of blood frequently takes place during the performance of historical totemic ceremonies; a number will do it and then with their thighs sprinkled with the blood, dance their vigorous backward shuffle until they are almost exhausted. It also occurs during initiation; some of the men go apart and cut or pierce their penes in sympathy, they say, for the young fellow who is to be circumcised or subincised. In another ritual in some tribes, some men climb up a pole or tree and cause the blood to drop down on the novices who have been placed around the bottom of the tree-pole.

[3] This idea of strength is in line with the use of blood for giving strength to the weak and aged.

THE MEANING AND SOCIAL FUNCTION OF THE RITES

The meaning of some of the rites, such as depilation and cicatrization and even tooth-knocking may be derived from the burial practices of the Aborigines or of other people who have been in contact with them, for it must be remembered that initiation is a transition rite through which the initiate passes from one condition to another. It is normally fashioned on the pattern of the greatest transition rite of all, namely, death; indeed, it is really a pre-enactment of death and of the rising which it is desired should follow death. That being so, it follows that the ritual pattern associated with death, burial and mourning should be acted out as far as possible in initiation. This pattern, however, becomes standardized in the secret organizations and therefore in the course of time it becomes difficult to correlate parts of the initiation death-ritual with the actual burial rites practised in the community, if the latter have changed. This difficulty is increased if the initiation ritual, or parts of it, has been introduced into the community, as, I believe, is the case in Australia. Thus, cicatrization and depilation may represent in ritual the removal of the skin and hair which does occur in burial ritual in some parts of eastern Australia, while the knocking out of a tooth may represent the ritual opening of the mouth of the corpse that the deceased may eat and drink and so live.

This, of course, is at present conjecture, as far as the interpretation of details is concerned, but I have referred to the matter for two reasons: in the first place to point out that a full understanding of the meaning of ritual customs requires a knowledge of their history, which, unfortunately, can seldom be obtained; and in the second place, to emphasize the difference between the meaning of such rites on the one hand, and on the other the social function of initiation and its significance for the individual. The latter begins his initiation progress with expectancy and also with some timidity: as he passes from rite to rite, ordeal to ordeal, revelation to revelation, he is disciplined and made of no account, and yet at the same time realizes that he is becoming of more importance and that his knowledge of secret matters is raising him above the status of children and women towards that of the elders; as a result his personality is being enhanced.

From the point of view of the tribe, the novice is being made, through a system of discipline and teaching, a worthy member of society and a future custodian of its sacred mythology and ritual. Moreover, the social sentiments on which the unity of society depends are being inculcated in his mind, and at the same time are being strengthened in the minds of all present at the ceremonies. These serve an important social function over and above the initiation of the candidate; in this it is similar to the totemic ceremonies, and indeed, the latter often form part of the initiation series, because they have to be shown and explained to the newly initiated in certain stages of his progress. This function is the participation by all present in common activities of a highly emotional nature which are closely intertwined with the beliefs, social behaviour and life of the tribe. The contemplation of the heroes and ancestors of the past through the chanting of the myths and the handling of their sacred symbols, the frequent self-infliction of bodily pain, the dancing and the tense atmosphere in which the main acts occur, all work on the emotions, and at the same time cause all present to feel themselves as one.

It is almost impossible for those who have not witnessed such ceremonies, to realize the important part they play in enhancing the individual and in strengthening the unity and sense of common purpose in the tribe as a whole. Indeed, the very possession of great secrets, won as the result of a difficult journey through initiation on the part of all men of the tribe, helps to bind the tribe together and to counteract any disruptive tendencies which may arise from the localized character of much of Aboriginal social and spiritual life. The groups are small and spend a good deal of time separated from each other wandering about gathering food, and though disputes and feuds arise between such groups, yet they know that they are bound together by a common membership of a secret life, and that every now and then that common life will be expressed by great ritual gatherings. This fact is, no doubt, the explanation of the custom that before the ceremonies are commenced at such gatherings, all grudges and complaints must be expressed and cleared up and all disputes settled. Those who have such complaints stand up and make their accusations; counter accusations are made; there soon develops a terrific cross firing of charges and counter-charges until at last missiles are thrown. To the outsider, a serious battle has apparently commenced which will prevent the holding of the initiation or other ceremony. But such is not the case; a few are hit, some blood is drawn; the fighting stops; apologies are made for hurting one another, and in the evening there will probably be a corroboree. Thus, the stage is set for the carrying out of the purpose of the meeting: repressions have been released, and all can enter the sacred realm in peace and harmony.

Such facts as these should make us realize how important is the ceremonial and secret life of the tribe. To undermine it is to jeopardize the unity of tribal social life. But to use it in civilizing and missionary work, is to build on a good foundation. Its crude and unseemly elements will need modifying here and there, but its theme and social effect are not objectionable; on the contrary, it enshrines that search for life both here and hereafter, which is the objective of all religious societies, secret or public.

INITIATION RITES

The general outlines of the series of rites are the same all over Australia, although we may distinguish between an eastern and a central and western "use", with, of course, local variations here and there. The eastern use is associated with a belief in a sky culture-hero or all-father who instituted initiation and now watches what is done, whereas in the central and western use, the culture-heroes who instituted the various rites of initiation, are totemic heroes who, after their course as incarnate totemic beings, went into the earth at definite places, from which they now, in some cases, watch over the ritual. This division, however, is not absolute; on the one hand, similar totemic heroes are recognized as living in localized natural features in north-eastern Australia, although they are not primarily concerned with initiation; and on the other hand, sky culture-heroes connected with the institution of initiation are found in the north-west and traces of the same are found in northern Australia in general. The main difference in the physical operations has already been mentioned; in the central and western use circumcision is the principal ordeal preparatory to receiving the first revelation of secret knowledge, whereas in the eastern use tooth-knocking, depilation or cicatrization constitutes this physical testing and preparation. This eastern use still prevailed in the south-west of Western Australia at the time of white occupation and was never ousted; the western use has only comparatively recently spread to north-eastern Arnhem Land where it is only gradually being integrated into the local culture.

The Stages or Degrees. During the course of initiation an individual passes through a number of stages, for each of which there is a special term; generally, too, the candidate is referred to by this term rather than by any personal name. These terms are usually common to a group of tribes—the result of taking part in each other's initiations. The terms used in the Broome-Sunday Island district will serve as an example. *Leminem* is the candidate for tooth-knocking and he is so called during the rituals which are performed for a week preceding this operation.

He is then a *Lainyar* until circumcision has been performed, usually a couple of days later; this makes him a
Palil and a few secrets are revealed to him. Later on he
is taken through an important blood ceremony, during
which he is called *Djurdu* and at the end of which he is
Djaminanga and is fitted to receive more advanced revelations. Some weeks or months later he is regarded as fit to
give arm-blood for ceremonial purposes; his arms are liga-
tured, the blood taken and drunk, and he is now a
Gambel; on a later occasion a wing of a bird is put in his
head band and he is called *Rungor*; when the pearl-shell
pubic pendant is hung on him he is *Bungin,* and finally
when he is admitted to the ranks of married men, he is
ceremonially painted and known as *Mambangan*. He is
now a man. Strangely enough, I could not find any special
terms to denote the subincised man or the man on whose
body cicatrices had been made. These were not regarded
as especially significant by the tribes of northern Dampier
Land. Elsewhere the latter usually give a status name;
indeed, the person is called by the term which denotes
the cicatrices. Thus, amongst the tribes of north-eastern
South Australia, these are called *Wilyaru,* and so is the
man who has the particular *Wilyaru* pattern of cicatrices
on his back; needless to say, there is a myth which sets
the pattern, and incidentally, the bull-roarer has the same
pattern cut on it. Subincision is almost always of less importance than circumcision, and only sometimes gives
status.

Although there are variations in details, the general outline of the initiation series is much the same everywhere.
The following is a brief generalized form:

(i) *The Taking of the Novice.* When the elders and the
father have decided that the latter's son is to begin his
initiation, the novice is taken from the camp in a prescribed ritual manner. The women cry and make a show
of resistance to the extent of using spears; the father may
even do the same. The lad is painted, in some parts with

red ochre or human blood; in one area a shell is hung around his neck as the sign of the step to be taken. In many tribes the novice is then taken round by messengers (sometimes the latter go alone) to summon the various local groups to the ceremony. In other words, he is presented to those already initiated for their approval and for their help in initiation. He may, before going out or else on the return, be tossed up in the air,[4] have his scalp bitten[5] and the septum of his nose pierced.

(ii) *Ceremonial Welcome and Combat.* As the groups come to the appointed place, they are ceremonially welcomed, generally in the public corroboree ground, after which they fix their camps on the side of the ground in the direction of their own country. A combat, ceremonial in nature, is a frequent feature and is usually connected with the settlement of grievances and disputes as already described. This is followed by a feast which in southeastern Queensland used to be cannibalistic in nature; the body of a person killed in the ceremonial combat was disposed of in this way.[6] In this region cannibalism was a regular feature of burial ritual.

(iii) *Preliminary Ceremonial.* The tossing of the novice up into the air may now take place. But more important are the ceremonies leading up to the chief bodily operation, such as tooth-avulsion or circumcision. One of the commonest features of these is their similarity to death-ritual. In eastern Australia, in particular, the candidate must act, and is treated, as though he were lifeless. He must not speak, and not even ask for what he needs, but just nod in reply to questions put to him. He is even car-

---

[4] Some say that this makes the lads grow tall, or it may symbolize separation from the women, more especially from the mother, and passing into the hands and rank of the men.

[5] To make the hair grow, it is sometimes said; but this custom must have some other meaning.

[6] The combat was possibly more serious in this area and may have been regarded as a means of providing a body for the meal.

ried about on some occasions as though he were helpless. In some tribes he is laid along the top angular space formed by two lines of men crossing their spears, and there he has to lie as though he had been killed by the spears, while the two lines move about, and the women cry. In north-western Australia, I witnessed several ceremonies, dirge-like both in the slowness of the movement and the type of chant; the novice was carried on the shoulders of two men, with his mother and other female relations hanging on to him and wailing.

(iv) *The Ritual Bodily Operations.* There is usually one of special ritual importance; if there are several operations, the rest are usually performed at any suitable occasion without the calling of a big meeting, and may be done in the general camp. Thus, in north-western Australia, the cicatrices are sometimes cut at any time and place after circumcision. I saw tooth-avulsion performed at the ordinary camp corroboree ground, though after several nights of ritual preparation and in a ritual manner. Circumcision, however, took place at sunrise one morning at the top of a hill and facing east, a long way from the camp. It marked the beginning of the candidate's period of seclusion and instruction. Likewise, in eastern Australia, where there was no circumcision, tooth-avulsion was, in many tribes, the supreme bodily operation; it took place in the secret ground after various ceremonies had been performed and symbols seen, all of which were as yet taboo to the novice. But after the operation, a beginning of revelations was made, but only a beginning, for here, as elsewhere, the period of seclusion was and is regarded as of prime importance.

Circumcision and the absence of a front incisor tooth can be an outward sign of having reached the threshold of the secret life, but it should be noticed that they only indicate entry on to the mystic path. Knowledge has yet to be gained. In some tribes the tooth was sent round various groups as a sign that the young fellow had advanced thus far; it was finally returned to him and generally buried in the secret ground. The foreskin is said by some to be changed into a bat which, incidentally, is associated with death—another indication that initiation is a "death".

I have already suggested that the cicatrices may have a similar "death" significance, but in any case, over large areas of Australia, they are a pass sign of a high degree; this is probably true also of those cases in which they are reported to be but "flash" marks. Normally, they are made late in the initiation series of rites or events.

(v) *The Period of Seclusion.* This is partly a continuance of the drama of death. The tooth-knocking, circumcision or other symbolical act "killed" the novice; after this he does not return to the general camp and normally may not be seen by any woman. He is dead to the ordinary life of the tribe. For the time being he is in the sacred world. But though ritually dead, he must eat and converse; he is, however, subject in both these respects to very severe restrictions. In eastern Australia he was, and still is, as far as possible in some parts, taken to many sacred grounds in the bush and gradually taught more and more of the custom and belief of the tribe, until such time as he is considered fit to pass through one of the higher ceremonies and see more of the symbols and rites of the secret life, and learn about the Great All-Father. This progress may take a year or more, though there are also shortened forms.

In Central and Western Australia, the youths seem to spend a good deal of their period of seclusion in pairs, thus assisting one another to get food; they must not come into the camp, but their parents may send them some food. Each novice has a special guide and instructor, a "wife's brother", who sees him from time to time and supports him in ceremonies and ordeals. They frequently have a special language code for their own use. This is in addition to the secret language, or code of words, which every initiate is taught and which can serve as pass-words. During the period of seclusion, the newly initiated are from time to time shown ceremonies and taught a little about them. In both cases, the newly initiated are warned not to reveal anything which they have experienced or seen.

(vi) *The Blood Ceremony*. In nearly all tribes from the west to the east and from the north to the south, at some part of the initiation series a blood rite is performed. It consists of anointing the newly initiated with arm-blood from the older men, or else giving them some of this to drink. The older men also anoint themselves or each other and drink blood. This blood is sacred; there is a secret name for it, and it is usually associated with some mythical hero's act. It gives life, strength and courage and so fits the candidates for the revelations which are to be made. At the same time it unites them to the elders of whose blood they have partaken; indeed, it does more; it unites them to the initiation heroes, for the blood taken under such conditions is the hero's or ancestor's life, and so to drink it, brings the initiated into the mythical world. A special song must be chanted while this blood is being drawn, and this changes it—consecrates it, as we would say, and gives it sacramental efficacy.

I have heard a missionary refer with loathing to this blood-drinking rite, but surely this is unreasonable for a Christian, especially one with strongly developed sacramental views. If we can no longer stomach blood-drinking, then we might at least appreciate the symbolism and recommend the substitution of such a liquid as wine, as is our own practice.

(vii) *The Fire Ceremony*. This also is almost or wholly universal. The candidates may have to sit round and stare at a fierce fire until they are almost dazed, or they may be dropped on to thick smoke fires, coals may be thrown on them or they and all the men may finally trample the fires out with their feet. I have known the fire ceremony to leave the greatest impression on the candidates throughout their lives, probably because the older men seem to be immune to feeling as far as the fire was concerned. The fire ceremony is certainly an ordeal, but is also frequently regarded as an act of purification, making it safe for the newly initiated to return to the world of everyday life. This explains why it is usually the final rite in the series.

(viii) *The Washing and the Return*. There may be one or more than one ceremonial return to ordinary life. This depends on circumstances—mainly economic conditions. Ideally there should only be one. The purpose of the washing is to clean off all traces of the sacred world—the blood and other materials used in decoration—before coming in contact with the uninitiated. Preparations are made by the women for the return which is carried out ceremonially. The newly initiated is welcomed as one returned from the dead.

(ix) *Revelation of Secrets*. Such is the briefest outline of the principal rites and events in initiation. The ritual, however, is not everything. There is also instruction and revelation. By positive teaching and through the acting out and explanation of the myths, the social customs are taught, and their sanctions or authority emphasized. The revelation is twofold; of myths and rites on the one hand, and of symbols on the other. The myths relate the institution of initiation and narrate the doings of the ancestors and heroes, most of whom are totemic in nature. The symbols are of two kinds, temporary and permanent. The first are made for the particular initiation or totemic ceremony and destroyed immediately afterwards. In Central and Western Australia these are mostly of the *waninga* and *nurtunja* types; the *waninga* is made of a main stick or piece of wood with one or two cross pieces, and parallel lines of string fastened around this frame-work; the *nurtunja* is more like a pole, but sometimes composite and adorned with blood and other materials. A mound may also be made and painted and a pole set up.

In eastern Australia, the temporary symbols were usually made of earth and represented culture-heroes, totemic and human.

The permanent symbols are of the bull-roarer and churinga[7] type, though in part of New South Wales definite patterns belonging to local territorial clans were carved on the trees around the initiation ground; these patterns symbolized myths and were explained to the initiated. We must also include in the class of permanent symbols certain natural phenomena such as outcrops of stones, hills, trees, etc., which are believed to be transformed heroes, human or other, whole or in part.

The bull-roarers are wooden objects which can be swung, mainly to warn off the uninitiated; but they are more than that. They symbolize the sky-heroes or totemic ancestors, are carefully looked after, and only shown to those who have been "prepared" to see them. The sight of them stirs the deepest feelings of reverence, akin to those experienced by the faithful when contemplating the Blessed Sacrament in some Christian churches. They are usually kept in sacred storehouses, and only handled with the permission of the headmen. No uninitiated person may go near the storehouses; even a hunted animal is safe when it runs near one of them, and so too is a human refugee. I know of nothing more impressive than to see a group of Aborigines sitting in a secret ground contemplating their sacred symbols and chanting the song versions of the myths appertaining to them.

Some of the objects of bull-roarer shape are not twirled; they may be very large—up to six feet and even more in

[7] The word *churinga* should be written *tjurunga* or *tjuringa*. Spencer and Gillen write it churinga. Its general significance is sacred. It is applied to all the sacred symbolic objects, especially of a permanent nature, referred to in this account. But the myths and rites are also churinga. It is an Aranda term; other tribes have their own terms. [The -ng in churinga is soft as in sing.]

length—and have designs incised all over one side.[8] These are found in Western Australia from Lagrange, the Fitzroy River and Eastern Kimberley south to Laverton and the Bight and up to the ranges near the junction of South, Western and Central Australia. Others of the same shape but smaller are made of stone. They, too, are incised and like the wooden ones are painted and greased.

In addition to the sacred symbols of bull-roarer shape, there are others, mostly made of stone, which are varied in shape, some being almost square or oval. Their significance is the same as the bull-roarers in the area where they are found. In several parts of Australia there are also small stones of different shapes which are shown and explained to the initiated, as representing some part of a hero's body. I have seen these in the far north-west as well as on the eastern coast. On the latter, too, in New South Wales, I have been shown carved pieces of wood, square or rectangular in one section and oval in the other, which are historical and totemic in significance, and indeed belong to the same cycle of myth as do the patterns carved on the trees.

In north-eastern Arnhem Land totemic objects are made which not only symbolize, but also partly resemble the totems with which the ceremonies are concerned.

The same sanctity surrounds or is inherent in all these various forms of permanent though movable symbols, whatever be their shape, size or material. Generally speaking, however, the older a churinga, the more it is valued, and a stone one is regarded as possessed of greater "virtue" than a wooden one, that is if the tribe has both types. This is a tribute to age—the older and more lasting the churinga is in nature, the farther back does it link the present with

[8] The bull-roarers which are twirled on a cord vary in length from about eight inches to three feet and from an inch to about four or five inches in width. Most are pointed at both ends. The large ones are about five inches wide. They seldom exceed a quarter of an inch in thickness.

the past, the nearer does it take the people of to-day to the great heroes.

THE DREAM-TIME

This brings us to the secret of the power of churinga and the veneration felt for them. They are revealed as symbols of the great heroes of the eternal dream-time. Indeed, they are means by which life and power are mediated from those heroes and the eternal dream-time. Therefore, to rub one on a sick person gives him strength. To take one when hunting ensures success, but the food thus acquired has become sacred, and only the fully initiated may partake of it, and that, after the observance of a small rite. To lend a churinga is to renew or strengthen friendship, and the latter is sealed with the sanctity which appertains to the dream-time. And finally, when the newly initiated man is allowed for the first time to see and handle these objects and is rubbed with them, he is brought into conscious touch with this eternal dream-time. Therein, of course, lies the real object of initiation: to make the individual sacred and a sharer of the sacred life of the tribal heroes and of nature. This explains, too, why in some tribes, perhaps in many, a separate churinga is associated with each individual (it may have to be specially made) and why the latter's spiritual double spends a great deal of time in the sacred storehouse with his churinga. In the same way, the life or spirit part of a totemic species is associated with a special churinga of wood or stone which must be cared for and used in increase ceremonies.

The term for this sacred time and state, symbolized by the churinga, varies from tribe to tribe; it is *Altjira* in the Aranda, *Djugur* in the Aluridja, *Bugari* around Lagrange and Broome, *Ungud* in the Ungarinyin, *Wongar* in north-east Arnhem Land, and so on. Moreover, this term not only connotes the eternal dream-time; it also denotes the churinga, the myths and rites through which the initiated enter into this sacred condition, and indeed, the initiated themselves. Therefore, to ask a man for his *Altjira* or *Bugari* is to ask him for *his dreaming*, that is, his cult totem, his share of, or link with, the eternal dream-time.

A sign of the individual's sacred or *altjira* significance is the new name given him in his initiation. It is usually taken from a sacred myth; in some tribes, it may be the name of a great dream-time hero. It is so sacred that it is never mentioned except in a whisper on the sacred ground. It is indeed, a pass word into the eternal, unseen world of ancestral and totemic heroes. Another sign of an initiate's sanctity is, in some tribes, the individual ownership of a bull-roarer or, in many New South Wales tribes, a small piece of stone, usually quartz; such a symbol must be kept secret and never lost, and as it partakes of the nature of the culture-hero or god it gives life and strength to its bearer. Thus by words, symbols and actions (rites), the initiate can pass into the sacred world, and we shall see in Chapter X, he must after death be accorded special rites which will ensure that his spirit returns to this world from which it came, there to remain for ever (be it in totem centre or the sky-world) or to await reincarnation.

Enough has been said to show that the sacred symbols are of vital importance to both the sacred and secular life of the tribe. In the first place they are used in three types of secret rites, initiation, historical and increase. The greatest revelation made at initiation is connected with them, and the spirit-life of the individual and the increase of the species is also associated with them (that is, in some tribes). In the second place, they affect secular life for they may be used in hunting (and in some forms of love-making), or to make, cement and renew friendships, and prevent fights and quarrels.[9] It is this social function of the

[9] They are in evidence at ceremonial times and after the preliminary settlement of disputes referred to, p. 176, there must be no quarrelling while the ceremonies are in progress or while the churinga are being kept near by. Every one is sacrosanct while near them.

churinga which led me to suggest in Chapter V that the lending or exchange of churinga might be substituted for wife-lending or wife-exchange. Certainly the whole cult of the churinga should be studied and respected and not condemned. It might well be made a useful symbolical means of retaining and imparting ideals and ideas of social and spiritual value.

THE VALUE AND FUNCTION OF INITIATION CEREMONIES

(i) The initiation ceremonies express the importance of the individual to the tribe, not so much because he makes an additional member, for a girl is not initiated and yet she also makes one more and a necessary one, but because he is an inheritor of the sacred rites, myths and symbols of the tribe, which are believed to be essential to its life and welfare.

(ii) The rites provide a safe and valuable transition during the period of adolescence, giving the youth that discipline, guidance and gradual feeling of enhancement which is so valuable in the development of character. In this way his social personality is developed; that is, his interests, ideals and hopes are enlarged to include those of the whole group as sanctified by the secret traditions of the tribe.

(iii) The rites, finally, have a positive social value for the tribe or group as a whole, for since the rites centre the thoughts and feelings of all on the common symbols, myths and hopes, and since they do this in a specially prepared setting and atmosphere, they create and renew feelings and experiences of social unity and cohesion; they ensure respect for the tribe's moral and social sanctions, and they sanctify hope for the future, both in this life and the life after death.

WOMEN'S SACRED LIFE

Although women are not admitted to the "inner sanctuary" of sacred rituals, yet, as we have known for many years, they do play a subsidiary role in most of them. They are in the "nave", and sometimes even in the "chancel". Their part varies in different regions and according to the ceremonies. For example, with regard to men's initiation, the women play quite a conspicuous part in the tooth-avulsion and pre-circumcision dances in south Kimberley, but are nowhere near the scene of circumcision and do not see the initiate again until his formal return to the camp after recovery. In southern Arnhem Land, however, while the women only dance inconspicuously during the pre-circumcision dances, a number of "sisters" are present at the actual operation, processing around the mass of men who completely hide the candidate. Indeed, I have seen women relatives bringing the initiate along behind the Songman to the place of the operation on the edge of the camp.

The secret life proper comes after initiation, and into that women are nowhere admitted in the same way and in the same degree as the men are. On the other hand they do possess cult totems, or "dreamings", as these are called, so that they are potential or threshold members of cult-lodges and the secret life. Their brothers, or whoever are the male members of their cult-society, perform the ceremonies for them. According to the myths of some tribes, women originally owned the ceremonies, but let the men take them and henceforth act on their behalf. They are also credited with introducing the stone circumcision knife in some regions, to replace the crude fire-stick "surgical instrument" which the men had been using. In the north-west of the continent they take a direct part in some rituals of increase for natural species which they gather.

To sum up: Women play a part in all important sacred rituals. It may consist of observing prescribed taboos while

the men are in the secret places; chanting; answering ritual calls; being present as observers or as minor participants in final scenes just off the secret ground or at the
general camp; and preparing food. The older women know
the sequence of rites as well as their own roles, and direct
the younger women in their duties and observances. One
or two old women may hold official authority over the rest,
although an old man is usually left in the camp to see that
all rules are kept.

We can therefore speak of sacred ritual proceeding simultaneously at two levels: the men's secret level; and the
camp level, the province of the women. The levels are for
the most part on parallel planes, but they meet from time
to time. This occurs more often in the tropical north than
in the arid interior. In the Maraian ceremonies of Arnhem
Land, for example, the men return every afternoon to the
camp where, still bearing on their bodies their painted ritual designs, they dance around two ceremonial forked
poles or "trees". The women meet them, and not only
dance in the background, but also join with them in some
scenes.

The Yabuduruwa of the Roper River district is even
more startling. It is marked by the beating of a wooden
gong, a sign that ritual painting or ritual drama is in process. Hearing the sound, half a mile off, the women instantly
stop talking, eating and smoking. In the evening, the men
return to the camp for food and sleep, with the designs on
their bodies for all to see, but if a woman or other forbidden person approached the secluded spot where the
painting and ritual took place, serious trouble would follow. The really striking convergence of the two levels occurs on the final night of the Yabuduruwa. The women
are brought after dark past the place of painting to within
ten yards or so of the secret ritual ground. No screen is
raised between them and the latter. They lie and sleep on
specially arranged earth "beds", facing away from the ritual place. A piece of rolled bark is buried superficially

under each woman's "pillow". It is referred to as the tail of the iguana—the central figure in the Yabuduruwa myth. They know about it, but do not touch it until they are awakened just before sunrise. Each woman immediately uncovers the piece of bark and they all proceed in a line past the bough hut in which the secret objects are kept, and around a special fire about ten yards from the "dance" place. At this very time an important ritual is in progress and the women cannot but hear the rhythmic breathing as well as the gong-beats. If they turned their heads as they jogged along they could see the actors. However, they light the iguana tails at the fire, and move off in a long sinuous line to the camp, conscious that they have played their part well.[10]

The conclusion is that although women are excluded from the greater part of sacred ritual and knowledge, they are not, therefore, merely secular beings. As the years pass by they learn quite a lot about the secret ritual and mythology. They know the great mythological paths, and the secret sites on them which they must avoid. They learn their own parts in the rituals, and they realize that the performances are for their benefit as well as for the well-being of the men. This is logical. Their own pre-existent souls come from the dreaming, and will eventually return to it. Moreover, they are the means or channels through which those souls, including those of men, will be incarnated; and in the northern half of the Northern Territory, the central theme of the principal cults is the fertility-mother or mother-goddess (Chapter VIII). They are, however, deprived of the conditions of being "twice-born" or ritually raised, and of the prestige and esoteric knowledge which goes with it. On the other hand, after death they

---

[10] Reference is made to this and other ceremonies in the concluding section of Chapter VIII. Another way in which women play their part is through ritual sexual intercourse, especially in those rites in which the selected women represent the fertility-mother and become the repository of the "shades" of the clan.

are accorded effective burial ritual, even if this is not always of the same "degree" or status as for initiated men. In the Roper River region, however, a deceased woman might be accorded a Kunapipi, or mother-goddess, ritual, although the Lorgan, a totemic painted coffin ritual, is more usual.[11]

WOMEN'S SECRET RITUAL

In addition to their role in the men's secret ritual, women in most of the Northern Territory and neighbouring regions of Western Australia have their own ritual to which men are not admitted. There are two main types. The first is known as Yowalyu (or some variation of this word). Widespread through the north-central arid regions, it is attributed to an ancestral being named Ininguru or Yuguruguru. His path is traced in the chanting and in the "dancing". Various natural species are also indicated in the singing and dancing and in the designs which are painted on the women. Thus, the whole complex is a representation of the myth, or the dreaming.[12]

Sometimes texts and meanings are incorporated in the Yowalyu to give it the effect of love magic. This, however, is not its primary significance. But both men and women in the arid region and farther north also, possess secret "love" song cycles. The most widespread are the Djarada. These belong to the same general region as the Kunapipi or Kadjeri fertility-mother ritual (Chapter VIII), that is from the Macarthur and Roper River districts on the one

[11] In 1952 I heard an old man suggesting that a Kunapipi which was just starting might be for the leading man's mother.

[12] The first reference to Yowalyu was in Dr Phyllis Kaberry's *Aboriginal Woman* (1939). A brief description was given by Mrs Catherine Berndt in *Women's Changing Ceremonies* (1950). In 1953 I saw, and recorded the singing in, two separate versions of the Yowalyu, the Wailbri and the Warramunga. The texts of the former belong to the same cycle as those noted by Mrs Berndt.

side to the Victoria River waters and the Kimberley border
on the other, and from Newcastle Waters or even farther
south to central and even northern Arnhem Land. Indeed,
the Djarada is an offshoot from the Kunapipi mythology.
The patronesses are the Munga-Munga, who formed part
of Kunapipi's band of followers, and who were both ven-
turesome and successful in love affairs. The chicken-hawk,
the crow and the possum are associated with Djarada
songs and rituals; they are considered to be accomplices
or helpers in sex assignations. The men chant their Djarada
but do not dance. The women both chant and dance, just
about out of sight of the men, but the latter, hearing their
singing, usually call out and swing a bull-roarer. The
women paint up and dance very gracefully. The sexual
motive is often obvious, just as it is in the words of the
chants. Through the singing, women hope to gain new
lovers, to make their husbands faithful and ardent, and to
bring absent husbands or sweethearts to them quickly. Behind this, however, is the dreaming mythological basis,
similar to that of the great cults. Further, the women's
Djarada, like the Yowalyu, is their own secret, and a secret
which directly expresses for them the eternal dream-
time.[13]

Appendix

The Secret Life and Missionary Endeavour. Some may
feel tempted to underrate the social importance of initiation and the secret life more particularly as a basis for missionary activity, or indeed for civilizing work, because the

---

[13] Throughout the western part of the Northern Territory and
the adjacent part of Western Australia, there are love songs and
ritual called Ilbindji or Yirbindji which are similar to the
Djarada. Where they overlap, they are confused with each
other. The Ilbindji is possibly only the Djarada under another
name. It reached East Kimberley in 1936 and was reported
from the south-western corner of the Northern Territory in
1929.

women are excluded from both. But we should remember that this is true of our principal and most widespread secret society, and that it is rare for women to be admitted to sacred positions in our religious organizations. In our own society, the Christian Churches in which communicant membership is open to women as well as men, exist along with secret societies of a religious nature, and there is no reason why the same should not happen in Aboriginal Australia. Indeed, we should encourage the men to stick to their secret life in spite of the fact that some modifications of it may seem necessary, and even though doing so may delay their conversion to Christianity. This delay, however, is worthwhile if missionaries succeed in christianizing Aboriginal secret life, and surely the whole pattern, symbolism and purpose of the latter should make this possible. The history of culture contact in Australia so far shows that the apparent conversion of men from their secret life is followed later by an attempt to return to the latter in which they then claim to find all that is worthwhile in the missionary teaching.

The men naturally think it strange (and so too, do the women) that women are admitted to all the mysteries of Christianity, and they may therefore believe in their hearts that it is a poor religion. But if we remind them that we have a secret life for the men, and also that they themselves really do believe that women's spirits are sacred before incarnation and after death, they may realize that on the first count, we are like them, and that on the second we are logical; for if a woman's spirit is sacred before birth and after death, it is reasonable to admit her to some form of the sacred life during her sojourn in the flesh.

However we tackle this difficulty, we can rest assured that the desecration or destruction of the secret life is not the way to success, but is rather the way to cause social disintegration, conflict of loyalties and psychological disturbance. Missionaries should not be misled by apparent success during the first two or three decades. The disillusionment will come and with it an endeavour to return to the old faith. True, the wise builder will try to help them then, but it would have been much better to have worked wisely, slowly and positively from the beginning.

Chapter VIII

ABORIGINAL PHILOSOPHY, RITES
AND BELIEFS

MOST of us would have to think long and hard if we were called upon to make an adequate presentation of our philosophy, for we spend our days without conscious reference to any systematized view of the universe, of man and nature, of life and consciousness, and of the processes of history. But that does not mean that we are not guided by some view of life, which is expressed in our daily conduct, in ritual and belief, and in times of individual and social crisis. In only a few cases, however, has the philosophy been thoughtfully worked out and applied to life's situations. We just grow into it, and leave the philosophical specialists to argue about its actual form. They look within and around themselves, back to the past and forward to the future, pointing out its consistencies and illogicalities, and finally present a more accurate and logical viewpoint.

The Aborigines likewise have, or inherit and grow into, a view of life and the universe, of the past, present and future, about which few of them speculate. But they do express it in rites, myths, conduct and in beliefs about themselves (their birth, sleep and death) and nature. They might even hold contradictory and incomplete theories, as we often do, but there is no doubt that the Aboriginal philosopher finds plenty of material on which to exercise his thought, his analytical powers, and his urge for systematic and logical construction. I shall take his place and endeavour to present a view of life and the world which is inherent in the conduct, beliefs and rites of the Aborigines of Australia.

This philosophy has three characteristics; it is spiritual, totemistic and historical, and is usually all three at once. The spiritual is totemistic in nature and historical in reference. In other words, these three are but aspects of one reality, as the following analysis will show.

THE SPIRITUAL VIEW OF LIFE

By spiritual I do not wish to convey the idea of an abstract conception of an all-pervading reality, non-material in essence; I am thinking rather of what is implied in the term "spiritistic". Indeed, Aboriginal philosophy might best be described as animistic. Fundamentally, all that part of the world, which is of interest and significance for man, is explained by the existence of distinct spirits; these are from time to time incarnated in human forms and also in the forms of natural species and phenomena; they can and do appear in dreams and visions either during incarnation or when they are discarnate. That is, they are never completely tied to their forms of manifestation. They may be symbolized by artificial or natural objects; indeed, their life may be mediated through these objects. This will be made clear by reference to their beliefs.

THE DOCTRINE OF PRE-EXISTENCE

The doctrine of pre-existence which is so widely held, is a good illustration. The spirits of the unborn sojourn in spirit-homes, usually well-defined sites; and after death return to these homes, though in some cases they go to the sky. The fate of the dead will be discussed later. The pre-existent spirits for the most part came into existence during the long-past dream-time as a result of some activity of a hero; according to some beliefs, however, they are made from time to time or brought into being by a creative hero whose activity was not confined to the past but is continuous. Indeed, man can take a ritual hand in this matter by performing a ceremony at a site sanctified by association with the hero's power of bringing into being, or making available, spirit-children. Such a ceremony is similar to those performed for the increase of natural species and phenomena, for the Aboriginal view of nature is the same as that which he holds concerning man. This is manifested in his mythology and totemism as well as in his ritual.

INCREASE RITES

Just as there are spirit-centres for human beings, so there are for natural species. Some heroes not only left human spirits at known places, but, in addition, made other sites, equally well known, to be the centres from which the life, or the spirits, of particular natural species would go forth and so cause the latter to increase in the normal manner. If the hero were connected, for example, with the kangaroo, having it for his totem and possibly being able to adopt its form, he might have performed ceremonies for the increase of kangaroos at one place and left a great stone not only to mark the site, but also as a storehouse of kangaroo life or spirits; another place on his journey might have been sanctified and made efficacious by the loss of some of his blood or part of his body, or by his body being transformed into stone. Such a site is henceforth sacred. It is a channel from the creative and eternal dream-time. The creative power is brought into operation and causes the increase, for example, in this case, of kangaroos, by the care bestowed on, and the rituals performed at, the site.

It should be noticed that the link with the eternal dream-time is ultimately a personal one, namely, the hero; even if the hero be pictured in the myth as an animal, he acts and speaks most of the time in a personal and human manner. This, as we shall see, is the characteristic of Australian mythology. It personifies natural species and phenomena, and thus explains them by a principle which man understands, that is, as manifestations of personal or spiritual beings like himself, though often endowed with greater powers.

It is not always easy to decide in what way the ritual of

increase is believed to accomplish its object. When the performer or performers say: "Let there be plenty of kangaroo here and there," and so on, they are obviously expressing their desire. But they also express their desire by action; in the simplest form they blow powder from the stone, throw stones from the sacred heap, or take a mixture of powdered stone or earth and blood from the sacred place and deposit it in the countries where an increase of the species is desired and should normally occur. Perhaps we could say that they are sending or taking out sacramental expressions of the ideas or conceptions of kangaroo, emu, or wallaby, or that they are actually (in their belief) transferring a portion of the life of the sacred stone and what it represents, to the country—and that that life will go into the species and cause it to increase. But whatever be our philosophical, sacramental and symbolical interpretation, we realize that the sacred stone or heap is not, for them, just stone or earth. It is in a sense animated; life can go forth from it, whether this be thought of as a generalized power which in one case will operate in kangaroos and in another in wallabies and so on, or as the abode or source of *individual* kangaroo spirits or lives which are ritually sent forth to be incarnated.

We must not dismiss the latter view even though it may not be held in every tribe, for it must be remembered that there are ceremonies for the increase of mankind of exactly the same type as those for the increase of natural species, and that in the former case, the effect is to make available for incarnation the individual spirits which exist in, or are supplied through, spirit-centres or children increase sites. The stone (or in some cases a tree) is painted, rubbed or struck and often a chant is sung or words spoken, and the spirit-children left there go forth to enter the wombs of women. Here, there is no thought of a generalized life-giving power overshadowing the women and causing pregnancy, but of the entry into their bodies of spirit-children thus sent forth; and there seems to be no reason for finding other interpretations for most of the increase ceremonies connected with natural species. The Aborigines think of the life and increase of man and nature in the same way.

KIMBERLEY CAVE PAINTINGS

There is another illuminating illustration of this in Northern Kimberley. The ritual means of increasing man and natural species already referred to and usually known as *talu*[1] or *intichiuma,* is practised there, but in addition, this increase is associated with cave and rock-shelter paintings. Except in the north-east of this region each gallery includes at least one painting of a personal being known as Wondjina, associated with the sky, rain, rainbow, the rainbow serpent, spirit-children and the increase of natural species. He is almost always represented as a human head with nose and eyes but without a mouth. He usually has a horseshoe adornment over his head which may represent the head band worn by the natives, but more likely represents the rainbow. If this painting is touched up by the men of the totemic territorial clan, rain will fall in due season, and the spirit-children who come from the rainbow-spirit and sojourn in water-holes near by, will be available for incarnation. Likewise, if the men paint or repaint representations of their totemic species on the gallery which is dedicated to a Wondjina, the species will increase. In one part of the Northern Kimberley the man who finds a spirit-child must go to the gallery and touch up the painting of the rainbow serpent, and even paint a representation of a spirit-child, so that the former will be

[1] In their epoch-making book *The Native Tribes of Central Australia,* published in 1899, Spencer and Gillen used the term *intichiuma* for the increase ceremonies in the Aranda tribe and it was therefore widely used to denote those ceremonies wherever found. But in the revised edition in 1927, under the title of *The Arunta,* the more general tribal term *mbanbiuma* was substituted for *intichiuma* which was then explained to be the term used by a strong local group. *Talu* is a Western Australian term.

able to keep up the supply.[2] Mythology associates each gallery with one or more distinct Wondjina hero, each with a personal name. There is no suggestion that the different Wondjina paintings are representations of one spirit of fertility. Painting and retouching them is efficacious because they are *ungud*; that is, because they were instituted in a past creative period, the "virtue" of which can be made operative to-day through such ritual action. It was in that period that the Wondjina entered the Northern Kimberley from the sea with their followers. When their wanderings were over, they (their bodies) became paintings, and their spirits went into spirit-home pools near by, ready to become active when their "bodies" were repainted.

USE OF BLOOD IN TOTEMIC CEREMONIES

A very common feature of increase ceremonies is the use of human blood, not only to paint the totemic emblems on the actors' bodies or to decorate some symbol, but also to anoint the stone which is the permanent symbol of the presence of the great hero (human or animal) associated with the particular species. This blood is, of course, sacred and is drawn from the arm or the genital organ. Now, just as human blood gives physical strength to the weak and aged, just as it gives spiritual courage and sacred life to the newly initiated, so in these ceremonies it gives life to the hero or to the totemic species. The stone is uncovered and cleaned, and in the midst of appropriate actions and chanting, the blood of chosen totemites is allowed to drop on it. Thus, they give of their life to their totemic partner in order that it may increase and give life to man. And whether the life or spirits of the totemic species benefit directly, or through the strengthening of the blood bond with the totemic hero or ancestor, it is at least clear that

[2] He uses the red ochre to make another spirit-child to replace the one "found" by him, and which is to be incarnated. Forrest River.

the life of nature and man is one in type and need. In brief, it is personal and spiritual.

This brings us to a problem raised by some totemic increase ceremonies. Does the ritual act directly on the life or spirits of the species or rather on the totemic hero or god who thereby causes the increase of the species? In the Wondjina cycle of ideas, the activity of Wondjina seems to be the purpose of the retouching of the paintings. In northern parts of Cape York Peninsula, the ritual is the way in which the totemites come into contact with the totemic ancestral-hero or god, who then "comes out", and causes the increase of the species which was associated with him in the heroic age, and for which he is responsible. It is not only in this region, however, but also in Central Australia and in part of northern and north-western Australia that we have evidence to show that the object of the ritual is to get the hero concerned to send out the life or spirits of the species now just as he did in the old dream-time.

EFFECTS OF DOCTRINE OF PRE-EXISTENCE

The doctrine of pre-existence has two important corollaries. In the first place, it explains the ignorance or denial of the causal relation between sexual intercourse and conception, and therefore of the physiological aspect of fatherhood. The spirit is already in existence; it has to be "found"; in the northern, western and eastern parts of the continent it is usually the father who does this, although the mother may also dream of the child; in the central area the mother plays the most important part in this matter. The child obtains its flesh and blood through the mother while the father provides it with a place in social and religious life. Here and there, however, sexual intercourse is thought to prepare the woman for child-birth, and in the northern part of Cape York Peninsula it is even thought to be essential; but even so, some superhuman and animistic agent is also necessary—a totemic hero or sky-god who makes the child which is to be put in the womb. It is difficult to decide whether this doctrine has prevented a knowledge of the physiological facts from being discovered, or whether this knowledge was formerly possessed and the doctrine has repressed it. At least, we know that either process would have been true amongst ourselves, and as far as the Aborigines are now concerned, it is the doctrine which prevents them from recognizing the facts.

This does not mean that the doctrine of pre-existence or special supernatural creation of the spirit could not be held together with a knowledge of the physiological facts. Such an association of belief and knowledge is held by many of ourselves, and we should aim, for the time being at least, at helping the Aborigines to understand the latter and at the same time to retain the former. To undermine their belief in pre-existence and the sanctity of spirit-homes is to snap a link which binds them to the spirit world, to their great heroes, to their country, and in the case of a group of individuals with the one spirit home, to one another. This would mean disaster to the tribe and should be avoided.

On the other hand, an acquisition or recognition of the belief in the causal effect of sexual intercourse, if combined with a higher view of the status and value of women than is usually attributed to the natives, might well lead to a modification or dropping of those customs in which women's sexual life is used for various purposes outside the family, referred to in Chapter V.

The second corollary has to do with nature. Until enlightened by us, the Aborigines believe that cultivation of the land, the sowing of seed and the careful mating of stock is unnecessary to ensure fertility. The ritual sending forth of the life or spirits of the species is man's part. This makes it difficult for them to appreciate our agricultural and stock-breeding activities. But suitable explanation of the processes of germination and crossing would enable them to appreciate what we do, while the association of religious ritual with those activities would link up agriculture and pastoral work with their lives. Missions have a great opportunity in this regard, if they care to use a little imagination and prepare rituals which will have meaning for the Aborigines and at the same time not offend Christian principles.

THE TOTEMIC VIEW OF LIFE

The discussion of the spiritual view of life has involved some reference to totemism, especially to totemic increase rites. The theme of totemism, as was shown in Chapter VI, is that man and natural species are brought into one social and ceremonial whole, and are believed to share a common life. In social totemism, the totem not only symbolizes the common relationship of the members of the human group, but also acts as their mate, friend, guardian or helper, and so is indeed their "flesh", while they, in return, respect it and refuse to injure it unless in dire distress. Likewise, in cult totemism, the totem is not only the emblem of the cult group or lodge; it also symbolizes the ancestor or hero whom the members commemorate, and the life of the species for the increase of which they are ritually responsible; moreover, this symbolism is based on the belief that man and nature belong to one order. Fundamentally, the ritual for increase of species is not an attempt to control nature by magical means, but is a method of expressing man's needs, especially his need that the normal order of nature should be maintained; it is a way of co-operating with nature at just those seasons when the increase of particular species or the rain should occur. It is not an attempt to bring about the irregular and extraordinary, but to maintain the regular. It is a system of co-operation with nature which is both economic and psychological in function; it expresses economic facts and needs and also provides confidence in the processes of nature (spiritually conceived and determined) and hope for the future.

Individual and assistant totemism is also based on this belief that man and natural species participate in a common life. Man and his totem get into personal touch with one another; the former depends on the latter for what can be described as personal services, and this is so, in spite of a certain amount of make-believe. The function of the totem in dreams is similar, for in this connexion it symbolizes the totemite, brings information to him and gives him strength. These facts show that totemism is a form of animism because it endows with spirits or personalities the natural species—that is, the totems. It also implies that the dream-life is an objective experience comparable to the events of the waking life. This is clearly illustrated in the Aboriginal view of the cult totem as "the dreaming"—as the door into the eternal dream-time—a time which is past and yet present, partaking of the nature of the dream-life, unfettered by the limitations set by time and space.

But the most interesting way in which the unity of man and nature is expressed is through classificatory totemism. As already pointed out, this may be a function of moiety, clan, section or local totemism. It amounts to a division and classification of man and all natural phenomena which are of any interest to man, under one system. In this scheme, human beings are not separated from natural species and objects, but grouped with them. Thus the moiety, clan or other group includes not only a certain number of men and women, but also certain natural species and objects. Thus, in the Port Mackay district, Queensland, where each tribe is divided into two moieties, the impression made on one who knew them was that the moiety division of nature was fundamental, and that man naturally was subject to it; as he also says: "The Blacks seem to have an idea that these classes (moieties and sections) are a universal law of nature, so they divide everything between them." It is often difficult for us to see the principle of division, but the native can usually say straight off to which moiety or other group kangaroo, bamboo, particular trees, grasses, or stones belong, just as readily as he knows the moiety or clan or section of his fellow tribesmen. The division or classification implies a relationship between the human beings and natural species and phenomena which are grouped together. For example, in the south-west of Western Australia, a member of one matrilineal moiety regards everybody and everything of that moiety as "his own family" while everything and everybody of the other moiety is "relation-in-law".

The moieties are always associated with other subdivisions, namely clans or sections: in all tribes in which totemism is a means of expressing the unity of man and nature as "one big tribe", men and women and all things are classified not only between the moieties but also between the clans or sections. In such case, we speak of multiple totemism and of sub-totems or subsidiary totems. For example, the clan totem may be kangaroo; it is therefore the totem of a human group, and, in addition, of a group of natural objects and species. Thus, grass, water, the Pleiades and so on are kangaroo, just as are certain men and women. To the latter, kangaroo is the primary totem, while grass, water, the Pleiades etc. are subsidiary totems; but though they are only secondary, they are objects of respect and can be expected to serve (warn and help) the members of the human kangaroo clan.

This same classification of man and nature amongst clans, local groups, sections or subsections obtains as a rule, even though there is no moiety division. The point is that totemism is so much a part of man's very being in Australia, that it enters into all his social and ritual groupings. Moreover, it does so not merely as a symbolical method of expressing the principle and purpose of those groups, but also as a means of expressing that common life which man and nature share and the mutual dependence of the one on the other. The result is that whatever be his form of social grouping, he must bring the whole of nature into it, for just as there can be no loose human remnants—that is, individuals—without clan or section, so also there can be nothing in heaven or earth in such a predicament.

Now, this is the way in which man can feel at home with nature, namely by bringing all its species, objects and phenomena into his social system, making it part of his own kinship, moiety, clan and other organization. He can then deal with it and expect to be dealt with by it in the same manner as prevails between the members of the various social and ritual groups of his human fellows. This amounts to humanizing, if not personalizing, nature in all its manifestations and brings us again very near, if not right into, the spiritual and animistic view of the universe. The same fact will be seen again in mythology which does personify, or rather personalize nature.

THE HISTORICAL VIEW OF LIFE

The Aborigines' view of life is not only animistic and totemic; it is also historical. Sanctity, sanction and life arise from the heroic and life-giving past. Conservatism and the maintenance of continuity with the past play an important part in the life of all societies and can never be ignored, except temporarily. This is true also of the Aborigines. The sanctuaries are life-giving and of totemic significance because of their association with the heroes of the past, and man's own spirit is a link with that same creative past because of its pre-existence. The rites for the increase of species are effective because they are performed in the old ways by actors who have been initiated into that secret life which is the door into that past. The great revelations made to initiates are of rites commemorating the doings of the heroes and ancestors of old. Likewise, the laws and customs which must be kept and the rites which are essential to the welfare of the tribe, are those which were instituted by the heroes or ancestors in this long past time. If a custom is not enshrined in a myth, it is regarded as merely man-made and of no great importance; on the other hand, if a new institution be developed or adopted or a new custom regarded as essential, it will find its way into mythology, and so be sanctified and become a sanction for conduct. The very word for cult totem, the "dreaming", includes the past in its connotation. Finally, mythology is the record of the doings of the ancestors, totemic and other culture-heroes in this past period of creative activity.

To the Aborigines, things are as they are, because of the personal actions of heroic beings in the past; customs are followed because they were the customs of, or were ordained by, these heroes; and life is possible for man and nature now because of their actions and life-giving powers. All that is, that must be and will be, is a matter of historical continuity with the heroic past.

But as already inferred, this past is, in a sense, also present: the culture-heroes and ancestors have not ceased to exist but are concerned with man's activities from age to age; initiation admits a person not only to a knowledge of that past, but also makes him a sharer and indeed, an embodiment of its life. This is particularly so during ceremonies; his blood is then the blood of the heroes; he passes into the sacred world of the heroes and for the time being lives a transformed life. This, however, is not all. It is not just a matter of bringing the past into the present or taking the present into the past by ritual action with its devotion and enthusiasm. The usual term for this past creative period, as we have seen, means also "dreaming". Various tribes or groups of tribes have their own terms: *altjira* [Aranda], *mura* [Dieri], *djugur* [Aluridja], *bugari* [Karadjeri], *ungud* [Ungarinyin]. A person's "dreaming" is his cult totem; in other words, this is his symbol and share of the long-past heroic age, and indeed his means of access to it. But it also implies, as already stated, that this age manifests the characteristics of our own experience of dreaming, namely, that the limitations of space and time are non-existent and that its actors are endowed with more than ordinary power and knowledge. It does not mean that the *altjira*, the heroic age, is the product of fantasy and unbridled imagination. The Aborigine does not believe that about his own dreams of to-day any more than do our psycho-analysts; they reveal to him events which have happened, are actually happening or which will happen. Likewise, the myths of the dream-time are to him records of history, which are associated with his geographical environment, economic pursuits, social order and personal experience. But the time to which they refer partakes of the nature of dreaming because, as in the case of the latter, past, present and future, are, in a sense, co-existent—they are aspects of the one reality. It is the eternal dream-time and is manifested in the past through the heroes, in the present through the initiated (especially in sacred ceremonies) and it will be manifested in the future, provided that the links with it are not broken.

Herein lies the importance of the secret life as was pointed out in the preceding chapter. The initiates, the myths, rites and sacred sites are the links; but desecrate and neglect the sites, break the succession of initiates, forget the myths and omit the rites, and the life which comes from the dream-time can no longer be obtained. As a result, the very existence of man and nature is in jeopardy, and the mere thought of this condition fills the surviving elders with a feeling of futility, while the new generation has neither an anchor in the past, a source of strength in the present, nor a sense of direction for the future.

As for ourselves, I hope that this brief discussion of Aboriginal philosophy will enable us to realize that the Aborigines have a view of life and nature, more or less logical and systematic, granted its animistic premises, which is a lantern to their feet and a guide to their paths, as they pass from birth to death and beyond. It is spiritual, totemistic and historical in nature, expressing the central facts of human personality, of man's intimate relationship to nature, and his tie to the past, all of which is carried over into a belief that personality is beyond space and time. We are very apt to underrate the philosophical powers of primitive peoples, but the absence of clothes and complicated economic systems does not imply an absence of thought. Primitive peoples have more time than we for contemplation, and we err in thinking that when an Aborigine is sitting, apparently idle, looking into vacancy, his mind is necessarily blank.

PSYCHIC LIFE OF THE ABORIGINES

The Aborigine has, in fact, developed the art of contemplation to a much greater degree than most of us. He may be taking part in general conversation or some activity when he experiences an involuntary movement in some part of his body. Then, as I have seen, he at once drops into a state of recollection and receptivity, lasting minutes, until he has realized who will be "coming along" in the near future. In many tribes, different parts of the body are regarded as indicating specific relations or groups of relations; in such cases, the meditation is guided along prescribed channels. On another occasion he may see a totemic animal belonging to his own or some close relation's group; once again he prepares himself to receive an intimation as to who it is and what is the trouble. The same procedure usually follows the sight of a smoke signal.

Many white folk who have known their native employees well, give remarkable examples of the Aborigine's power for knowing what is happening at a distance, even hundreds of miles away. A man may be away with his employer on a big stock trip, and will suddenly announce one day that his father is dead, that his wife has given birth to a child, or that there is some trouble in his own country. He is so sure of his facts that he would return at once if he could, and the strange thing is, as these employers ascertained later, the Aborigine was quite correct; but how he could have known, they do not understand, for there was no means of communication whatever, and he had been away from his own people for weeks and even months. The Aboriginal psychologists would no doubt speak of telepathy, if they had such a term, and emphasize the reality and reliability of the dream-life. We would no doubt seek other explanations, but at least we must admit that psychic experience plays an important part in their life and it involves thought—the processes of meditation, recollection and reception. In any case, granted their animistic and "dreaming" philosophy, they are quite logical, and what is more, they act on their logic and apparently seldom find it wanting.

The Cure of Sickness

Their psychic experience, however, is not only receptive in function; it is also positive and active. Thus some individuals, especially old "wise men" believe that they can influence other people at a distance causing them to come or go or have some experience or other; they regard this as very difficult work for it requires a great amount of concentration. Such men understand quite well the power of faith and the influence which can be exercised by the mind over the body. They realize that their manipulation of a patient's body (sucking, extracting bones and stones) is only the external means of gaining the patient's confidence and restoring his faith in life. The final test is often a command to the sick person to get up at a certain time and go somewhere (perhaps down to the creek for water); if he obeys, he will get better; if not, then there is no hope. Most of us, too, have heard of cases of Aborigines dying because a "bone" has been pointed at them or some other magical rite has been performed in order to cause their death; what is so startling about this phenomenon is that in cases examined, there is no physical explanation of the process of dying and often too, neither hospital nor medical treatment is of any avail. The point is that while we admit that even we can be cured and live by faith, we doubt the possibility of dying by faith. The Aborigines, however, have no doubt about it, and prove the truth of it by dying in spite of all our efforts. This is one explanation of their lack of resistance to many illnesses which should not be fatal, and that quite apart from introduced diseases to which they have not built up an immunity. They know the physical aspect of these illnesses, but to them this is only the symptom of the real trouble which is animistic (spiritual or magical) in nature. Someone has "pointed" or "sung" them, or some taboo has been broken and they are suffering the penalty. There is only one final cure, and it must be animistic or spiritual in nature. Their own medicine-men know it and without our psychological training, they work psychologically, and get rid of the animistic cause of the illness, producing tangible evidence of it if necessary, either in the form of blood, stones or bone, or by feigning to throw it away. Some of our own medical practitioners know the experience of actually curing a sick Aborigine of all the symptoms of his illness, and yet, in spite of all their efforts, being unable to restore the patient to health. As a consequence, they conclude that there is something about the Aborigine's attitude to sickness which they cannot fathom. Such is the fact. It would therefore be worth while allowing Aborigines to have the help of their own medicine-men as well as our own. The other alternative is to call in the assistance of a priest who has an adequate knowledge of Aboriginal psychic life; he may be of real help.

In all I have been saying about the psychic life, I have been thinking of civilized Aborigines as well as those on the fringe of settlement or the "untouched". Whatever customs are dropped, these psychic beliefs hang on and indeed seem to be almost ineradicable. In any case, many of us play with the ideas of telepathy and of curing disease by thought alone, and it has taken a long time for the germ-theory of disease to be accepted.

MYTHOLOGY

The Aborigines do not limit their thinking to times of special happenings only; they are provided with an ever-present theme for contemplation, namely, the dream-time itself, the mythological representation of which they can carry about in their minds. We should try to realize the psychological effect made on the candidate during the course of his initiation when after disciplinary and other preparation, he is first admitted to a knowledge of the dream-time. Let us think too, of the suppressed eagerness with which he must look forward to the occasion when he himself will be entrusted with the custody of some part of it—a myth, a site, a sacred symbol—and will be called upon to assist in the performance of a sacred rite. But not only does he learn the myth in its prose and more exact poetic forms, he also in time comes to understand its significance—its relationship to the country, to the ritual and to social life. All this demands thought, directed and reverent though it be. His interpretations may usually be the same as those of people before him, but just as new customs arise or are adopted, so new mythological sanctions and interpretations come into being either through contemplation and thought in waking life or through dreaming and consideration of the significance of the dream.

What is Aboriginal mythology? It is not a mere collection of stories concerned with the sun, moon and stars and various natural features, though these do figure in myths. We are apt to get a wrong idea of mythology from books, large or small, which give us lists of such stories quite unrelated to the social, economic and religious life of the tribe. The natives do possess make-believe and "just-so" stories, but mythology is a very important institution. We have already noticed how it describes what are believed to be historical events and processes and that it provides the authority for present-day social and ritual life. Indeed, so important is mythology that cult societies or lodges are or-

[13] *Top*, rock-shelter painting associated with the clan hero, the increase of natural species, and with "burial". Northern Kimberley. *Bottom*, bark-painting: Songman and Didjeridu player. Western Arnhem Land.

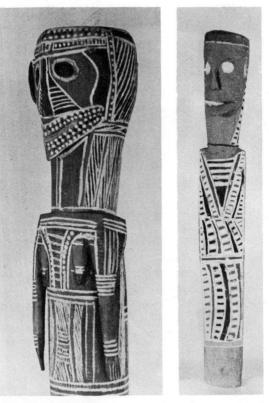

[14] Carved wooden figures of mythological persons. North-eastern Arnhem Land.

[15] Bark-painting: Macassan Prahu. North-eastern Arnhem Land.

[16] *Top,* scene from peace-making ceremony. Points removed from spears. North-eastern Arnhem Land. *Bottom,* mission girls "dancing" at burial ritual. Goulburn Island.

ganized to be responsible for its transmission, interpretation and application. This reminds us that mythology is not just a matter of words or records, but of action and life, for the cult societies, the totemic lodges, do not spend their time at meetings reciting and chanting only; they also re-enact the myths, and do so because the heroes and ancestors were, in their belief, actual persons and totemic beings; what they did in the course of their labours must now be done in ritual, and the places associated with them must be visited and cared for. In this way the myth is lived out. The purpose of this is to ensure the well-being of the tribe by keeping in living touch with the creative dream-time. In other words, *the myth is life-giving.* For the most part, the details of any myth are only important because they enable the present-day men to walk the path with fidelity, which leads into the sacred dream-time, the source of life.[3]

An examination of the details of myths shows that subsidiary functions are performed by them and that they are intimately related to the Aborigines' social and economic life. I give three illustrations of myths, all from the northeast of South Australia. The first is a myth of the Arabana tribe on the western side of Lake Eyre.

[3] We may, of course, give explanations of the life-giving significance of these acted myths, which differ from those given by the Aborigines. We may claim that while individual and social benefits are derived from the rites and while general well-being is established by them, the source of such virtue is not in the dream-time or the mythical age, but in the very nature of the ceremonies themselves. The contemplation in unison of symbols, myths and rites which are surrounded by a halo of sanctity, the sacred and tense atmosphere of the proceedings, and the great intensity of emotion reached by the singing, dancing and infliction of pain—all contribute to an experience of exaltation, courage and well-being and also to an accession of strength arising from the experience of common purpose, action and feeling which characterizes all those taking part. Of course, all this is true and remains true whether we accept or reject the Aborigines' traditional interpretation that strength and life are derived from contact with the dream-time.

An old woman who was looking for food at Maluna near Lake Eyre, saw a big kangaroo (*kungara*) which she desired to kill, but a boy, Wilkuda, sprang out of her inside —apparently like a young marsupial springing from its mother's pouch—and chased the kangaroo in a westerly direction across what is now Lake Eyre. He camped near the site of Peake Station homestead. Next morning he managed to kill the kangaroo and put it on the fire at Ngurupana; this is the place of the tail, for *ngurupa* means tail; it is near Keckwick's Pile. Wilkuda then went to sleep, but when he woke up, instead of finding a cooked kangaroo, he discovered that the kangaroo had got off the fire and run away. He chased it into a mob of kangaroos near Kununa, up Arckaringa Creek, but managed to cut it out of the mob, for he had to catch this particular kangaroo.

Coming to Tondina, he saw his *ngauwili*, a classificatory father's sister, who happened to be his own mother's cross-cousin; he had sexual intercourse with her; as she resented his action, he killed her. Incidentally, this incident expresses the resentment felt in the tribe towards such sexual intercourse, which is a form of incest.

Continuing the chase, he grew very weary. At this stage, an old man who was hunting with a dog came along, and seeing the big kangaroo, and thinking it was just an ordinary kangaroo, caught it with the help of his dog, and killed and skinned it. Wilkuda at length came up to the old man and told him it was his kangaroo, adding, "you can eat the flesh, but give me the skin."

Wilkuda then went off with the skin, making back east. Arriving at a spot near Guduna (Goodana Creek), he contemplated making a lake there with the skin, but a little bird, the Yuriilya, told him not to do so, as people had to walk about there. So he rolled up the skin and walked down the Nulkuna (Nilkinna Creek). The bird again stopped him from making a lake, telling him not to put the skin down Anna Creek way. Passing to a spot east of Anna Creek he threw down the skin which became Lake

Eyre, while he himself turned into stone; his knife and bag in which he carried the skin can also be seen there in stone, and, strangely enough, the kangaroo is likewise there in stone. As far as I know, this stone is not the abode of kangaroo-spirits. There is also a heap of kangaroo-stones at Maluna where the kangaroo started from.

This myth records and sanctions a sexual prohibition, reflects the value of dogs in hunting, gives an explanation of various natural features, such as Lake Eyre, and also shows that in the heroic age, there was a distinction between ordinary animals and those, which, like the big kangaroo of the myth, possessed special virtue.

The second illustration comes from the Wongkonguru on the north-east of Lake Eyre. Fire is the name or "dreaming" (Ularaga) of a cult-clan, a fact which witnesses to the great social importance of fire and fire-making. The method of making fire is by twirling, but the success of the process is bound up with a dream-time song which must be preserved by the men who inherit the fire dreaming from their fathers.

The maker of fire in the Ularaga was a Yigauara, a native-cat man who belonged to the country to the north-east of Macumba. He is sometimes called Makatakaba. On one occasion this man tied his hair up with string. Being laughed at by the blacks, he made fire and burnt them all up, and on another occasion did the same to a group at Macumba; indeed Macumba River and Station gets its name from this myth, for *maka*, is fire (Makamba); the myth is here associated with a mass of black stones which are said to be the remains of the blacks who were burnt. There are also said to be two standing stones leaning one against the other at Ururuwora, which represent two snakes, or two women (perhaps these are the same), who were caught by the fire as it travelled. The myths evidently describe the sudden starting up of a bush-fire (probably as the result of the sun's heat at the end of a good season when the grass and herbage have dried up), and the fierce but sometimes insidious manner in which such fires travel. Thus, the fire is said to travel inside the ground, and to come out a long way off at Wiluumanga, and so, whenever fire breaks out suddenly and unaccountably, it can be attributed to the fire started by Yigauara. From there, the fire spread towards the south-east, and then back to the place where Yigauara made the fire, and then it spread east burning man and dog. Two of Yigauara's brothers were carrying the skins of Kanmari, the mythical water snake, when the fire overtook them with the result that it lifted them and their snake-skins up to the sky where they can be seen as two black marks in the Milky Way, while Yigauara himself is also up there, a third black mark.

The song for making fire by twirling is:

> *Neka (Maka) takaaba   balu rari inya;*

Neka or *maka* is fire, and *takaaba* refers to the twirling of the sticks; the other words are "the song". Another song which must be sung when recounting the Ularaga and which also refers to the making of fire is:

Anbalu	*radi*	*maka*	*takaaba*	*andana*
Lightning goes up,		fire,	twirling	"song"

Other songs commemorate Yigauara's doings at fire-making and fire-spreading. Thus, when he saw the fire light he sang *Aruringa anpalpiwa*, to make it spread, and *Arelina aletaterpa*, to make it go higher, while the following song tells its own story:

> *Maltdja kura argura namba aruribara,*

the free translation of which is that the firestick slipped out of his (Yigauara's) hand, and as the wind covered the track, he lost it, and then growled. (*Maltdja*, hand; *kura*, blow out track; *argura*, lost; *namba*, slipped; *aruribara*, he growled.)

This myth provides an historical and personal explanation of the colour of certain stones at Macumba, of certain black patches in the sky and of outbreaks of bush-fire. It enshrines the widespread belief in the mythical water-serpent who is often identified with the rainbow and is a means of access to the sky. Finally, and most important, it expresses the conviction that such a social necessity as fire has an "other-world" source. Life without the firestick is unthinkable: to sit down or to sleep by day or night without it is almost impossible. It is often used as the symbol of marriage; the burning points of two fire sticks are made to touch and are kept touching until the sticks are both burnt away; this symbolizes the common fire of man and wife and also their common life. The newly circumcised youth, as I have seen, is left with his fire to mark his attainment of a distinct social personality, with the implication that henceforth he may make and be responsible for fire. Now, it is just because fire means so much practically and symbolically that it becomes the central feature of a myth and its very making is a sacred ritual action. In other words, the myth and rite do not merely provide an explanation for the making and appearance of fire, as though mere friction were not sufficient of itself; they also witness to its great social importance and to the necessity of guarding it most carefully, on the one hand against its careless use, lest bush-fires should be caused, and on the other hand, against loss.

The third myth comes from the Dieri on the east of Lake Eyre. Paltira, a wind *mura-mura*, or dream-time hero, stole a pounding-stone and also a large stone dish, but as he could not lift the latter, he sang a song which caused a wind to blow and lift the stone on to his head. He then carried it down to Parachilna. The songs which he used are still sung to make the winds blow, different songs for different winds, cold, hot and dusty ones. It is only the men with the wind for their *mura-mura*, or cult totem who are privileged to sing the songs or who can do so effectively. This myth, through its totemic context, brings such apparently fortuitous phenomena as the winds into the social order, not only by the personification of a power which caused the winds in the beginning, but also by enabling a special totemic group to adopt such a ritual attitude towards winds that some sort of control or, at least, some understanding of them can be established. The taking of the stone dish to the Parachilna district explains, by the process of personification, the presence there of suitable sandstone for use as a nether millstone; it may also reflect some comprehension of the fact that the sand of which such stone slabs consist, is the same as that which is constantly blown about by the wind in the north-eastern part of South Australia. Incidentally expeditions went annually from the Dieri and other north-eastern tribes, even as far off as the Yantruwanta on the Queensland border, down to the Parachilna district on the western side of the Flinders Range to obtain these stone slabs as well as for red ochre. The latter is the theme of a long series of myths and rites which, unfortunately, cannot be given here.

These are typical Australian myths. They belong to the cult-life of the tribe, and therefore to its sacred literature. They are usually associated with certain features in the landscape which are thereby rendered sacred, and taboo to all but the fully initiated; even the latter must approach them in a prescribed manner, and according to my informants, they are emotionally stirred when they do. But, in addition to being doors into the dream-time and means of life, myths perform several functions, though any one myth does not necessarily perform them all.

They do provide an explanation of the origin of natural phenomena, objects and species and also of institutions and customs. This is sometimes referred to as the aetiological function of mythology. Two points about this are worth noting. If we were to examine all the myths of the Aborigines, and we are familiar with the subject matter of many hundred, we would find that almost all of them are concerned with natural phenomena and species in their normal form; only a few seek to explain the extraordinary, the catastrophic and terrifying. As with totemism, so with mythological explanation, the Aborigine's concern is with the normal and regular. The other point is that the mythological explanations are by personification. As a result of certain activities of heroes, ancestors and animals in the mythical past, the various natural phenomena took their rise; for example, according to the Wongkonguru fire-myth, a heap of black stones represents the transformed bodies of men and women who were punished by being burnt; or, as in the Arabana myth, Lake Eyre was made by a hunter throwing down a kangaroo skin. In the same way, these and other myths provide historical and dream-time sanction for customs, rules and rites on which the cohesion and well-being of the tribe is believed to depend. This means that the myths, while providing explanations of origin are at the same time "historical".

In this regard we should not ignore the possibility that these sacred myths do often enshrine actual historical events and sequences, even though these may be somewhat symbolized and distorted. The myths of the culture-heroes who introduced circumcision and the stone knife into tribe after tribe in the central parts of Australia, and those recounting the movements of the sky culture-heroes of eastern Australia as they travelled from the north-east to the south and south-west introducing elements of culture, are examples of such historical myths. In these myths, the appearance of certain natural features are accounted for as in the myths quoted, but it is just possible that in such references, it is not so much a case of explaining natural features as of sanctifying them by making them memorials of the deeds of heroes and ancestors, and of the latter's ritual and social teaching. In some tribes, the natives, even to-day, set up stones to mark important events.

Mythology reflects the value and social importance of animals, plants, objects, natural phenomena, events, and institutions, and does so either directly or indirectly. It is not everything which becomes the theme of a myth, but usually only those things which affect society for good or ill. These are edible species, ceremonial objects (e.g. red ochre, pearl-shell, churinga), important natural phenomena like the moon, sun, rain, flood, wind and fire; insects and small birds which play some part in social life, either directly by their association with man (mosquitoes) or as representatives of natural phenomena (e.g. in Central Australia, the spur-winged plover enters into ritual because of its association with rain, being a forerunner of the latter); objects of material culture (axes, nets, etc.); social institutions, and finally, another set of occurrences which are of great significance to the tribe, namely, man's origin, birth and death.

Thus, the Aborigine does not try to explain the origin of everything in the heavens above and the earth beneath, but only those things, natural, manufactured, personal and social, with which his life is concerned. In this he is, of course, like most of us. But, even so, he is not primarily concerned with the origin of things except in so far as this provides a sanction or pattern for daily life. His real problem is life in the sense of living. The life of the food-gathering Aborigines is, as we have noticed, a matter of adjustment to and utter dependence on nature, its species, objects and phenomena. They cannot adjust themselves to these nor control them by applied science, for they know but little of the laws of nature. Moreover, they recognize that they cannot control the contingencies of life nor maintain the regular and normal order of nature's seasons and products by material arts and crafts. They have, however, an alternative which prevents them from being helpless and listless, namely, to regard nature as a system of personal powers or beings who can be brought into their own moral and social order, an order of which they, as members of society, have intimate knowledge. They do this in mythology by the process of "personalizing", and then, just as they take up definite attitudes towards one another, so do they act towards these personalized objects and species; they regard them with respect and adopt various ritual attitudes towards them.

This brings us again to totemism, though we should remember that, quite apart from totemism, the Aborigines observe various taboos, mostly of a temporary nature on some natural species in connexion with age, sex, childbirth, initiation and mourning. But in totemism, the ritual attitudes are based on definite and permanent bonds of a kinship or ceremonial nature, which are believed to exist between man and natural species and objects, and at the basis of this is the mythological principle of personalizing or personification. In other words, mythology provides the fact or explanation of this process, while totemism brings the natural world into orderly relationship with the human world by grouping both together into moieties, clans, or sections. Totemism implies that there is a common life shared by man and nature; mythology says that this life is a personal or quasi-personal one.

So once again, we are brought to the Aborigines' view of life which is spiritual (animistic and personal), totemistic and historical—a view which enables them to work out their destiny free from any overwhelming fear and uncertainty.

THE SKY-HEROES

When mentioning, in the preceding chapter, the differences between the eastern and western initiation ritual uses, I referred to the belief in sky culture-heroes as being part of the former. This belief demands special mention for it undoubtedly exercises a definite influence over those who hold it. Moreover, it seems to be connected especially with initiation ritual on the one hand, and with the making of medicine-men on the other. It stood out above all other beliefs and myths in most of Queensland, New South Wales and Victoria. The sky-hero, Baiame, Daramulum, Nurunderi, Bunjil, Goin, Biral—to give some of the names by which he was, or is, known in different regions—was often pictured as the hero who led the tribe to its present habitat, and made the natural features as they are to-day. In addition, he bestowed on men their various items of material culture, gave them their social laws, and above all, instituted the initiation rites. It is in the latter that the initiates first gain any real knowledge of him, and learn his secret name; even to-day civilized Aborigines will not breathe that name to the outsider. Though he sees and knows all, he is in the sky, a place often pictured as possessing much quartz crystal and fresh water. The secret initiation ground in New South Wales, especially the smaller Bora ring, represents, I believe, this sky world. The newly made wise man, usually known as the medicine-man, can visit this sky land and see something of Baiame; and finally, the departed go there as they are entitled to do by reason of their initiation.

As far as I can see the matter, and I have discussed it with initiates, this sky-hero corresponds to the hero of religious secret societies, the mysteries of which go back to the old mystery cults of a few thousand years ago, and with which I am prepared to believe that this cult is historically connected, by whatever incidents it was brought to the Australians. Initiation and the secret life spread all over Australia and though now in central and northern parts of Australia, the belief in the sky-hero of initiation has either ceased to exist or else has been pushed into the background by the totemic heroes whose spirits are tied to the earth, yet a careful survey of the evidence suggests that initiation there, too, was possibly, in former days, a means of gaining knowledge of the sky-hero and access to his world. In the north-west, the heroes who taught the natives how to make the bull-roarer, and who introduced initiation ceremonies, belong to the sky. In an important and widespread Central Australian myth concerning incompletely formed beings, which I think refers to an initiation rite performed on candidates, the hero and operator came from the sky.

In the Kaitish belief (a tribe just north of the Aranda), a sky-being is very interested in the swinging of the bull-roarer—the symbol of the sky-hero in eastern Australian ritual; moreover, he is said to conduct initiation in the sky-world—no doubt the prototype of the rites performed on earth. Amongst the western Aranda and Loritja, the dream-time heroes are said in some myths to have had formerly associations with the sky-world and access to it by way of a mountain. The sky-hero, however, caused this to sink and so the dream-time totemic heroes had to remain on earth. In Kaitish mythology, the sky-being existed before this dream-time. This possibly represents the historical sequence in that area and indeed in all the central, northern and north-western regions. Initiation was at first admission to the beliefs and rites connected with the sky-hero, but later it included also admission into cult-totemism with its myths of the dream-time heroes, which in many tribes, as far as our knowledge goes, ultimately overshadowed the former belief and associations.

There is no need to pursue further the evidence for the existence of the belief in the sky-hero, or to study the complex of beliefs and rites. The problem of the diffusion of these two sets of beliefs does not concern us here, nor do we need to go into further detail regarding the belief in the sky-hero, except to say that he was usually referred to as father, or all-father, that the bull-roarer was his symbol, and that he was and is the sanction for essential laws, customs and rites. Just as in central or north-western Australia, to say a custom is *altjira, djugur, ungud,* etc., that is, dreaming, is to give it final and unimpeachable authority, so in eastern Australia, to say of a custom, "Baiame say so" is to provide the same kind of sanction. Finally, the myths in which the sky-hero figures, perform the same aetiological, historical, and sociological function as do those of the dream-time heroes, and through their representation in symbol and rite, entry is gained to the sacred, life-giving world—but this time it is in the sky.[4]

THE "MOTHER-GODDESS" CULT

Over forty years ago Professor Baldwin Spencer recorded a myth of a mythological woman from whom the tribes of western Arnhem Land arose, and in 1937 Professor W. L. Warner published an account of myths and rites in north-east Arnhem Land in which certain women and a great serpent were the leading figures.[5] However, it is only during the past decade that we have begun to understand the significance of the great myths and rites of the northern half of the Northern Territory. These express two main concepts—the fertility-mother or -goddess and the rainbow serpent—which tend to coalesce. In the Alligator rivers region, western Arnhem Land, the basic myth is of "our mother from earliest times". She came from the islands to the north with her husband, and as she moved about on the mainland left spirit-children to become the ancestors of the different tribes. She allotted them their languages and countries. The myth varies, but there is only "one mother for all people everywhere". The chanting during the sacred ritual of the Ngurlmak relates her journeying through the tribal countries. A hollow log, the *ubar,* which is prepared and beaten continuously during the ritual, symbolizes her womb, and the "drum" beats represent her voice calling the men to the sacred ground. In some versions, this ground is the mother's womb, and the ritual is one of rebirth. Moreover, she becomes identified with the female rainbow serpent, for the ritual-myth is concerned with a man who turned into a rainbow serpent and hid in

---

[4] The two sets of beliefs co-existed not only in Central Australia but also on the north coast of New South Wales.

[5] B. Spencer, *Native Tribes of the Northern Territory* (1914), a record of field-work in 1911. W. L. Warner, *A Black Civilization,* (1937) based on field-work in 1927–9.

a hollow log, so as to bite a woman who, though "promised" to him, refused to be his wife.

Much more widespread is the cult of Kunapipi. It entered north Australia by way of the Roper or of the Victoria River and has spread east and west, both directly and also in a great southerly curve by way of Borooloola, Newcastle Waters and the Upper Victoria River branches. In addition, during the past three decades, it has spread almost all over Arnhem Land—even to the Fitzmaurice and to the vicinity of Darwin, as well as to the far north-east. Parts of the mythology and ritual connected with this cult have spread in recent years through East Kimberley to Forrest River (the Tjanba cult) and to the North Kimberley coastal tribes (the Kurangara ritual—modified).

Kunapipi, also known as Mumina and Kadjeri, and exoterically as "the Old Woman", travelled across the land with a band of heroes and heroines (the Munga-Munga). She gave birth to men and women, and by her ritual acts caused natural species to appear. Her way was prepared by the rainbow serpent. This symbolizes the storms which clear a road through the trees and cause the streams and creeks to find their way to the river and the sea. This serpent is also the maker of the road along which a pre-existent spirit-child enters its mother's womb.

In the ritual a curved trench represents Kunapipi's womb, and two rainbow serpents, a male and a female, are engraved on the walls. In addition, a serpent is painted in red on a tall, elongated, pointed object which is erected on the ceremonial ground to be the sanction of the teaching and discipline which the initiate receives. At the end of the ceremonies this object, the Yermalindji, is burnt on the side of the trench and collapses into it. The blackened, charred form can be seen for weeks later. The initiate, too, is made to go into this "womb", from which he is later "reborn". In addition, he is given a bull-roarer to swing; as he does so, his spirit-double, or ceremonial or "wood shade", enters it, for this piece of wood symbolizes not only the mother's voice, but also her womb. On his rebirth the initiate leaves this bull-roarer in the trench, along with his "wood shade". When the wood disintegrates, his "shade" or double goes to his spirit-home, there to wait for his "flesh" soul. His two "souls" are reunited following a Kunapipi, which is performed for him some time after his death by a son or other relation.

Similar concepts are expressed in the great north-east Arnhem Land cycle of the Djanggawul. These heroes and heroines came to the land from Beralku, the Island of the Dead far to the east. They brought sacred sticks, called *rangga*, which represented the iguana tail and trees. With them, the leader, Djanggawul, caused water to flow and natural species and trees to grow. The *rangga* were kept in a large conical-shaped mat which symbolized the womb. Moreover, the people to whom the Djanggawul sisters gave birth were the *rangga*; and as people's bones are now likened to these objects, they must be ritually disposed of after death. The rites, which are mainly concerned with fertility in man and nature, are now carried out by the men, though originally they were the possession of the women.

Another important mythological cycle, which belongs to the eastern groups along the Arnhem Land north coast, is about the Wauwelak sisters and a female rock python, Yulunggul. Fitting into the same general concepts, it adapted the Ngurlmak (or Ubar) for one of its rituals, and the Kunapipi for another. There is too, the very "high" Yabuduruwa of south-eastern and south-central Arnhem Land and of the region south to Borooloola. Amongst the striking features of the ritual are the complete absence of singing; the use of wooden gongs; impressive scenes representing the lifeless coming to life; a beehive-shaped hut, the "mother" or "queen", in which some sacred symbols are kept and solemnly revealed; the presence of women sleeping on the edge of the secret ground on the final night, with iguana "tails" (of bark) for pillows, and their return to the camp at dawn carrying these pillows as flaming torches.

The concept of the mother-goddess or fertility-mother is more marked in some of these cults than in others; it is especially clear in the Kunapipi and the Ngurlmak. Moreover, a careful study of the rituals and the mythology, of the symbols and the meanings, of the emphasis on birth and rebirth, and of the "mystery" which is scrupulously guarded in secret, shows that we are once again in the presence of a religious complex similar to that of the ancient mother-goddess cults. These spread east and southeast as well as west from the eastern Mediterranean many centuries ago.

The fertility-mother concept was probably an importation into Arnhem Land from across the sea, as the myths suggest. In spite of its great appeal it was confined to about the northern half of the Northern Territory, well within the tropics, the Macarthur and Victoria River waters constituting its southern limits. Possibly it is to be correlated with the regular fertility and fecundity of the tropical wet seasons. In any case, all these cults are of high import, into which persons are initiated at no little cost. But the cost is not too high, for the man who has been through the Kunapipi, Ngurlmak, Djanggawul and the Yabuduruwa knows that the same ceremony will be performed for him after his death, ensuring the continued existence of his soul and the possibility of rebirth. Indeed, he tries to provide for this by seeing that his son or someone in a comparable relationship is admitted to, and versed in, his cult before his death. Thus, an elderly Djauan tribesman, a friend of mine, who is a "past-master" in the Kunapipi, is at present (1953) anxious to put his big son through the Kunapipi so that the son will be in a position to hold the ceremony for him after his death.

This is true also of the basic cult of Arnhem Land—the Maraian. The myth relates the journeyings of cult-heroes, often in animal form, in particular of a great python, the rainbow serpent or its representative. This serpent put forth at various water-places the spirits of members of the local clan and the first forms of the local species. These places and the mythological roads are known and followed in actual pilgrimages and also in the order of chanting and singing during ceremonies. The Maraian ritual may best be likened to an All Souls' festival. Shade places of boughs are erected on the secret ground, in which symbolic objects representing the great serpent and various totems are painted and stored in readiness for "exposition", handling and teaching. And into these shade places, the "shades" of the departed, the spirit-doubles of living but absent clansmen, and the "shades" of the Maraian heroes, are summoned by ritual calls. Totemic scenes too, are danced daily in imitation of the dances performed by the "shades" of animals, reptiles, insects and birds in their "shade" places. For in this, as in all the great cults, the same philosophic doctrine explains natural species and man.

I was admitted to the Maraian in 1949 by the south-central Arnhem Land headman, who held the ceremony for the purpose of handing it over to his son, for he felt that his own death was near. He died a year or so later, and in 1951 the son, now headman, held a Maraian for his father.[6]

VARIETY OF RELIGIOUS CULTS AND DOCTRINES

Looking over Aboriginal Australia we see that the cult of the sky-hero or god predominated in the east; the Wondjina cult in the far north-west; the mother-goddess or

[6] There are normally two shade places on the Maraian ground, one for each of the two ceremonial moieties into which the tribe or tribes are divided. In this case (1949), there was a third shade. Looking in it I saw a long painted wooden symbol of Muitj, the serpent through whom living creatures came to the region. Two old men, who were guarding it, said it was for me. The invitation to me to be at the Maraian was made during a conversation with the old headman in 1948.

fertility-mother and serpent cult in most of the northern half of the Northern Territory and latterly in Eastern Kimberley; and the totemic hero cults throughout the whole of the arid regions from the Bight to Broome, and from Broome east into western Queensland. There has been overlapping and coalescing, for cults received or developed in one region spread into others, although at different rates. The mechanism for diffusion is to hand in the secret life, while receptivity is made easy by the common theme of all the cults—the problems or "mystery" of creation, of birth, death, life.

Probably the cults of the sky-hero, the fertility-mother and Wondjina are later than the totemic heroic cult with its basic concept of "dreaming", or the eternal dream-time. Before the Wondjina was the *ungud* and its clan totems, though the Wondjina are now *ungud* (dreaming) and the totems are increased by Wondjina ritual painting. The sky-hero, Baiame, is credited with the totemic system, and in the few places on the east coast where some of the pre-European culture could be recaptured—north-eastern New South Wales and the neighbouring part of Queensland— totemic "dreaming" rites, similar to those of Western Australia, were formerly practised. On Cape York Peninsula there are similar rites and also hero cults. The latter suggest some Papuan influence. Finally, fertility-mother cults include imitative and representative totemic ceremonies. Apparently, the more recent cults have been combined in myth and ritual with the older indigenous ones, either in juxtaposition or else by assimilation. No contradiction was, or is, felt. The totems, for example, can be attributed to an act or feat of the mother-goddess or sky-god: and in the north of the Northern Territory it is quite normal for an individual to possess, or belong to, not only a totemic cult dreaming, but also a "Big Sunday": the Kunapipi, Yabuduruwa or Ngurlmak.

The Rainbow Serpent. The evidence suggests that totemic philosophy and ritual were fundamental and primary in Aboriginal thought and religion. Even sky phenomena were brought under this category. The most significant of these is the rainbow. It is always thought of as a great snake or serpent, a link between earthly water-places and the world-on-top, the sky, to which he raises himself. Quartz-crystals in the east and pearl-shell in the north-west are his symbols and contain something of his power. Through their ritual use rain can be made and the medicine- (or doctor-) man exert power. Coming with showers and storms which fall from above on a thirsty land, the rainbow serpent is credited with a causative role in rain, and in the appearance of life, which follows the rain and depends on it. In the western deserts he, Wonambi, guards the water-holes where, it is said, pearl-shells are stored, and there too, he kills and restores to life those who would be medicine-men. No doubt the migrating groups from the north-west coast brought the doctrine with them. Also under the name Galaru, a rainbow serpent cult has spread from South Kimberley into North and East Kimberly. In the former it has become integrated with the Wondjina cult, and has given its name to a local clan, Galarungari, which is especially concerned with rain; Galaru has taken its place as a painting on Wondjina galleries, as well as on separate galleries. But the concept was not new there, for the dreaming term *ungud* denotes also big water python and rainbow snake, part of the doctrine which the Wondjina found in the region. In East Kimberley, Galaru, as in many regions, is the maker of rivers and rain, the giver of spirit-children (for they sojourn in water places), and the sanction of marriage laws. In spite of the wide diffusion of rainbow snake beliefs, however, and their association with medicine-men, no distinct cult of the rainbow has been reported; it seems only to enter into cult and ritual when associated with another concept—the fertility-mother, the Maraian or Wondjina. It was an integral, though striking, element in the totemic philosophical view of the world which, for the Aborigines, was basic to all their ritual.

Chapter IX

ART AND RITUAL

An Artistic People

Officials and other persons moving beyond the confines of the first settlement at Port Jackson saw no native gardens and only slight indications of permanent habitation. Soon, however, they came across rock-engravings and cave-paintings and, a few decades later, settlers and explorers pushing west of the Great Dividing Range and on the North Coast found trees engraved with elaborate geometrical patterns. In the very early years, too, some of the newcomers saw Aborigines performing corroborees which were marked by rhythm, song, mimicry and interpretative dancing. Moreover, weapons and implements were seen to bear artistic designs. Thus, however primitive the Aborigines were, however savage were some of their actions and dances, and however crude were their rock-paintings and -engravings, they were obviously not devoid of aesthetic sense.

Gradually, similar reports came from other parts of the continent. One of the most startling in those far-off years was the discovery by George Grey in 1838 in the northern Kimberley of remarkable cave-paintings, the Wondjina, the meaning of which was not unravelled until ninety years had passed (Chapter VIII). By 1876 Mr R. Brough Smyth summed up the information to date by saying that

the practice of ornamenting caves, rocks, and trees, and cutting figures on the ground by removing grass, is characteristic of this people. Their pictures are found in every part of the continent, and also on the islands adjacent to the continent to which they had access. A large number of references could be given illustrative of their love of art, but a few will suffice to induce the reader, perhaps, to regard with a higher interest the first attempts of a savage people to imitate the forms of natural objects, and to portray, though usually in no very durable form, incidents in their lives."[1]

Since these words were written, our knowledge of Aboriginal art has increased immensely. We have studied it as a living element in the tribal culture of several regions, and have come to understand much of its meaning and of its function in the context of Aboriginal social life, religion and philosophy. As a result, the term "savage" seems inappropriate except in the technical sense of denoting a people who depend solely on food-gathering and hunting for their existence; make implements of wood, bone and stone, but not of metals; have no pottery and do not live in hamlets or villages. For, although on the one hand, some of their cruder paintings and engravings on rock may be likened to the first artistic attempts of a savage people, on the other hand much of their artistic endeavour is neither crude nor savage. It wells up from long tradition and is expressed with great skill and with sureness of purpose.

The Aborigines' forms of art are varied. Of these, engraving in stone and shaping or painting figures of earth are the only ones no longer practised. The others are engraving in wood and shell; carving and painting wooden figures in the round; making and decorating composite ceremonial objects; painting on stone surfaces (the walls and roofs of caves and rock shelters), on bark "canvases", and on the human body; ritual re-enactment of mythology; ballet and imitative dancing to the accompaniment of rhythmic tapping or beating (of sticks, boomerangs, "gongs" of solid or of hollow wood, or of cupped hands

[1] R. Brough Smyth, *The Aborigines of Victoria,* vol. i, p. 291.

on thighs), and usually also of singing or chanting; and the use of poetic imagery and rhythm in song-making.

ART REGIONS IN ABORIGINAL AUSTRALIA

Aboriginal Australia may be divided into eight art regions, though a complete analysis would require some subdivisions.

(i) *The South-Eastern Region.* This, the first known to us, was characterized (a) by mainly angular (with some curved), conventional designs on ceremonial tree-trunks, on weapons, on wooden symbolic objects, and, in some districts, on the ground in ceremonial places; (b) by temporary naturalistic moulded earth figures associated with initiation and the revelation of "secrets"; (c) by rock-engravings, generally referred to as "carvings": in the two New South Wales extensive "galleries" (Port Jackson-Hawkesbury River, and north of Broken Hill). Apart from some symbolic markings, the majority of these last are naturalistic in design, representing human beings, cult-heroes, animals, reptiles, birds and fish, but in eastern South Australia and through south-western to eastern Queensland, they are mainly geometrical and symbolical, with possibly some conventional designs; and (d) by rock-shelter and cave paintings, of animals, weapons, the sun and symbols, together with stencilled hands. Polished stone axe-heads (some very large) and polished stone ceremonial objects[2] were also particular features of the region. Very little is known of the ritual apart from some observers' accounts of parts of initiation, and we have no worthwhile texts of native songs and chants.

[2] These were the cornute-shaped stones of the Darling River area, which were also found in north-eastern South Australia. In 1935, on the north coast of New South Wales, I first came across a dumb-bell-like stone symbol; during the next few years a few more came to light. In 1950 I saw similar objects in the Central Highlands of New Guinea, where they are thought to be of recent archaeological origin.

(ii) *North-East Queensland.* Art is here limited mainly to painting weapons, implements, and bull-roarers and other ceremonial objects. The colour is thickly applied, usually in stylized patterns. The latter express or symbolize myths and sacred meanings. Carving has not been reported, but in part of Cape York Peninsula logs and pieces of wood, which show resemblance in forms to certain natural and totemic species, are painted for use in ceremonies.

Dancing and the ballet are well developed. Papuan influence by way of Torres Straits Islands is evident in the north of the Peninsula in the decoration of dancers (including the use of masks) and in the drum used in some "dances". The mythology which is re-enacted in the ceremonies and represented in the art centres is that of totemic cult-heroes, some of whom are ancestral in character.

(iii) *The Lake Eyre Region.* This country of moving sand and of sand-hills, but no rock-masses and caves, did not lend itself to rock-engraving and rock-painting. During the periods between the floodings of the great river system (the Diamantina and Cooper on the east), and the erratic rains on the west, life was hard, and tribes had to move about in small groups, gathering their food. This probably explains why their art was mobile and not rich. Short sign-posts, called *toa,* were shaped and brightly painted in designs to symbolize the journeyings of the ancestral heroes, the *mura-mura*; they were used to indicate the destinations of persons setting out from a camp. Weapons in this region, like the large boomerang-shaped club, were incised with designs, mainly of shuttle-type curves. Finally, some ceremonial objects were painted to represent the deeds of mythological heroes.

Tribes of this cultural group, who share the same type of social structure and mythology, spread along the Flinders Range, where there are some galleries of paintings and of rock-incising and intagliation. The designs are geometrical and symbolical, but nothing definite is known about their meaning. Moreover, we do not know whether these tribes were responsible for this art, or whether it was done by earlier tribes, perhaps moving across from far-western New South Wales.

(iv) *The Southern and Western Arid Region.* This region which extends from about the Quorn-Oodnadatta railway line on the east to the Great Victoria Desert in Western Australia, has been, for the most part, the scene of migrations of small groups moving from the north-west from water to water across the arid country looking for a better land. Central ranges like the Warburton, Petermann, Musgrave and Everard could hold them for a time, but then, under pressure of numbers or of failing food supply, some had to move on towards the Laverton area, Boundary Dam and Ooldea, and eventually the Great Australian Bight, or in recent decades, the Transcontinental Railway, a less bleak prospect. Such a life did not encourage art. There are almost no local art forms, and ceremonial objects have been imported from the north-west in Western Australia, whence the immigrants themselves came. The art is typified by incised angular patterns—concentric squares and rhomboids, zigzag, meander and key. These designs prevail from Ninety Mile Beach, south of Broome, south-east to central Western Australia, and have spread to Laverton and Ooldea.

Temporary ceremonial objects of the Waninga type (Chapter VII) are made for ceremonies and dances. Actors are painted and decorated for totemic ceremonies, but all traces of this adornment are removed immediately the ceremony has been performed. The acting in these ceremonies is simple, relatively slow in movement and conventional, with some imitation of "dream-time" heroes and creatures. In any case the actors, whose adornment and role have been chanted on to them, as well as put on and adopted, represent the heroes and creatures of the dreaming. The effect is often startling. The singers jump up, draw bood from their genital organs, and with both arms bent at the elbows (the upper arms horizontal in line with the shoulders and the forearms perpendicular), they slide backwards in quick jerks one behind the other, until they are exhausted. This part of the ritual reflects the hardness of life in the region.[3]

(v) *Central and North-central Region.* This region, which extends from about the South Australian border northwards to the vicinity of the Victoria and Roper rivers, is poorly developed in pictorial art. There is, however, an aspect of stability in both the tribal organization and the mythology. Tribes were settled in their territories and were not ceaselessly in a state of flux and migration. The mythological heroes finished their courses or performed important feats at definite and fixed sites. In the central tribes ceremonies were performed at these places, so that they partook somewhat of the nature of pilgrimages. The sites were approached by the mythological paths, and identification of the cult-group with the ancestral heroes and the dreaming through the sacramental nature of the symbols at the sacred place or sanctuary was continued by ritual acts. Once again, these were not energetic and demonstrative, but rather sacramental and contemplative, centring around both the permanent object or symbol at the mythological sanctuary, or on the sacred *churinga* (*tjurunga*) produced from hidden store-houses for the occasion. These rites were believed to result in the increase of species.

In addition, in all of this region, "historical" ceremonies were, and in some areas are still, performed at selected

[3] I first saw these ceremonies in 1930 in the Musgrave Ranges, in the far north-west of South Australia near the Central Australian border. Having inquired about the "dreaming", I suddenly found that my camp was made a secret place; the men camped near by for a week and performed these ceremonies each morning, afternoon and night. They were Pidjindjara people from the Petermann Range.

In 1953, when on a visit to Areyonga in the Krichauff Ranges, Central Australia, I saw the same type of ceremonies performed by Petermann Range tribesmen who this time had migrated east, instead of south-east. I recorded some of the chanting.

sites. A few actors, often only one or two, are painted and decorated according to a traditional design, and then move on to the cleared ground (or "stage") in a prescribed fashion, do their brief act and sit down. In the central tribes no particular order is observed, but in more northern tribes the historical (mythological) sequence is carefully followed.[4]

All these totemic rites, with their aspects of body painting and adornment, traditional representative acting, and the accompanying rhythm provided by tapping boomerangs on sticks, and sometimes also by singing, can be included under the term art. The art is in the service of ritual; the ritual is expressed through art. The texts of the chants which accompany the painting and acting, where they have been studied, are poetical in form, imagery and feeling. Only deep knowledge of the language and of the meaning of the chant texts can bring this out.

The honey-ant totemites, taking the place of their ancestral heroes, tearfully chant as their old home Tjaba passes from view:

> *Enfolded by plains lies Tjaba;*
> *Beyond the far horizon lies Tjaba.*
>
> *Enfolded by plains lies Tjaba,*
> *Dimmed by the enveloping mists.*

The headman of Ulamba, his fighting done, and death near at hand, plods slowly over the intervening miles so that he might begin his final sleep there:

> *High in the heavens shines the afternoon sun:*
> *His heart is filled with yearning to turn home.*

Pushing on, he at last sees Ulamba:

[4] See in particular Spencer and Gillen, *Native Tribes of Central Australia* (Chapters VI–IX) and *Northern Tribes of Central Australia* (Chapters VI, VII, IX). The Wailbri (Yuendumu to the Granites and east to Philip Creek) still perform these ceremonies (1953).

My own home, my dear home,—
O Ulamba, rugged, chasm-cleft.[5]

Pictorial art in this region is poorly developed. Cave-
and rock-paintings, which are not numerous, are usually
of conventional designs. The naturalistic paintings are
crude. Both wooden and stone sacred objects (the *churinga*) are usually incised with concentric circles, U's, arcs
and parallel wavy lines. The same design may have different meanings for different groups; that is, it refers to different traditions.

This poverty of local pictorial art in Central Australia in
particular, provides a justification for the lines taken by the
Aranda "school" of water-colour artists. They have deserted nothing, for there was almost nothing in their own
art tradition which could be developed. It was therefore
most fortunate that Albert Namatjira, a product of Hermannsburg Mission, was attracted by the work of a visiting
white artist, felt the urge to paint, and was given encouragement and help. For the most part his landscapes are in
the orthodox tradition of many leading Australian painters,
but at least two of the other dozen Aranda who have followed his lead, do express Aboriginal feeling and emphasis
in their pictures. In any case, they know the region, its hills
and gorges, and its ever-changing moods and colours.
Their better work expresses their experience, and the many
successful exhibitions and continued demand for their pictures show that people far and near want to share in that
experience. The criticism that they should not just represent on canvas nature as they know and feel it, but some-

[5] T. G. H. Strehlow, *Aranda Traditions*, pp. 31–2. This
whole chapter (I) should be read. Mr Strehlow gives only a
few examples of translations. We may hope that he will publish
full texts and translations of many of the chants. One, "The
Song of Ankotarinja", has appeared in *Oceania*, vol. iv, no. 2,
1933, pp. 190–2. The biggest contribution in this regard yet
made is *Djanggawul*, by R. M. Berndt, the translation of a long
series of chants in north-east Arnhem Land. See next chapter.

thing primeval, is baseless. These artists are not primeval people, but persons of the twentieth century brought up in an Aboriginal-European context in the Alice Springs district of Central Australia. Equally invalid is the criticism that they should show in their water-colours "the subtlety and force of conviction which are in "the wonderful bark paintings of Arnhem Land". Namatjira and his fellow artists had never seen these bark-paintings, which are about nine hundred miles away, and if they did, might not see their force and subtlety. Probably their best work will more and more express some unique emphasis, shading and colour which only an Aboriginal Central Australian could effect. Out of their store they will bring treasures new and old.

(vi) *The South-west*. Little is known of the original culture of the south-western corner of the continent, though a few galleries of stencilled hands and simple linear designs have been found in it. For the Murchison-De Grey River area, however, we have some information about the social organization and also the art. Weapons and ceremonial objects bear rectangular designs, incised in parallel arrangement. Stencillings, mainly of hands, and a few stylized geometrical painted figures occur on rock surfaces in the Murchison district, while in the Gascoyne and De Grey districts petroglyphs, but not paintings, are numerous, especially at the Port Hedland gallery. These include both linear and outline engravings and also surface intagliated designs. They depict stylized geometric figures and naturalistic subjects.

(vii) *The Kimberley Division*. This far northern region of Western Australia, especially the rough mountainous North Kimberley, is remarkable for its many galleries of paintings, the great majority of which contain one or more representations of the Wondjina cult-heroes (Chapter VIII). The design is constant, from the King Leopold Range in the south to the Drysdale River in the north. The head is always, and the shoulders often, depicted, the trunk

and legs sometimes. The full-length paintings, which usually show the Wondjina lying on his side, vary from about
four to seventeen feet in length. The eyes and often the
nose are shown, but the mouth never, for the Wondjina's
body or skull is now lifeless and speechless. The colours
are white (pipeclay), red (ochre), yellow (ochre), black
(charcoal) and, in one small area, blue (obtained from a
powdered mineral). On the same galleries natural species
and objects, all of totemic significance, are also depicted.

In the southern and south-eastern Wondjina galleries a
great serpent is represented. This is an intrusion from the
south of the mythology of the rainbow serpent, Galaru,
who is associated with rain and the sky. So far, no Galaru
paintings have been reported from the South and East
Kimberleys, although the cult was important there. He is,
however, depicted on the big gallery at Forrest River near
Wyndham, which is almost in East Kimberley and just outside the range of the Wondjina cult, and on a gallery at
Mount Anderson Station on the border of South Kimberley.
Probably more will be revealed.

Thus the Northern Kimberley, a country of caves and
rock-shelters, provided permanent "canvas", of which full
advantage was taken to paint the most startling series of
pictures found in Australia—the Wondjina and the Galaru.
Of course, the presence of the appropriate rock-surfaces
and ochres would not necessarily lead to these paintings,
nor to any paintings. The inspiration came from the two
cults, which commemorated the origin of the tribes and
totemic species and ensured their continuation. In the same
area there is no rock-engraving, and none but the crudest
attempts to paint material possessions.

Very little rock-painting has been found in the South
and East Kimberleys, but in the former, weapons and sacred wooden objects are engraved either with the meander
and key pattern (La Grange district), or with parallel
straight lines, in some cases taking an angular bend about
the centre. In the east, the concentric circle design of Cen-

tral Australian *tjurunga* occurs on some sacred and secular objects. Love bull-roarers are sometimes engraved with realistic or conventionalized human figures.

(viii) *Arnhem Land.* The richest art area in Australia is Arnhem Land, using that term in its earlier geographical reference to the total northern part or peninsula of the Northern Territory from about the lower Victoria River and the Roper River to the Arafura Sea.

Spears amongst the coastal tribes were elaborate works of art both in the varied shaping and grading of their barbs, and in the application of colours to these. Indeed, in many cases, utility was sacrificed in the interest of beauty and form, as when the barbs were cut so far into the stem that the latter would snap if thrown. The whole weapon was cut out of a single piece of wood. Such spears were used ceremonially and are now seldom made.[6] Clubs and baskets were also highly decorated with painted geometrical and conventional designs. Other examples of their art are very ornate mourning armlets and painted burial posts in the north-west corner (including Melville and Bathurst islands); and in the area east of the Darwin road, long hollow log coffins, painted with naturalistic totemic designs, and also various carved and composite ceremonial objects.

Arnhem Land's fame in this sphere, however, rests not on the adornment of weapons, utensils and ceremonial objects, but on its rock- and bark-paintings, to which we should add its sculpture, music, poetry and dancing.

Rock-engraving and rock-painting are rare in the far-western side of the Arnhem Land Peninsula: Delamere and Willeroo in the mid-Victoria River district provide the only important galleries so far described, but others are slowly

[6] Iron was known to the coastal Aborigines before European contact. It was obtained from the Macassans, who visited the region regularly to fish for trepang. Iron points were attached to the fighting and hunting spears. Inland, flaked stone points were used.

being made known. The former include some intagliated and also painted naturalistic designs, some line-grooves only a few of which suggest patterns, and above all the famous polychrome painting of the Lightning Brothers, and Kananda, the elder brother's wife. This picture is at a great rain "dreaming" or mythological rain centre, and is retouched ceremonially by persons who are the reincarnations of the heroes. They are represented with a gecko-lizard aspect, a creature associated with lightning.[7]

Probably the most profuse cave-painting area in Australia will prove to be in the western part of the Arnhem Land Aboriginal reserve, particularly in the Oenpelli or East Alligator district, with an extension south to the Katherine Gorge and the Roper River. The country east and south of the Alligator Rivers becomes hilly and rocky, and indeed rises to a stony tableland, the Maielli or "stone country" as the Aborigines call it. It contains many rock-shelters and caves and, as in Northern Kimberley, the Aborigines have taken advantage of the suitable "canvas" to express their ideas by painting in ochres and pipeclay. A thorough search has yet to be made, but many galleries have been located.[8]

The impression of profuseness is increased by the mass of material in any one gallery. The drawings overlay one another. This suggests that satisfaction lies not so much

[7] The lizards come out of a tree which has been struck, and so are given credit for breaking and cracking it.

[8] Only two have been adequately examined and described in southern Arnhem Land. This year (1953), I made the first preliminary examination of four more, three of them very large galleries, and three not previously shown to white men. These were in gorges. In addition I saw, not far from Katherine, four small rock-shelter galleries in as many quartzite residuals standing up from the level country. The designs belong to the same "school" as the others in southern Arnhem Land, mainly in Djauan tribal country. The most surprising find was made in one of these small galleries. It consisted of well-executed intagliated figures of a bird, a fish, bird-tracks and symbols.

in admiring the finished picture, as in the act of painting it or in some practical desire it expresses and in some result it will effect. The fish a man sees in the stream is painted on the gallery; next time he goes spearing he will get that fish. He paints a conventional figure to represent some person from whom he wants some satisfaction, or whom he desires to injure, by magical means; and he believes that this "ritual" act will bring about the desired result.

The most distinguishing feature of the rock-paintings of this district is the intellectual approach to the majority of subjects, resulting in what is usually called X-ray art. The artists depict not only the outward form of the animal, reptile or bird, but also part of what they know is inside that form, but which is not seen until dissected. The backbone, lungs, intestines and other organs may be shown. This means that most of the exterior—scales, fur or feathers —is not represented. As these creatures are sought for food, the interest in their interior is understandable, but it is a problem why no Aboriginal artist started a similar style elsewhere in Australia. This approach has such a hold that it is frequently adopted in painting mythical creatures and malignant spirits, and also in expressing magical themes. This type of painting is found from Oenpelli to Roper Valley just south of the Roper River.

In addition, Oenpelli cave-paintings include mythological beings and totemic and magical representations which are not X-ray in style. In southern Arnhem Land too, ceremonial objects, often called *maraian* and *rangga,* are depicted; and about forty miles south of Roper Bar (the head of the Roper River tidal water) is a gallery of beautifully coloured paintings, clearly of ceremonial and mythological significance. One striking type of design in some rock-galleries in the Oenpelli district is characterized by thin and almost line-like drawings in red of human subjects. They show much action. They are referred to as *mimi* and as the work of *mimi* spirits in the bush. This means probably that they, or their prototypes, were drawn by a tribal or clan group now extinct.[9]

The only other cave-paintings in this northern region are mainly naturalistic, and some conventional, polychrome designs on Groote Eylandt and other islands off the north-eastern corner.[10]

BARK PAINTINGS

All the tribes from the Alligator River district around the coast to Groote Eylandt paint on bark, a "canvas" not used elsewhere in Australia. Rectangular or square sheets are stripped from the stringy-bark eucalyptus-tree, bent flat over heat and then under stones. The rough external surface is removed and the inner surface smoothed in readiness for painting. The red and yellow ochres and the pipe-clay are mixed with water and sometimes, too, with oil from an appropriate swamp root, or with juice from crushed orchid-stem. Pieces of green stick, roots, or bamboo shoots with one end frayed—usually by chewing—serve as brushes. They vary in size according to the breadth of stroke required. Small brushes are also made from human hair.

One obvious difference in design between western Arnhem Land (Oenpelli) and north-eastern Arnhem Land (Milingimbi and Yirrkalla) bark-painting is that in the former there are blank spaces on the "canvas" between and outside of the figures in the design. In the latter, however, the whole of the bark is nearly always covered with the design. Some of the dots, lines and dashes and areas of colour may seem to us only fill-in to complete the

[9] This has been an area of much tribal movement and displacement. Thus, at Oenpelli station itself the Mangari almost died out and were replaced by the Kakadu from the north-west; and now for some years, the latter have been almost extinct and replaced by a Gunwinggu group from near by, on the east.

[10] On Groote Eylandt small pieces of paper bark are used for brushes.

"panel" and give balance to the total picture. This is partly true, but to the artist every mark has meaning, it is part of the myth, incident or object being represented. It is, for example, cloud, or rain or flowing water, or the banks of a stream. The design is frequently depicted in two or four panels, the viewer, like the painter, moving around the bark as it lies on the ground.

There is also some difference in subject-matter and purpose between the bark-paintings of the two districts. In the Oenpelli area, one group, mostly X-ray in type, is painted as part of magico-religious ritual for the increase of species. Another group illustrates religious myth and traditional and contemporary incidents; while a third group serves the purposes of magic and sorcery. In the north-east, however, the main use of bark-paintings is sacred, namely, to represent clan designs which are themselves based on mythology. When painted they are kept in secret shelters, to be shown and explained to initiated and duly qualified persons. The latter reward the artist. The same designs may be painted on the body, generally on the chest and abdomen and thighs, of the person who is being admitted to a clan's "dreaming", its mythological and ritual heritage. Indeed, it is possible that the latter was the primary custom. Certainly in Central Arnhem Land, where there is no bark-painting, clan designs are painted on the human body. They are, however, painted in both districts on the clan's secret emblems.[11]

The use of bark-painting in the Oenpelli district for secular and magical purposes is extensive, but in the north-east this use is desultory and of little importance. The subjects are those of everyday interest, common objects, or a

[11] This body-painting is done most meticulously. The person being painted may have to lie perfectly still for three or more hours, while every line and dot is applied. Chanting accompanies the painting. When this is finished, the person is "raised" ritually. Before the design is begun the skin is rubbed with grease or vegetable gum, and red-ochred.

burial ceremony; of sorcery very seldom, and imitative magic only by implication. Outside the sacred sphere the north-east Arnhem-Lander paints because he wants to, because he takes pleasure in the work and in its result. Moreover, he is free to experiment with his design, but, strangely enough, the painter of secular subjects is not regarded as an artist, and receives no payment for this work.

The Groote Eylandt bark-paintings are more like those of Oenpelli than the nearer north-eastern type. The bark is not completely filled by the design. Turtle, crocodiles, snakes and so on are depicted, and the rest of the canvas is left with the colour previously applied as the ground. This is frequently black, though red and white grounds are also used. In the other two areas the ground is uniformly red. Sometimes the "canvas" is divided into two panels in the north-eastern manner.

Carvings and Composite Figures

Throughout most of the Arnhem Land reserve ceremonial objects, often naturalistic in form, are carved out of solid wood and then painted with clan mythological designs, to be used in sacred ceremonies. These designs are the same as those painted on the living bodies of initiands and performers, and in the north-east also on bark "canvases" and on skulls of the departed at the time of the final burial ceremonies. Frequently, in the eastern part of the region these objects are elongated, round and pointed pieces of hardwood of varying thickness. They are kept for months or years between ceremonies in river or billabong mud, being cleaned and painted afresh for each ceremony.

The most striking of these objects, however, are the sculptured and painted human figures of wood which are carved out of round pieces of soft wood for special ceremonies in the far north-eastern corner of Arnhem Land, and nowhere else. They are painted red to give them personality and then clan designs are carefully applied.

When all is over they are thrown into a water-hole where they disintegrate.[12]

Quite apart from the meaning and function of the designs on bark, on emblems, and even on the human body, the paintings are of great artistic interest and merit. Skilful composition, good balance, clearness of line, almost pulsating movement, pleasing variation and also striking contrast in colours, and the use of areas of colour, are amongst the features which mark this region as truly artistic. Each subregion has its own traditional patterns within which the artist works, but not slavishly.

With this background, we may hope that the Aborigines will develop a school or schools of art which will be a positive contribution to Australia's cultural heritage. It will be a great loss if they lose their art, and leave it to white artists to use or develop that art without understanding its significance—its relation to life.

In Arnhem Land, and wherever we have sufficient knowledge of the facts, painting, carving and engraving (of some of the figures) are an integral part of religious life. Designs are not only painted on; they are also sung or chanted on. In this way they are endowed with meaning, and indeed made "dreaming". They are symbols and sacraments of the cult-heroes and fertility-mothers who gave the land its form and brought the natural species, and generally too, the pre-existent human spirits, to their habitats.

The myths and doctrines are preserved in poetic versions which are chanted during the painting, and explained to those admitted. These explanations and elaborations are the prose versions of the myths. The poems, however, are

[12] About thirty of these were given to a field-worker, Mr R. M. Berndt, who was present during the ceremonies. They are now kept in the Department of Anthropology, University of Sydney. So too are several hundred bark-paintings and a number of the secret and sacred *maraian* and *rangga* emblems. The significance and meaning of each of them was obtained.

beautiful in themselves, both in form and in imagery, particularly in the north-eastern corner of Arnhem Land, a subject which will be discussed later (Chapter X), along with the music and dancing of the region. The wealth and variety of music, ritual performances, ballet dancing, and cults in Arnhem Land have to be experienced to be appreciated. The various songs, dances and cults criss-cross each others' paths as they spread from tribe to tribe, and in doing so sometimes adopt or adapt features from one another. The population was comparatively dense and living conditions good. Groups, both clans and tribes, could and do associate a great deal, and enjoy each other's dances and learn their rituals. Thus, there was time and encouragement for thinking and meditating, and to let ideas find their expression in verse, song, dancing and painting.

DOCTRINE IN ART

The foregoing is a brief survey, in some cases and aspects a mere indication, of Aboriginal painting, engraving and carving. More attention has been given to the northern regions than to the others because more is known of their art, and also because it is richer and is still functioning.

What then is Aboriginal visual art? It is an expression of Aboriginal philosophy in form and colour and in design which has an aspect of beauty according to the tradition of the tribes concerned. It is not primarily an attempt to produce the beautiful for its own sake, though it does reveal aesthetic appreciation. Aboriginal art is first and foremost a ritual activity, correlated with chanting, dancing and acting—the other components in most rites. Chanting over the "pretty" patterns of a secret bull-roarer in the Flinders Range of South Australia; greasing and devotionally rubbing the grooves of the designs on Central Australian *tjurunga*: chanting while the actors are being painted to "become" the Dreaming heroes in the western desert of South Australia, or while the initiated are being painted to participate in a clan's "dreaming" in Arnhem Land; painting and retouching the Wondjina cave-paintings of North Kimberley to make their Dreaming power effective again; painting mythological designs on bark, emblems and carved human figures to bring the "dreaming" present: these are expressions of the belief that by representing the "dreaming" or creative heroic past which is still present though unseen, the tribes and natural species are again brought within the effective influence of that creative past. The painting is the visible sign and sacrament of the "dreaming", just as the chanting is its audible sign, and the acting by the painted and transformed actors is its dramatic form.

Man and all that is has two aspects: the material which is seen, and the "shade" or soul which is not seen—at least usually. Neither can be ignored. The heritage of knowledge of the environment and of skills deals with the one; the heritage of art and ritual channels the other. This latter is the ordered arrangement of symbols, symbolic actions, designs and sounds, in an attempt to express in outward forms the "shade", the inner life and meaning, the permanent element, in man and the world in the present, past and future.

Here, too, lies the significance of designs on weapons, implements and ornaments. It comes as a surprise to see on these objects the same designs engraved or painted, which are associated with sacred symbols and emblems, and treated so reverentially on secret ritual occasions. The point, however, of secret ritual, which is performed as it were in the world of the "shade", is to make the unseen effective and active in the everyday world. Therefore, these designs often come forth from the sacred life of mythology, of doctrine and belief, from the "world of the shades", and so provide for the "shade", for the unseen and contingent element in the use of those everyday objects which bear their mark.

But while ritual is a source of the art it does not set

impassable bounds to its practice. Some individuals do draw and paint for the sake of doing so, though the amount of this is slight, when compared with the use of art in the service of religion and magic. Moreover, such art for art's sake is within the pattern set by tribal tradition and ritual.

VARIETY OF ABORIGINAL VISUAL ARTS

The Aborigines are one people. Their tribal languages, in spite of differences of structure and vocabulary, have a common base. Likewise, the economic and social organization of all the tribes, being based on food-gathering and hunting, perforce have much in common. Australia, however, is a vast land of varied and, indeed, contrasting environments. In some regions food-gathering involves long, toilsome and uncertain search. In others neither hardship nor uncertainty is involved for the person with knowledge and skill. In some regions, too, nature adequately supplies materials for making equipment needed in gaining a livelihood, and even provides for other than mundane activities and purposes—namely for religion and aesthetics. In others, however, she is most niggardly. The less favoured tribes have managed to overcome some of their handicaps by "trade" and by recognized expeditions to natural sources. Desired types of wood and stone, weapons, ceremonial objects and ochres have been, and are, obtained in this way. This, however, does not affect local adaptation to natural conditions, nor alter the density of population, nor the degree to which the local groups can associate.

Variety in Aboriginal visual art needs to be viewed against this ecological background. Particular designs and methods, although traditional, have arisen from individual inspiration and urge. Artistic activity and ideas, however, were conditioned and limited both by what nature provided in the way of material capable of being used for aesthetic purposes, and also by the degree of effort, of ease or struggle, and the amount of time required for ensuring existence.

Permanent forms of visual art cannot be practised in regions which lack appropriate surfaces. Such are the large central, north-central, and arid regions from the Lake Eyre basin across South Australia into Western Australia. There are no outcrops of sandstone suitable for petroglyphs (engraving and intagliating), as there are in the Port Jackson-Hawkesbury, Broken Hill or Port Hedland regions. There are few, if any, thick-trunked trees such as were engraved in parts of New South Wales. In these parts, too, caves and rock-shelters in which paintings could be entrusted to protected walls and ceilings, such as are found in Western Arnhem Land in particular, are rare. There are some galleries in this vast area—Ayers Rock is an example—but the environs are such that a clan or other group could only spend a limited period at it in exceptional seasons, so that there was no continuity of practice and the technique remained crude. We cannot know whether the Aranda tribe of the less uniformly harsh region of the Finke River and Hermannsburg district would have painted or engraved on rock surfaces if these had been suitable. As it is they confined themselves to conventional and geometrical designs on portable media, expressing mythological themes. This possibly created a barrier to freer and more realistic designs. Even the designs painted on the body and on the ground in central and north-central tribes were trammelled in this way. The snake pattern, which easily fits into the geometrical design, is almost the only aproach to realism.

Geometrical and conventional patterns are engraved on hard-wood shields, boomerangs (in some tribes), clubs and wooden ornaments throughout large regions of Australia. With the available engraving tools any other patterns would be difficult, as the crude attempts on some love-bull-roarers in the north-west show. Soft-wood shields, however, are painted (north Queensland), or else left bare (Northern Kimberley).

In the northern regions, where seasonal rains seldom fail, the sources of food adequate and constant, life less nomadic and the population comparatively dense, the artist had time to learn, to work and to improve. He could be, and was, supplied with food and rewarded. In other words, the opportunity was present. So, too, were the media. The caves of Northern Kimberley and Arnhem Land became galleries of mythological, ritual and magical themes, rich in variety and number. In the latter region other media were also used. This profusion and blossoming were not automatic. The conditions of time, of living, of material and of mythological and ritual context allowed the artist to realize his inspiration and to express it.

The ecological explanation, however, must not be pushed too far. There are suitable trees for engraving geometrical designs beyond the limits of central and northeastern New South Wales, and the conditions of life were much the same to the north and south of that region. These patterns represent paths to set the soul on its way from here to the world "on top" where Baiame, the cult-hero, is. Apparently an artist-mythologist was inspired to represent the relationship of the two worlds in this way. So, too, the felt need for permanent visual memorials of their mythology and doctrines resulted in artists of the Hawkesbury and of the far west of New South Wales engraving these in the rock surfaces around them. Moreover, the skill was at hand. New South Wales was a region in which the craft of making stone axes by grinding and pecking was well developed. The artist used the same skill for engraving the outline or for pecking out the area of his subject on the rock surface.

Looking over the whole field we see, in addition to scattered rock-paintings and engravings, in some cases desultory, a number of areas of concentration of artistic endeavour. In each case a particular style or method has been developed. In other words we can speak of a school of tree-engraving in New South Wales; of two schools of

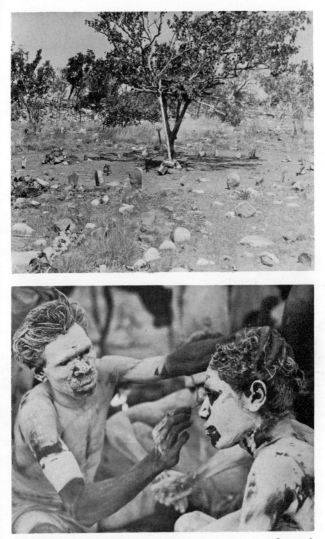

[17] *Top*, tree-stage burial, with inquest stones underneath. North-western Australia. *Bottom*, painting-up in pipe-clay: initiation ritual. Southern Arnhem Land.

[18] Bone-pointing. Central Australia.

[19] Preparing coffin for bones. Goulburn Island.

[20] Warramunga and Wailbri tribes. Decorated with wild kapok and colored with pipe-clay and blood for totemic ceremony North-central Australia.

rock-"carving" in the same State, and another at Port Hedland on the other side of the continent; of schools of rock-painting in the Northern Kimberley, in western Arnhem Land and in the coastal and island regions of eastern Arnhem Land; of three schools of bark-painting in Arnhem Land; of a school of carving human wooden figures and related bird figures in north-eastern Arnhem Land; and of a school of making composite ritual figures, naturalistic and conventional, in northern Arnhem Land.[13] In addition, as stated, body-painting and also the painting and adornment of sacred emblems are practised in this region as it is or was throughout the Northern Territory and elsewhere.

These localized schools of visual art are evidence of the aesthetic impulse and drive of the Australian Aborigines. An individual feels the urge to express or represent his doctrines, myths, desires or experience through and in media which are to hand. It is appreciated. He may be a strong personality who draws some disciples, or he teaches his son or nephew. In the course of time his method and range are improved; the style becomes determined, and the "school" established. We see this in the sureness of touch, the confident sweep of line, and the obvious mental grasp of the whole and final design, which are displayed by the artist at work, each in his own "school".

[13] Human and animal figures are moulded out of beeswax for magical purposes in Arnhem Land, and formerly, at Oenpelli, human heads and busts were moulded in clay, for purposes of sorcery.

Chapter X

MUSIC AND DANCING

THE PROBLEM OF RECORDING

ABORIGINAL music and dancing has been treated rather casually until recently. A few brief transcriptions, and some recordings (rather poor in technical quality) were made in the past, and some quite inadequate descriptions of dances were written. Systematic study of the music had to wait until good portable recording apparatus became available, and until students of dancing and choreography were willing to undertake field-work. Cinematography could be a means of bringing the dancing to them, but dancing, filled with zest and meaning, almost always occurs at nighttime. This presents lighting and technical difficulties and costs which are too great for research-workers. Aborigines will on request, though somewhat reluctantly, dance in the daytime for the cinematographer, and some useful material has been obtained in this way. The results, however, are artificial and forced compared with spontaneous evening dancing.

Another reason for this gap in our knowledge of Aboriginal culture is that, except for the field-work of Spencer and Gillen forty and more years ago,[1] no systematic research was undertaken until 1927 amongst tribes whose culture was a living reality. Emphasis was then placed on analysing and understanding social organization, ritual and mythology, magic and religion, though some attention was

[1] B. Spencer and F. J. Gillen, *Native Tribes of Central Australia* (1899) and *Northern Tribes of Central Australia*, (1904). B. Spencer, *Native Tribes of the Northern Territory* (1914).

given to the visual arts, especially cave paintings. In recent years, however, as our understanding of Aboriginal culture as a whole has grown, interest in native art has increased, and now includes the dance and music.

Fortunately, the opportunity remains to satisfy this interest. The visual arts, if of permanent form, can at least be described and analyzed, even after they have ceased to be practised and their meaning lost. But Aboriginal music and dancing must be recorded and studied while it is a functioning element in a living culture. This is still the case in parts of Arnhem Land, and in a more varied and striking form there than elsewhere.

From 1927 on I had seen corroborees, with their singing and dancing, also ritual chanting and acting, but it was not until I made a survey in 1946 almost around Arnhem Land that I realized the vitality and richness of the singing and dancing of that region. I therefore determined to make permanent records as soon as possible, so that musicians and dancers would be able to hear and see this part of Aboriginal culture, even if only at second hand. In 1949 six hours of Arnhem Land music and ritual were recorded, in 1952 eight and a half hours, and in 1953 a further three hours. In 1949, too, an hour of 16-millimetre Kodachrome of corroborees and of a sacred ritual was taken, and in 1952 a Kodachrome "short" of dancing.

SACRED CHANTING

Sacred rituals are part of totemic and heroic cults. They include dramatic acting, occasionally with a "ballet" element. In most cults chanting goes on throughout the preparation of the actors, but not necessarily during the act. This music creates an impression of seriousness and reverence. Nothing could be more impressive than the Byzantine-like solemn chanting in iambic measures by male voices in unison of parts of the Kunapipi—the mother-goddess cult of the central north. The tempo and accent are provided by the tapping and "rattling" of pairs of

boomerangs. The central Arnhem Land Maraian "hymns"
too, full of poetic expression, which impart the "dreaming"
and end with an amen-like *e-i*, leave no doubt of their sacred character. They are sung to the rhythm of stick-beats
during the painting of the dreaming designs at the secret
ground, and also at night in the camp during the ceremonial period. On the latter occasion the women "dance"
quietly in the background. Indeed, two series of these
"hymns" are then sung at the same time, one by each of
the two ceremonial moieties or groups. The words and
melodies of the two series are different, but hearing them
suggests a way in which counterpoint could arise. The
Ngulmag (Ngurlmak) of western Arnhem Land includes
another type of sacred (and secret) chanting; it can be
best likened to the chanting of the historical and ritual
psalms in the Book of Common Prayer. With special in-
troductions and endings, the series relates the travels of
the fertility-mother from the north coast inland, and also
ritual details. It is usually accompanied by a didjeridu and
tapping-sticks, and the beating, at set points, of the *ubar*,
a hollow-log drum.

So, too, although twenty-three years have passed since
I first witnessed totemic cult rituals amongst the Aluridja
groups in the Musgrave Ranges, between the sandhills near
Ooldea, and in the Laverton region, the impression still
remains of the zest with which the chanters, sitting in two
rings, beat the earth with sticks to mark the tempo and
sang with determination and at times with almost fiery
energy. The "owner" or head of each series or section of
the chants stood and started the singing.

Much sacred singing is secret; on the other hand, especially in Arnhem Land, a lot of it is sung in camp at appropriate times, and some is sung both on the secret ground
and at the camp. Generally speaking, however, greater
secrecy attaches to what is *done* on the secret ritual
ground than to what is *chanted* or to the calls (invoca-

tions), shouts and gong or "drum" beats.[2] Moreover, some camp corroboree chants include words of deep secret significance, only understood by those well up in the secret life. In addition, some camp singing is definitely sacred, but not secret. Thus, the Arnhem Land Mulara and Ngorunapa series for the final burial ceremonies, connected with the disposal of the bones in the totemic coffin, relate in poetic and psalm-like form the clan dreaming, the journeying to the Home of the Dead. So too, the Waranggan corroboree of the Upper Roper River tribes, though performed in the general camp, is sacred. It is based on the secret myth of Kunapipi, the fertility-mother, who travelled with her warriors and her women (the Munga-Munga) throughout the Macarthur, Roper and Victoria River regions. She left spirit-children who, being allotted languages and localities, became the ancestors of the different tribes. In addition, by her rituals the fertility of natural species was ensured. Her cult (as we have seen in Chapter VIII) includes a ritual of return to the mother's womb and a rebirth, which ensures life after death, provided that a Kunapipi is performed for one's soul. The Waranggan is a secular introduction to, and acknowledgment of, this cult. Esoteric words are sung, and at times, the men huddled in a close circle tapping their boomerangs and chanting vigorously, are transported in spirit to the secret ground, while the onlookers are concentrating on the Munga-Munga "dancing" women and the male actors performing some legendary scene. In this way, the secret, the sacred and the secular dovetail. This is logical, for the pattern and sanction for everyday behaviour are found in the sa-

[2] In 1949 the old headman of the very "high-" ceremony, the Yabuduruwa, would not allow any photography of the painting of the actors or of the acts; but he said there was no objection to recording anything which could be heard. However, there was no chanting, only gong beats, imitative animal cries, and loud rhythmic breathing. The Kunapipi includes chanting which must not be heard by those who have not been through the ceremony. This is also true of the Ngurlmak.

cred, and ultimately in those "mysteries", mythological possessions which are so fundamental that they must be
guarded in secret.

Musical Instruments

The most interesting Aboriginal musical instrument is
the didjeridu, but it is only known in Eastern Kimberley
and the northern third of the Northern Territory. It is an
unstopped hollow piece of bamboo or wood, usually the
latter, about four or five feet long, and two inches or even
more in internal diameter, with a mouth-piece made of
wax or hardened gum. The player blows into the instrument in trumpet fashion. The precision and variety of
rhythm produced on the didjeridu are very striking. Sometimes it sounds like a deep bourdon organ stop being
played continuously; at other times like a drum beaten in
three-four time, and so on, varying according to the type
of song and dance which it is accompanying, and indeed,
"carrying". The tongue lies flat, with the lip at times projecting into the mouth-piece. The continuous nature of the
sound is most remarkable. The diaphragm rises as breath
is taken, or "snapped", through the nose. It is emitted
through the didjeridu. Two quick breaths are usually
taken, and the next over a second later, but some of the
incoming air is kept in the mouth to be blown into the
instrument while a quick intake is being made. Glass-
blowers may understand. Didjeridu playing is learnt when
young. A good player, or "puller" as he is called, produces
two pitches, one usually a tenth above the regular one,
but it is always a short sharp sound, with no suggestion of
didjeri. I have not seen more than one didjeridu played at
the one time.

The percussion sounds are made in several ways. In most
parts of the continent, women sitting and watching, hit the
inside of one thigh, sometimes over the space between the
closed thighs, with a cupped hand. The other hand is
usually held over the striking hand, or else on the wrist,

thus adding firmness to the blows. In parts of Queensland and of south-eastern Australia, a solid skin ball or a piece of skin tightly stretched across the thighs was hit with the hand. The Melville and Bathurst islanders strike their buttocks with cupped hands as they dance. These various drum-like sounds keep the tempo of the song, didjeridu or dance.

In central regions the singers frequently hit the ground with a stick, while both there and throughout the Northern Territory the leading singer or singers use, for certain songs, pairs of tapping or rhythm sticks. The lower of these is generally cut from a hard resonant wood, and the upper or striking stick from a softwood. The principle is that of the gong, the full development of which is seen in the secret Yabuduruwa ceremony of the Roper region; a thick length of resonant wood is held shoulder-high, lying across one hand, and is struck with a striker a little more than an inch in diameter; it emits a remarkable gong-like sound which carries about half a mile. In north Central Australian totemic ceremonies a shield may be hit with a stick to direct the tempo of the actors' movements. In western Arnhem Land a length of hollow log is hit in a secret ceremony; the ends are left open. The Papuan type of handdrum with the ends closed with iguana skin, has been introduced into Cape York Peninsula. In many parts of Australia pairs of boomerangs are tapped together in secular as well as in sacred music.

SECULAR MUSIC

In addition to sacred and secret music, which may or may not be accompanied by dancing or dramatic acting, the Aborigines possess much secular or "everyday" camp music. It is usually part of what is known as the corroboree. The latter is a complex of singing, percussion sounds, didjeridu notes where it is used, dancing, and the dancers' calls, shouts, sibilant and other sustained monotoned notes.

Corroboree themes are usually based on everyday experiences and incidents, both recent and traditional; they include the ways of birds, animals and fish; the movements of the storm, the flood and the sea; gossip, or the doings and escapades of both sexes, though the allusions are indirect, and the dancing generalized; and the Aborigines' experience of, and interest in, European and other non-native objects and pursuits, such as tobacco, the meal-gong, kitchen, engines, aeroplanes, soldiers, stock-work, and card-playing.

Indeed, we can detect in some of this last group a protest against, or an attitude of casualness towards, the people who usurped their country. A most striking example comes from the early days of settlement in southern Queensland. The rhythmic dancing represented Aborigines spearing cattle, whites galloping in and shooting and dispersing the natives, and the ultimate rally of the latter who drove the whites away.

According to European observers the Aboriginal onlookers groaned whenever a blackfellow fell, cheered when actors representing whites were "knocked" down, and were overcome with delight at the final defeat of the "whites".[3]

Card-playing with its accompaniment of gambling is the subject of many tuneful songs in the north. Some refer to the widening of the "ring" to admit a white player who, in this position, loses his own self-conceived superior status. Some soldiers, who gambled with the natives, found that they also lost their money. The songs do not reveal any attitude of inferiority. Moreover, whites, Malays, Koepangers and any other non-natives are classified together as groups from whom tobacco and other desirable objects should be obtained. Indeed, we see in these "songs of contact", the Aborigines in the stock-camp or in the kitchen, in the garden or in the boat, using the contact situation and European articles for their own personal and social ends, almost as though white men as such did not exist.

[3] G. S. Laing, *The Aborigines of Australia* (1865).

MUSICAL PATTERNS

The song structure varies in different regions and within a region according to theme. The northern part of the Northern Territory will serve as a good illustration, for many recordings of it are available.

Melville and Bathurst islands are characterized by loudly intoned recitatives, mostly in monotone, and chanted by one man, while other men slap their buttocks and shout. Along the coast from Darwin south to the Lower Victoria River, the melody starts on a sudden, uncertain high note, as though the voice were breaking into falsetto; it then descends in regular intervals to a low pitch, after which the Songman just beats his sticks to the accompaniment of the didjeridu; twenty seconds or more later the melody is sung as before, and so the singing may go on for a long time. This is the Wongga. It is sung in connexion with the circumcision ceremony, as well as on less formal occasions.

Western Arnhem Land is marked by a similar, but more ornate, song structure. The basic pattern consists of four descending glides from true upper notes, each starting from, and ending on, a lower pitch than the preceding one. In between each phrase the didjeridu and sticks are played. Definite words are sung in this Gunborg type, whereas the Wongga phrase often consists solely of syllables, such as *a: na: la:*. The structure of the Walaka is similar. This corroboree belongs to the Wadaman and other tribes on the south-west of Arnhem Land, and is performed when tribes meet to exchange goods and to arrange marriages. The time is four-four; the dancers take three even steps, and pause for the fourth beat. They also shout, sometimes sustaining the shout on a high note, out of which the Songman's glide seems to descend.

North-east Arnhem Land is rich in music. The rhythm is varied and most striking, and the melodies often pleasant to our ears. Multi-part music is also a feature. It is mostly based on the style of the canon or fugue for two or three voices, but not on the construction of chords. Another feature of most of the song structures in this region is the concluding recitative. This recites, frequently in monotone, the general subject-matter of the verse to which it is suffixed. If there are two or more singers, all sing the recitative in "round" fashion, but the chief Songman always finishes. Here too, in most of the song forms, such as the Djerag, Waramiri, Kamalanga and others, often grouped together as Bunggal, the word texts are fairly full and grammatical, as in the case of European songs. In western Arnhem Land, on the other hand, they are usually very short, consisting of four or five words which provide a key to the meaning, or rather meanings, for these may be both patent and latent. This type of short text is widespread in Australia.

A somewhat different type from either of these is found in north-east Arnhem Land. The text includes a number of "key" words, and lacks a final recitative. The most interesting feature, however, is its structure. The didjeridu and the Songman with his beating sticks commence and the dancers advance on to the dance ground from the side opposite the musicians; when they reach the centre the didjeridu makes a break and a change in the rhythm, the dancers stop in their steps and stamp one foot, and the Songman ceases except for making such sounds as *ge: ge:*; after about three bars the previous rhythm is reintroduced and the dancers advance, while the Songman takes up his song again, generally with the words *mardji mardji*, meaning proceed. This type of corroboree is called Djedbangari, a word which appears in nearly all the song texts along with a number of other constants, *lima lima, wolang, gumur djarg, mardji mardji*, and a few variants. But the same words can be interpreted differently by the same Songman at different times. The reference, however, is always to something which starts, stops, and then goes on again, such as the waves rolling in, pausing as they hit the shore, and then washing up on the beach; or a child running, falling, and getting up and going on again. The use of the constant words shows that the musical content and form are the significant factor; the dancers and on-lookers put the interpretation into them. This helps to explain, too, the commonly reported fact that Aborigines sing and dance to words which have come from other tribes or from the past, the meaning or translation of which they cannot give. They do, however, read a meaning into the total performance.

The central Arnhem-Landers have a corroboree called the Ginbir in which the melody is of limited range, but the rhythm varies according to the part of the "totemic" or mythological series being sung. The dancing, however, is representative and interpretative, according to the subject of the song, and the dancers add to the effect by their imitative calls and noises.

In this same area, too, as mentioned above, an interesting stage in the development of harmony is illustrated. Several times during the course of the camp singing, connected with the Maraian, a kind of All Souls' festival, two ceremonial groups, sitting about fifteen yards apart, sing simultaneously, but independently, each its own series of mythological chants; the words, melody and rhythm differ in each case. Listening to this from a distance, or to the recordings, we get the definite impression of counterpoint and almost of harmony.[4]

The secret sacred chanting of Arnhem Land includes the Ubar (or Uwar) or Ngurlmak; the verses begin with *a: ga: la: la: la: la:* on a high note, and the long texts, referred to above, are chanted, mainly in monotone, some-

[4] This was first recorded in 1949; about ten singers in each group took part. Three years later I got a pair of singers from each group to sit about six yards apart, and to sing their own group's "hymns". With fewer singers the result was not only less confusing, but illustrated more clearly a possible origin of counterpoint.

what in recitative fashion. The final word of each verse is *didjeri-bom*, a reference to the didjeridu which accompanies the chanting, and which symbolizes the womb of the fertility-mother. Another type is that of the secret Kunapipi, to which reference has already been made. Each chant consists of about four words, slightly modified and rearranged in the course of singing. The melody, chanted by men in unison to the accompaniment of boomerang tapping, has very limited range, and strongly suggests monastic chanting. The Kunapipi background of the Waranggan has already been mentioned. Similarly, it supplies through the mythology of the Munga-Munga women the background of the Djarada chants (Chapter VII). These women represent not only desirable sex-partners, but partners who defied established rules with some impunity. The structure of the text and music is similar to that of the Kunapipi and Waranggan.

We may compare the women's secret Yowalyu (Chapter VII), which is found farther south, from Tennant's Creek to the Kimberley border. It is based on "dreaming" of the totemic cult type. As in the Waranggan and Djarada, each chant-verse consists of only a few words which are repeated in a variety of ways, but always to a definite rhythm. The melodic range is usually very limited. One interesting feature appears, particularly in the Wailbri women's chanting: this is a rise and fall in volume, caused by an overlapping of voices on a tile-like system. Just as the chorus becomes low, a number of the singers start afresh, usually on a higher note, while the others are still chanting. This both increases the volume and produces incidental harmony.

This is similar to a feature of the secret chanting of the Pidjindjara men of the south-western corner of the Northern Territory. Just as the singing seems to be dying down, some of the singers start up with fresh zest, and so give an impression of rising and falling, and of increase and decrease, which is continuous and eventually hypnotic. This effect is increased by the simultaneous chanting by the two ceremonial groups into which the singers are divided in this region.[5] Sitting a few feet apart, the two groups sing without any apparent concern for each other. However, the frequent lack of synchronization of the stick-beats and rhythm, and the rising volume of one group as the other decreases, suggests "multi-part" music. Another feature of this chanting is the use of combined accent and staccato, in which there is perfect synchronization.

THE SONGMAN

The variety of musical patterns in the northern quarter of the Northern Territory is especially marked. This can be associated with the institution of the Songman, just as the special development of the visual arts in the same region may be correlated with the recognition of specialist-artists. Further, as already suggested, this specialization may be correlated with the good ecological conditions of the region. Food-searching over large areas was not necessary. Moreover, the specialist could be "paid" or well rewarded for his work, and he was and is.

The Songman is not simply a man with a good voice, but one who has been taught by, and inherited his position from, his father or uncle, and so on in a lineal succession. Up to twenty names in such lines have been recorded. The Songman is the owner of his heritage of songs and of those which he composes, and no one can sing them without his consent and without "paying" him. He composes both words and music, and the dance which goes with it, although there is room for a virtuoso dance-leader to express himself.

In many parts of Australia corroboree singing is done by a number of men, but that seldom occurs in Arnhem Land—apart from certain sacred "hymns" and secret chants. The Songman, however, may be assisted by one

[5] The division is on the principle of alternate generation lines (Chapter IV).

or two other Songmen who have learnt from him. In some cases, especially in western Arnhem Land, they sing in unison. In central Arnhem Land the singers tend to follow just behind the chief Songman, and so give a somewhat discordant effect. In the north-east, however, the fugue has been developed, at least by one group, of whose singing I recorded a great deal. The rhythm, order and plan of entry were discussed before the song, although all three seemed to introduce extempore variations. Further, as the verses of series progressed, they usually worked up to a climax in attack, tempo and pitch.[6]

A Songman is a great acquisition to a camp. Once he starts tapping his sticks, and his didjeridu accompanist takes up his position, a group gathers around. The active men dance and make the appropriate noises and calls, while some women beat time in the background and others unobtrusively get up and "dance" just where they stand, moving their feet, legs and arms, and often holding a piece of string stretched between their hands and probably making a "cat's cradle" with it. The older folk watch and silently beat time, while their thoughts sink into the dreaming, the unseen world of belief, of faith, and of hope. So all are bound in word, action or thought to the dreaming and to one another. A silent camp may be one in which something is amiss. On the other hand, all is well in the camp in which the fires blaze up, the singing goes on far into the night, the dust rises high with the stamp-stamp of dancing feet, and the resounding calls of the dancers announce the end of movement after movement.

The Dance

A volume could be written on Aboriginal dances, especially if we include those scenes in secret ceremonies which

---

[6] In some parts of the continent corroboree songs died away at the end, becoming softer and slower: e.g. C. W. Schurmann, "The Port Lincoln Tribe", in J. D. Woods's *The Native Tribes of South Australia*, p. 242.

are performed rhythmically to the accompaniment of beating sticks and often, too, of singing. There are occasions when the song or chant is not also "danced": for example, the mother crooning over her baby; the Songman chanting for the initiand who is absent journeying from group to group; men chanting the appropriate sacred series of "psalms" while the actors or dancers in secret acts and ballets are being "painted up", or while sacred objects are being revealed; and a man, away from his own country, thinking of the home of his spirit, quietly sings his totemic songs, or simply, "Poor fellow me; my country."

On the other hand, in many secret ceremonies, as in the central and southern parts of the continent, the chanting provides the background and meaning of the acts, but does not set the rhythm. In Arnhem Land, however, the rhythm of the mimetic "dances" is controlled by the stick-beats and other noises. The Maraian secret dances, for example, performed by twenty or thirty men at a time, are remarkable for their precision and for the excellent representation of animals and birds.

In my experience the best ballet dancing in Aboriginal Australia belongs to central Arnhem Land. It is both mimetic and interpretative. The base of the corroboree structure is the Songman's sticks which beat like a metronome, though both the rhythm and tempo may be changed at various points. Next comes the didjeridu played to the same rhythm, or at times to a separate one. On top of these is the Song, which frequently coincides with the rhythm of either or both the sticks and the didjeridu, but may go independently, even of the Songman's own stick-beats. Then come the dancers, with light unceasing movement, running, springing, hopping, gliding and turning to the accent of stick-beats, though not necessarily so. But even though there are two or three rhythms and marked syncopation in progress, the effect is not one of disorder, but rather of massiveness and depth. Actually, all is controlled by the Songman and the dance-leader.

There is no toe-point work, and little twirling, but there is planned foot, arm and body movement, and a good deal of stamping with one foot. In some cases there is sufficient mimetic action to make clear what is being danced, but in others it is a matter of interpretation. The waves rolling in, or the spirit leaving its earthly resorts for its spirit-home are examples of the latter. In a yam dance three dancers approach the Songman with slow, long leaps, followed by a group of four doing the same. Then all stride around clockwise looking on the ground, then counter-clockwise, and once more reverse again, after which they go off with great bounds. Digging up yams was the interpretation of the strides. The leader then threatens the ground with a roll of bark which he carries, and one of the dancers does the same with a spear-thrower. The former hops twice on the same foot, and then hops on to both feet. The whole scene is then repeated at a faster tempo. The leader waves his bark roll from side to side with a wrist-movement and finally runs around the other dancers.

Individuals earn big reputations for their dancing, and deservedly so. Kwialbuma in central Arnhem Land is such a one. Mosek of the Wadjigin at Delissaville near Darwin was another; by his dancing and singing the whole settlement gained a big name for its corroborees. The Delissaville style has fewer mimetic features than in central Arnhem Land and is marked by very precise, often machine-like motions of arms and legs, bent at "right angles", and of the head from side to side. The Melville and Bathurst islanders are noteworthy for their outstretched arms in line with the shoulders, the throwing back of the head and the high lift of the knees as they do their buffalo, shark, crocodile and other dances with great vigour.

As we move around the tribes we recognize that there are schools of dancing as well as of painting. We think of the graceful, gliding, lithesome, light-stepping mimetic and interpretative style of central Arnhem Land with the dancers in loose and free formation; of the precise, angular traditional style of Delissaville with dancers massed together; and of the boisterous solo dancing of the Melville and Bathurst islands in an arc of stamping, shouting participants; and so we could go on.

Women, too, have their dance patterns and their reputations. Most commonly some of them stand and "dance" quietly in the background of the audience, but in view of the Songman. Their knowledge of the feet and hand movements associated with each dance, and their skill in execution are duly, but unobtrusively appraised. In most dances they do not lift their feet fully from the ground, but only move up and down on heel and toe, or glide one toe in front of the other foot. In some, however, they lift their feet up and down quickly and vigorously, although not shifting their position, and at the same time move their two arms alternately up and down, in some cases touching the top of the head as they do so. It is in their own secret dances, however, which the men do not witness, that they exhibit much grace of action and expression, particularly in the rhythmic movement of the arms and body in the Djarada. They still do not raise their feet, but they do move over the "stage". In time with the stick-beats and the singing, they slide and shuffle in jerks, keeping the two feet together. In the Yowalyu of north Central Australia, there is the same shuffling and sliding in jerks, both forwards and sideways, but the dancing is a type of acting to represent the doings of totemic and other characters. Some of the actions by good dancers cause much merriment and appreciation.

Variety and the Individual. Dance-forms vary, but this is not merely a matter of regional separation. It is the result of individual inspiration and ideas. A Songman sees, or dreams, something. Words, tune and actions "come" to him. He works it over in his mind and then quietly hums it. A new song is born, perhaps one with a definite variation in pattern. Keeping the rhythm with his sticks, he sings it to his didjeridu player if he is in a didjeridu region, and discusses his dance pattern with a leading dancer. If, during a performance, the dancers do not grip the idea, he may get up, teach and lead them.

Such "compositions" mostly fall within the traditional regional pattern, but they are not just reproductions. A Songman is expected to produce new songs and dances, and he does. So, too, leading dancers introduce variations in actions either during a dance or as a result of previous planning. In other words, in music and dance the significance of the individual is not blurred. He transmits, modifies and produces. The Songman, in particular, is a symbol of individuality and originality. But didjeridu players and dancers are also valued for their individual skill and virtuosity, and have opportunities to exhibit their powers. We can therefore speak of a tradition of individual gifts, skill and ownership. This is distinct from leadership in secret chanting and acting, which is determined by hereditary cult-headmanship or by recognition as "master" of a particular cult-performance, not by musical powers or musical heritage.

DIFFUSION OF MUSIC AND DANCE

In every region at some time in the past an individual or individuals must have been responsible for its peculiar song and dance patterns. Corroborees and ceremonies, however, also spread from tribe to tribe. Initiation is seldom a one-tribe event. The candidate is taken around groups in one or more neighbouring tribes, members of which later attend the ceremonies. On such occasions new rites and variations in old rites are discussed and often introduced; in addition, the visiting groups perform their corroborees and are entertained at those of the local groups. Sometimes the corroborees—that is, the songs and dances—are exchanged along with presents to the Songmen and others concerned. Such exchanges may also occur when groups meet for other ceremonies or just for trade. In this way rituals and corroborees pass from tribe to tribe. One of the most spectacular examples is that of the Molongo or Molonglo. Dr W. E. Roth reported that wherever its origin was, it spread from the Worgaia at the head of the Georgina to the Yaroinga by 1893, to the Pitta-Pitta of Boulia by 1895, and the Miorli of the Middle Diamantina in 1896. From there it passed on to the Dieri near Lake Eyre by about 1900, and Penong on the Great Australian Bight by 1915. At some point it turned north, for I saw it performed by Aranda and Loritja men at Horseshoe Bend, Central Australia, in 1930. Likewise a turtle dance seen at Broome was later seen at Boundary Dam on the border of Western and South Australia.[7] The Waranggan sacred corroboree of which Baldwin Spencer heard on the Upper Roper River in 1911 and which I saw performed by Djauan and Yangman people in the same region in 1949 and 1952, includes chant texts which trace the movement of the corroboree from East Kimberley to Newcastle Waters and thence north to the Upper Roper.

Today, corroborees are often performed at long distances from their place of origin, not because they have been "traded" or diffused, but because of migrations arising from official and non-official action. Individuals or small groups gain employment on cattle stations or around townships far from their own tribal country; or they move in to a government or mission aboriginal settlement. They sometimes learn and "buy" local songs and dances which they later take back to their own country. On the other hand, as happens often, they tend to remain in their new surroundings, and if there is a Songman amongst them their own corroboree becomes part of the local camp life.

[7] W. E. Roth, *Ethnological Studies among the North-West-Central Queensland Aborigines* (1897), pp. 117–18. A. W. Howitt, *The Native Tribes of South-East Australia* (1904), p. 416. See also pp. 413–16. Mrs D. Bates, "Aborigines of the West Coast of South Australia", *Journal of the Royal Society of South Australia,* vol. xlii, pp. 165–6.

It is possible to hear on a large government settlement three or four different corroborees in progress at the one time—a few hundred yards apart, each maintaining its own identity.

A survey of Aboriginal music and dancing shows that secret ceremonial chanting, acting and rhythmic dancing are persistent in detail through time and space and, moreover, tend to be widely diffused. Corroborees which have a sacred or mythological base are also persistent in structure and detail, and spread widely. The Waranggan, Djarada, Yowalyu and the Molongo are examples. So too, are the Mulara and Ngorunapa of Arnhem Land; these are associated with delayed burial ritual in which painted totemic coffins figure. On the other hand, corroborees based on everyday incidents, never mind how popular at the time, become replaced by more topical compositions, and gradually pass into oblivion.

POETRY

Both chants and corroboree songs consist of series of words arranged to impart impressions and meanings. Those texts which are limited to four or five words do not readily suggest poetry to us, although the singing version with its accent, rhythm and repetition and with its variation in accent and rhythm may do so. Moreover, each word or, in some cases, the total verse gives rise in singer and audience to ideas, pictures and emotions, which can best be translated in poetic form. An excellent example was given in the preceding chapter.

The missionary George Taplin, an early observer and student of the language of the Narrinyeri tribe on the Lower Murray, was impressed by the use of imagery and simile in Aboriginal songs. He translates one text, "The Railway Train", as follows:[8]

[8] G. Taplin, "The Narrinyeri", in J. D. Woods's *The Native Tribes of South Australia*, p. 39.

You see the smoke at Kapunda,
The steam puffs regularly,
Showing quickly, it looks like frost,
It runs like running water,
It blows like a spouting whale.

Accuracy of description together with an ability to find ways of conveying impressions is a characteristic of song and chant texts. The black plover soars down like a falling star and circles around the drifting timber, on which it will settle. The saw-fish jumping out of the water cleaves it as it dives down to chase fish which scurry off among the rocks. The thunder roars, and the rain falls making a noise on land and water; the river runs and rises; the water sweeps grass and sticks into heaps; fresh surges rush along, bubbling and frothing—swirling here, and quiet there; and the great paperbark trees are undermined and at last fall on the water. The bush-fire, burning all the way, spreads along the grass and sets the bushes and trees alight, leaving a trail of burning charcoal and ashes; the smoke rises and the frightened quail fly before the travelling flames; little fires appear ahead as the fire flies on to fresh spots, blazing all the way.

Such are a few prose summaries from parts of northeast Arnhem Land chants. From a great wealth of beautiful poems the following about the moon is a good example: In the dream-time, Moon, a man, and his sister, Dugong, lived near a large clay-pan in the Arnhem Bay plains country, which, during the rainy season, becomes a billabong. There they used to collect lily and lotus roots which became the Evening Star. Leeches made the place so uncomfortable that Dugong went into the sea to live. For his part, Moon went to the sky, saying that when he became sick, thin and only bones, he would follow Dugong down into the sea, where he would leave his bones to be washed up on to the beach in the form of the nautilus-shell. Moon added that after three days he would become alive and gradually regain his strength and size by eating lily and lotus roots. This myth gives the background of the following verse of the Moon-bone song:

Now the New Moon is hanging, having cast away his bone:
Gradually he grows larger, taking on new bone and flesh.
Over there, far away, he has shed his bone: he shines on
* the place of the Lotus Root, and the place of the*
* Dugong,*
On the place of the Evening Star, of the Dugong's Tail, of
* the Moon-light clay pan . . . .*
His old bone gone, now the New Moon grows larger;
Gradually growing, his new bone growing as well.
Over there, the horns of the old receding Moon bent down,
* sank into the place of the Dugong:*
His horns were pointing towards the place of the Dugong.
Now the New Moon swells to fullness, his bone grown
* larger.*
He looks on the water, hanging above it, at the place of
* the Lotus.*
There he comes into sight, hanging above the sea, growing
* larger and older . . . .*
There far away he has come back, hanging over the clans
* near Milingimbi . . . .*
Slowly the Moon Bone is growing, hanging there far away.
The bone is shining, the horns of the Moon bend down.
First the sickle Moon on the old Moon's shadow; slowly
* he grows,*
And shining he hangs there at the place of the Evening
* Star . . . .*
Then far away he goes sinking down, to lose his bone in
* the sea;*
Diving towards the water, he sinks down out of sight.
The old Moon dies to grow new again, to rise up out of
* the sea.*[9]

[9] R. M. Berndt, "A Wonguri-Mandjikai Song Cycle of the Moon-Bone", *Oceania*, vol. xix, no. 1, pp. 19–20, 46. Mr Berndt also gives the native texts.

SONGS AND CHANT CYCLES

It may be thought that because the Aborigines have no system of writing, their chants and songs would be short and unconnected. This is true of many everyday corroboree songs, but not of the sacred and secret "hymns" and "psalms". Whether the text of the individual chant be of the brief four- or five-word type, or of the full explicit type, each is usually part of a series or cycle. These cycles have a mythological-historical basis. They record the travels, experiences and actions of heroes, ancestors, founders, explorers and even "goddesses". These journeyings took a long time; so do the chanting and singing. The "roads" or routes must be followed and everything of significance sung, because the past is perpetually and causally related to the present. So whether we are in the Petermann Ranges of the Centre, on the north-east of Lake Eyre, in the Kimberleys or in Arnhem Land, there are occasions when the whole "local" epic or cycle must be sung. Headmen of the cult in each clan or tribal country may lead in those parts of the cycle which concern their country, but all present may join in. In other circumstances the headman or "master" of the cult or, if it is not secret, a song-leader, may lead and conduct the full cycle. In central Arnhem Land each of the two ceremonial moieties sings all night its cycle of the hero's experiences as he journeyed from the north coast south and then back again north. There is therefore geographical and temporal sequence in the order of the songs and chants, and this is an aid to memory. Discussion often takes place regarding this sequence so that the chanting will be in order. While a Songman was chanting unfalteringly, and without notice, the Ngurlmak (or Ubar) ritual psalm-like chants for half an hour's tape-recording, a headman sitting near by commented that the Ngurlmak, according to the text, was now in that country, then in another place, and so on, ever coming nearer until at last it was just where we were making the recording.

The north-east Arnhem Land Kunapipi ritual cycle includes 129 chants, the texts of which have been written
down. I have recorded on tape over forty of the Waranggan chant-series, half an hour to an hour of the Ngorunapa, Mulara, Ginbir and of other series, but these are only
samples of each. One of the most astounding yet studied
is the Djanggawul cycle of north-east Arnhem Land. It is
an epic in poetry and song of the journey of the two
Djanggawul heroines and their two men from Bralgu
(Beralku), the island of spirits across the sea to the east,
until they land at Port Bradshaw, and then walk around
the neighbouring country, giving rise to population and
establishing rituals and sacred symbols. Its poetic expression is beautiful and its whole conception inspiring. But
what is probably startling is its length: 188 songs, the
fairly close poetic translation of which covers over ninety
printed pages, and it is all chanted in one great ceremony!

Although I leave Bralgu, I am close to it. I, Djanggawul,
    am paddling . . .
Paddling with all the paddles, with their flattened tapering
    ends.
Close I am coming, with Bildjiwuraroiju,
Coming along from Bralgu. We splash the water as we
    paddle, paddling wearily,
With Miralaidj, undulating our buttocks as we paddle.
We paddle along through the roaring tide, paddle a long
    way.
I am paddling along fast, through the rough sea . . . .
Beside me is foam from our paddling, and large waves
    follow us.

With Bralbral, we move our wrists as we paddle, making
    noise as we go through the sea . . .
We, Djanggawul, are paddling along, lifting our paddles,
    slowly going along . . . .
All the way we have paddled. I rest my paddles now, as
    we glide.

*On the sea's surface the light from the Morning Star shines
    as we move,*
Shining on the calmness of the sea.
*Looking back I see its shine, an arc of light from the Morn-
    ing Star.*
The shine falls on our paddles, lighting our way.
*We look back to the Morning Star and see its shine, look-
    ing back as we paddle.*

*Close is the Morning Star, stretching from its pole, extend-
    ing out from its string . . .*
Shining from Bralgu, as we paddle through the sea.
*Bubbles rise to the sea's surface; our canoe is carried on
    the crest of waves. Ah, "waridj" Bralbral!*
*Sound made by our splashing paddles, and the sea's roar
    as we rise to the crest of the wave!*
*We make our paddles sound, with the noise of the sea,
    sound that is heard far away at Bralgu.*
*We, the Djanggawul, make sound with our paddling,
    make spray as we paddle fast . . . .*
*The salty smell! The roaring sea, and its foam! Its wide
    expanse behind us!*[10]

OF LIKE MIND

The first contact with a people who neither wear clothes
nor build houses, who neither till the soil nor tend flocks
and herds, and who have apparently no appreciation of
western culture and its economic system, may lead many
of us to think that such a people is very different from
ourselves and, indeed, inferior. Further acquaintance reveals that they have a social structure and some simple
economic arrangements which are sufficient for their simple manner of life. But there still seems to be a barrier
between them and us—probably impassable. Such has been
the reaction of many to the Aborigines and their way of
life. Possibly, however, as we learn more of, and come to

[10] R. M. Berndt, *Djanggawul* (1952), pp. 63–4.

appreciate, their artistic life and attainments, their artistic achievements, their best painting, dancing, music and poetry, we shall realize that we and they are "of like mind". We shall realize that above, as well as in, social and economic structure and activity, we and they alike seek "the things of the spirit". In song and dance, in poetry and painting, we find our common humanity, reaching out and up to the spirit which is eternal—"the dreaming".

Note. The recordings referred to in this chapter were made on the first occasion with wire recorders and on the second with tapes. The best equipment available was used and an expert technician employed. Power was provided by wet batteries. In Sydney the recordings were transferred to 16-inch long-playing (33⅓ revolutions per minute) discs and masters made. The results are excellent. Pressings are available at about cost through the Department of Anthropology, University of Sydney. There are twenty-nine double-sided 16-inch records, giving about fifteen minutes a side.

In addition eleven 12-inch long-playing double-sided records have been prepared from recordings made in 1953 in the Northern Territory on a small portable tape-recorder run by a hand-wound spring and dry batteries. The results, particularly of ritual and speaking, are very good. This is true also of some of the singing, but in other cases, when the tape is played on a big recorder of high fidelity to be transferred to the disc, a wave or flutter appears. In other words, this machine gave inconsistent results. Some important ritual material discs are available.

Both the Australian Broadcasting Commission and the Postmaster-General's Department gave invaluable help in recording. A set of three double-sided 12-inch micro-groove records is planned, to provide a two-hour edited selection of the music.

The Australian Broadcasting Commission also possesses twelve 12-inch double-sided standard discs (78 revolutions per minute) containing samples of singing and ritual sounds from Oenpelli and from far-western Arnhem Land (the region near and south of Darwin). Further, in 1952–3 Dr Waterman, a musician from Northwestern University in Illinois, spent some months at Yirrkalla in north-east Arnhem Land, recording music. The results are not yet known.

Copies of the long Kodachrome films (two reels, one corroboree and the other, the Maraian) with sound-track of words and music can be obtained through the Department of Anthropology, University of Sydney.

See A. P. Elkin, "Arnhem Land Music", in *Oceania*, vol. XXIV no. 2, pp. 81–109, for an introduction to these records.

Chapter XI

MEDICINE-MEN AND MAGIC

The Sorcerer

THERE is no more interesting type of person in Aboriginal life than the medicine-man and no more interesting phenomenon than the beliefs held by and concerning him. The term is usually applied by whites, unfortunately, to two kinds of magician, namely, the sorcerer and the medicine-man proper. The former is the worker of evil, the taker of kidney-fat, the stealer of the soul, and a cause of death. He is, however, very rare. Whole regions lack such an individual or the belief in such, and in some others where the belief exists, the professional worker of black magic is always to be found in another tribe; the latter might be proud of being referred to in this way, but it would usually be impossible to find any individual who would be designated as the sorcerer. Still, there are exceptions. In some tribes such men are known and openly admit they possess the powers attributed to them. They have even given to investigators details of their successful magical operations. These are not only gruesome, but also so contradictory in nature that they could not have actually been performed. For example, after putting a halter around the neck of the sleeping victim and dragging him unnoticed out of his camp, the sorcerer makes an incision in his abdomen or side, through which he extracts his kidney- or caul-fat; then, inserting some grass or other packing, he closes up the wound so that no mark is visible, and restores the victim to consciousness. The latter returns to his camp, and is in perfect health for a day or two but generally dies on the third day. In another area, after preliminary acts the sorcerer opens the victim's side between the ribs, and pushing his hand in, pierces the heart with a pointed stick and lets the blood out. He then closes the wound, and restores the victim to consciousness. As before, the latter is perfectly well for a day, but sickens and dies in about three days.

Needless to say, such a succession of happenings is impossible. Had the operation been performed, the victim would have died at once, or certainly would not have had an invisible wound and been in good health for a day. Yet in cases of serious illness and death in the regions where such powers are attributed to sorcerers, this magical operation is regarded as the cause; moreover, the procedure supposed to be adopted is widely known.

Two problems arise: in the first place, to what extent do the sorcerers really believe that they have performed these operations, and in the second place, what is the explanation of the particular forms of operations? With regard to the latter question, we need to consider the belief that the fat attached to the internal organs is regarded as a special source of vitality and strength; if applied to a spear, it ensures unerring accuracy; if put near a waterhole it attracts fish, birds and animals to that spot, and if applied to the body, it gives strength. Likewise, the heart's blood (in the form of dried resin) has similar properties, for it is the life, and indeed, "the seat or vehicle" of the soul. The details of the "unperformed operations" could arise from the logical necessity of making the incisions in order to obtain fat or blood and of explaining the fact that there is no wound to show that these vital materials have been extracted. As a matter of fact, the fat is sometimes taken after death, but very seldom before death.[1]

[1] Although it would be necessary to make incisions on the abdomen, or side or between the ribs to get the fat or blood, it does not necessarily follow that all the details and the general pattern of the operations have been thought out, though not

The first problem is difficult, although no doubt the sorcerers speak as though they believed that they really performed these gruesome and very remarkable operations. If they did, it must have been in a dream or vision which occurred after a death and was induced by an accusation of fat-taking or blood-drawing. In any case, the method which is constant, is handed down from sorcerer to sorcerer and so the form of this vision or belief is controlled, and probably in time, a sorcerer does believe that he has caused the death which is attributed to him.

A sorcerer's lot is not a happy one. He seldom differs from other people in his clan and tribe and leads the same kind of family, social and secret life as they. His malpractices are reserved for members of other tribes, or occasionally for a distant group of his own tribe. But to have a reputation for successful sorcery is to be a marked man. Such a man knows that sooner or later he will be designated as the "murderer" of some person or other, and that either magical retaliation will be taken or else a revenge expedition will be sent to kill him. He has, therefore, to be especially watchful and possibly the consequent anxiety is a cause of the sorcerer's belief in the reality of his supposed powers and actions. At any rate, there is no reason for attributing to him complete duplicity and sheer lying. The worker of black magic is after all, part of an institution.

---

practised, merely to explain the obtaining of the fat or blood without leaving a mark on the body. They are probably modelled on some other operation on the human body, alive or dead, most likely the latter, seeing that the purpose of these magical operations is death. The insertion of extraneous material into the wound made for the extraction of the fat needs explanation. Likewise, there is a very strange part of the supposed heart-blood operation which seems to have no necessary connexion with its object. A length of the intestine is said to drop out and has to be made return to its proper place. Needless to say, this does not actually happen, but that makes the feigned procedure all the more significant.

MAGICAL CAUSE OF ILLNESS AND DEATH

This institution arises from a belief that illness and death and even accidents are caused by magical or animistic actions. The Aborigines know nothing about the germ-theory of disease and scarcely recognize natural causes of sickness and death or even of accidents. In the case of the death of a very old person or a baby they seldom bother to seek a cause, and for some ordinary aches and pains (e.g. colds, sore eyes, headaches, yaws and festering wounds) a magical cause is not sought and ordinary medical treatment is applied.[2] But for all serious disturbances of a person's health and life and, therefore, of the well-being of his group, a cause must be sought and dealt with. Their explanation of such occurrences is logically connected with their general spiritual and animistic view of life, and not with such "unknown" agencies as germs and laws of nature. It is found in causes which they can understand, namely men (and sometimes women) or else spirits.[3] In both cases, the agents use magical methods to cause the illness and death. The agent may be a sorcerer and in addition to using such absolutely fatal methods as fat- and blood-taking, he may also use more ordinary methods of sympathetic magic. But he has no monopoly of the latter; generally speaking, any adult member of the tribe (including women) can practise some forms of black magic, and this is true whether they are supposed to be sorcerers or not. The old men are usually more proficient than others in magic for they have had more opportunity to become acquainted with the correct ritual methods and the chants to be sung.

[2] The Aborigines use mixtures, poultices, steam-baths, liniments, bandages, heat and cold. Some of their treatments are definitely of curative and medicinal value, though they frequently endeavour to ensure their efficacy by combining magical practices with them.

[3] In less serious cases, illness may be brought on by breaking social or food prohibitions.

The types of magic vary, though they are similar to those practised elsewhere. One form is *contagious* magic; by the performance of a rite on a person's footprint or something which has been in touch with his body, damage can be done to his health. This, however, is not a very powerful or much dreaded form of magic in Australia. People do not go about in fear lest some of their personal leavings or belongings will be used magically to do them harm. *Imitative* magic is also practised; that is, the desired result is pre-enacted in some manner or other. Thus, one method used in western Queensland and the Northern Kimberley is to make an "image" of the person out of straw and to mete out to it the experience which the performer intends to be the lot of the victim. For example, the image may be put on hot coals and then stabbed with a pointing-stick to the accompaniment of the appropriate chant; the belief is that as the image is burnt up and dies, the victim will be burnt up inwardly and so die.

The third form of Australian magical procedure is the most powerful, most feared and most wide-spread. It consists of "singing" alone, or "pointing" accompanied by "singing", and may be referred to as *projective* magic. By this I mean that the performer desires to project something into his victim without the aid of anything previously associated with or representing the latter. Of course, all magical performances are in essence projective, and imitative magic does rely almost wholly on the act of will. In any case, the personal image or object only focuses the expression of the desire. But Aboriginal pointing and singing are usually purely projective.

The best known projective method is *pointing* or bone-pointing. Probably the bone had originally to be a bone taken from a dead man's body, for then it would have in it the power of death, and so would best express and mediate the performer's wish. This is still the ideal instrument in some tribes, but a kangaroo bone or a properly prepared pointed stick may be, or is, used instead. When being used for its fell purpose, great care must be taken lest its power rebound on to the performer. Thus, in north-eastern South Australia, the latter must see that the sun or moon is behind him and that there is no waterhole in front of him, or else he will be struck himself. If he starts to tremble at the end of the rite, he realizes that this has happened, and his only hope of warding off the threatened illness is to jump at once into a waterhole with the bone in his hand.

In pointing the bone, the performer or performers adopt the correct ritual attitude, chant the prescribed song, and then usually point or jerk the bone in the direction of the victim.

I came across an interesting illustration of the use of the pointing-bone in north-west South Australia. The "bone" which is called *kundela* is said to have been introduced from the north-west. It was formerly made of stone but now consists of a piece of wood about nine inches long and half an inch thick, pointed at one end, and with some human hair string fastened with gum to the other end. The string acts as a tail and causes the bone to go straight, while the effect of the gum is to burn the victim after the bone has entered his back.

A man must be specially qualified before he can throw a *kundela*. The qualification includes a physical preparation: possum teeth are inserted into the postulant's nostrils for the purpose of extracting a little bone. *Kundela* are inserted into his upper arms, through both palms and some distance into the chest. Strangely enough, these operations do not cause any bleeding. When a person has been thus prepared and can also hit a thin mulga-tree at a distance of about eighty yards, he is shown the use of the pointing-sticks and taught the chant. After this he is a man with *kundela* power and may throw a pointer at any time, though midday is the usual time. He has to sing the *kundela* chant, incorporating in it the victim's name, while he dances round and taps two of the sticks together; he then goes on top of a rise and throws one of the sticks forward and towards the victim. The latter has only one chance of being cured of the serious illness caused in this way, namely, the successful extraction of the stick by a medicine-man.

This example shows that the pointing-stick is a kind of spear which can travel invisibly and for a very long distance with unerring aim. In some cases an actual spear is supposed to be used. The best illustration is the procedure of *kadaitja* (*kurdaitcha*) magic which was reported from Central Australia over forty years ago, but which is also well known in western South Australia. I quote from notes made in the latter area in 1930.

The term *kadaitja* refers first to the shoe which is made of marsupial fur string and emu feathers, and secondly to the men who perform magic while wearing them. These shoes are not seen by women, presumably to heighten the mystery surrounding them and also because sacred blood from men's arms is put inside them before they are worn. The man who wears them must undergo a painful ordeal, having his little toe treated with a hot stone and then dislocated. This toe acts as an eye, seeing any roots or other obstacles which would cause the wearer to trip. A man goes *kadaitja* at the request or command of another person, usually a headman; such a request being made in prescribed ritual manner, can only be refused on pain of death. The person in making the request, accompanies the *kadaitja* and there may be two or three others, one of whom is a medicine-man. All the members of the party must have had the little toes dislocated so that they can wear the shoes. Incidentally, the latter must be put on a person's feet by another man standing in a prescribed ritual relationship.[4]

When the party gets near the intended victim, the slayer sneaks up and spears him in the middle of the back. About

[4] He must be *tanamildjan* to the wearer; that is, he must belong to the generation one above or one below. See Chapter IV.

an hour later, the medicine-man heats a white (magical) stone which he applies to the wound causing it to heal up without leaving a mark. He also inserts something, perhaps a spirit-snake, in the victim's inside, which has the effect of giving him life, at least, temporarily. The medicine-man then causes him to get up, starts him on the way to his camp and restores him to consciousness. The victim makes back as though nothing had happened, but he dies in two or three days. If he does not die, the *kadaitja* party, which has been watching all the time, goes up one night and kills him. In any case, the young folk in the camp are prevented from seeing the victim. The expedition then returns and the shoes are put away.

This magical form resembles the fat-taking in that the victim is killed and then restored temporarily to life. Like the latter, too, it probably never happens, though the belief in its possibility, and indeed imminence, is very real and sometimes frightening. It is, however, a possible explanation of deaths and of strange noises and marks in the vicinity of the camp; moreover, the shoes do exist and so do the dislocated toes. But the interesting point is that the spear is supposed to be thrown, and usually it is endowed with special virtue from the sacred churinga which are carried by the *kadaitja*. Actually no mark is made and the spear does not touch the victim's body. In other words, it works in the same way as a pointing-bone, which, as already explained, is an invisible spear. Incidentally, one Central Australian tribe uses a certain kind of quartzite spear-point in exactly the same way as a pointing-bone.[5]

The power of medicine-men in south-eastern Australia

[5] This point is said to come from a tribe out to the west. The illustration given by Spencer and Gillen (*Northern Tribes of Central Australia*, p. 463) suggests that it is a spear-point made by pressure flaking, an industry peculiar to the Northern and Eastern Kimberleys and adjacent country. Its very difference in workmanship from the local spear-points would, no doubt, suggest that it was endowed with magical efficacy.

to project substances such as pieces of quartz into people to cause certain illnesses, is analogous to the use of the pointing-bone; the cure consists in the extraction of the substance.[6] In central and northern tribes, too, there are objects, usually standing-stones, associated with the afflictions (boils, blindness, etc.) of heroes of the dream-time. A person can now, by rubbing or striking the object and exhorting its evil magic to go forth and strike his enemy, cause the latter to have the affliction formerly borne by the hero. A realistic form of this projection is used in some Northern Territory tribes; the magic power resides in certain small stones which have a dream-time origin. In addition they are "sung" by the two tribes in whose country they are found. To injure an enemy, a person powders a little off one of the stones and manages to drop it on the former's body while he is asleep.

The simplest form of projection is that in which the procedure consists solely of *singing*. The chant is, of course, traditional, but through it the singers express their wish. This form is commonly adopted by the group when meting out punishment to some person for having acted in an anti-social way, such as breaking an incest rule. There is no cure for an illness caused in this way, and that for two reasons: in the first place, the singing did not involve the insertion, though invisible and in belief only, of a tangible bone or other object which can now be extracted by a medicine-man. In the second place, very few individuals are able to resist a social judgment and penalty, especially when this is expressed through a magical procedure.

[6] Examples of such projection practices are given in the works of Howitt, Spencer and Gillen, and Roth. A similar magical practice is spreading up the eastern shore of the Gulf of Carpentaria. Various substances, many of European origin, are manipulated by the performer in such a way as to project malign influence into the victim. This form is much dreaded, and in this disorganized society, the old men are seizing upon it as a method of restoring their authority.

FUNCTION OF BLACK MAGIC

In the last case, we see that black magic can be of social value, but as for the rest, be it fat-taking or blood-taking, sympathetic or projection magic, it is hard for us at first glance, to do anything but condemn it. We would probably argue that it is surely antagonistic to the well-being of individuals and society for the former to believe that they are in constant danger of being pointed or sung, etc. And it is true that in some regions natives are seldom at ease, especially when away from their accustomed haunts. There is, however, another point of view: as already stated, the Aborigines do not understand that serious illness, accident and death can be explained by natural causes. The only causes they understand are personal and spiritual, and some such cause must be found for that profound disturbance of the well-being and equilibrium of an individual and his group which is associated with his illness and death. He is maladjusted to his environment and can no longer do all that he normally should do. Moreover, his clan or tribe recognizes this, and is itself weakened thereby. Now, the first step in regaining equilibrium for the individual and for the group is to understand the cause of the disturbance. If the person's condition were the result of a wound received in a fight, his group would understand it and also would know what steps to take, especially if he died. If his condition, however, were not caused in that external way, it must have been caused in a similar way—the only difference being that the spears and missiles were invisible and were projected by magic instead of by physical power. In other words, the black magic put into operation by definite persons is the cause of the illness, death and social upset. On the basis of this knowledge, the group knows what steps to take. Usually certain types of affliction and death are caused by particular forms of black magic, and in any case the medicine-man can be summoned to decide the type and, if possible, withdraw it from the sick person; if necessary he may try to recapture and restore the latter's soul. If, however, a cure cannot be effected, the medicine-man finds by "inquest" who worked the magic, and then the group can adjust itself to the new situation by mourning, and above all by seeking satisfaction for the death in accordance with prescribed form. In these ways, the individual or the tribe or both are restored to a condition of well-being.

We should remember that under normal conditions, the natives are not going about in abject fear of black magic, and generally speaking, there are very few who practise it. Its existence only comes into consciousness when the ordinary course of a man's life has been interrupted by illness, accident, misfortune or death. Then the animistic and personal explanation of magic is resorted to, and he and his group know how to react so that peace of mind may be again established.

The foregoing explanation of the actual function of black magic does not mean that the latter is innocuous and fundamentally necessary for social stability. Eventually, the belief in it will be undermined, but derision, force and jail cannot get rid of it. Such treatment only makes it more secretive and convinces the natives that we really believe in its power. The belief and associated practices will only be discredited by education—that is, by the attainment of a truer understanding of the causes of illness, disaster and death. Even this will be a very slow process, but it will eventually be successful.

The Danger of Magic

A feature of black magic is that it is fraught with danger to the person who brings it into operation. It is a power or force which must be handled with great care, and only by those duly qualified. Whatever be the origin of this belief, it acts as a protection to society. If magic could be handled with impunity as far as the performer is concerned, the only control over its use would be the forceful reaction of the community or tribe to any person who made too frequent use of it. Fortunately, this is seldom necessary, though the fear of being designated as the cause of another person's illness and probably meeting with severe punishment, does prevent the use of magical procedure except after careful thought or under extreme provocation.

But this fear is backed by a greater sanction, and one which cannot be escaped, namely, the fear lest error or oversight in the ritual should involve the performer in the evil influence of the magical power; such an error might also cause damage to persons whom one has no desire to hurt. I remember a native in the far north-west, who, after demonstrating the use of the pointing-bone and image, was truly afraid lest he might have been seen, for if any one in the camp took sick, he would be blamed, even though he had not intended harm. In other words, to use the bone ritually, though without specific intention, might bring the magical power into operation. In west-central Queensland, a triangular piece of pearl-shell is often used instead of the pointing-bone in a magical rite introduced from the Northern Territory. The assailant approaches his victim while asleep, as closely as possible, and holding the weapon by one corner at arm's length in the direction of the victim, he makes two horizontal and two vertical passes, symbolizing the cutting of the throat and the ripping up of the abdomen respectively. But so dangerous is this procedure that special precautions must be taken lest any innocent person be hurt by the too great extent of the horizontal sweep; the performer therefore holds up his other forearm so as to limit this sweep.

Spencer and Gillen give an interesting example of the great awe felt for pointing-sticks. After much persuasion an old man was induced to show how one particular type was used. Another native who was with them promptly retired to a safe distance, and the performer himself, after jerking the stick in the proper manner towards an imaginary victim, was himself rather upset and said that some of the evil magic had gone into his own head. He only gradually regained his equanimity after he was assured that the investigators' medicine-chest contained sufficient magic to counteract that which was contained in the pointing-stick. The old man's great worry arose from the fact that he had not made and sung the stick himself, and so he did not know what magic was in it. This may be compared to those magic stones found here and there in some territories, which will affect adversely any one coming near them. The only way to prevent this magical power issuing forth is for every one who passes by to throw a stick on the stone; sometimes an old man takes this precaution on behalf of the rest of the tribe.

Now, such facts as these explain the great care with which magical ritual is performed, the feeling of awe which is experienced while doing this, and the concentration of the whole personality which is involved. Moreover, the power to use black magic is not easily come by. In addition to learning the correct procedure and "song", the performer must usually have passed through some physical preparation and maybe also a spiritual experience. As we have seen, the *kadaitja* man has his little toes dislocated, and the *kundela* pointer has an operation on his nose and at least a ritual operation on his hands, arms and chest. In other cases, a vision, sometimes gained while sleeping on a grave, is a prerequisite. No doubt, if we could get full information with regard to the preparation of a person to use bones and practise the more serious forms of magic, we should find that the physical and spiritual preparation is much more general than we at present realize. As we shall see later, it is universal in the case of medicine-men.

This much is clear, however, that in performing magic, the native believes that he brings into operation a power over which he does not possess complete control, and which exists independently of himself. Indeed, this is natural, for the mythology connected with magic reveals that

[21] *Top,* recording Nyindi-yindi corroboree at Delissaville, Northern Territory. Microphone fastened to tripod. *Bottom,* the anthropologist learns. Far North-eastern Arnhem Land.

[22] Raising four visiting young men after being painted with local clan designs. Arnhem Land, 1949.

[23] Casting spears at fish from a tree.

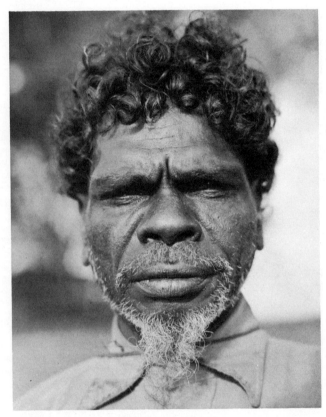

[24] Facing the future.

it has its source in the powerful dream-time or in the sky-world. Therefore, to use it with safety to himself, the performer must use the ritual and sing the chants that have come down with it and which mediate it. In other words, black magic derives its efficacy not only from the general belief in it as an explanation of illness and death, but also from the spiritual and historical philosophy which pervades all aspects of Aboriginal life.

MEDICINE-MEN AND SORCERERS

In spite of the distinction made at the beginning of this chapter between medicine-men and sorcerers, the fact remains that in some regions, notably the south-east of the continent, the former do sometimes act as sorcerers, taking "fat" and projecting magical substances for the purpose of causing sickness and death. Needless to say, such a malign medicine-man usually belongs to another and hostile tribe. But the belief shows that the source of power, be it good or bad, white or black, is in either case superhuman. It is not man-made, but as it arose ultimately from personal beings, the totemic or sky heroes, it can be understood by man and brought into operation by man.

FUNCTIONS AND POWERS OF MEDICINE-MEN

The functions of medicine-men as distinct from those of the sorcerer or from their own power of sorcery, if they possess it, are threefold: to diagnose and cure illnesses, to hold seances, and to conduct "inquests". In the case of some illnesses, medicine-men are not summoned; homoeopathic remedies are used. But in others which are associated traditionally with magical practices, the medicine-man is called in to diagnose and treat. The type of magical affliction can easily be recognized by the symptoms of the illness; thus, in one region rheumatism is the result of bone-pointing; local internal pains are caused by the projection of pieces of quartz; and sickness almost unto death shows that the patient's soul has been stolen or has strayed away, or maybe his kidney-fat or heart-blood has been taken. But having diagnosed the illness, the medicine-man begins his treatment. This sometimes consists in part of methods and materials which are of some medicinal and curative value, but in addition or without these, he uses magical ritual and formulae which have no such virtue; they are, however, of psychological value. By sucking in the region of the pain, he produces the bone, quartz or other substance which had been magically inserted. In another case, he may rub the afflicted part and produce the offending substance, or he may just move away from time to time with his hands seemingly full of something, the badness, and throw it away with great solemnity. He may, instead, send his familiar, a spirit lizard or snake, into the patient to clean out and extract the badness; or he may cause this badness to pass along a string from the patient's mouth into his own, whence it is spat out with blood. Finally, he may go in search of the dying person's soul and if successful in catching and restoring it, he has worked a cure.

The value of these and other methods is that when the medicine-men perform with assurance and apparent success, the patient believes that the trouble has been removed, or that his soul has been returned, and that therefore he can be at peace with himself and assured that all will be well. He therefore normally recovers. Thus the medicine-man's task in life is to restore faith in life where that faith has been lost, and so restore a sense of well-being. He does this by making the expected animistic diagnosis, and then performing the accepted rites in a thorough manner and in an atmosphere of dogmatic certainty. So the Australian medicine-man cultivates the requisite bedside manner and indeed often looks preternatural —as, of course he should, seeing that he is assisted by spirits and familiars unseen by others, and that he has a fund of knowledge and bluff which is not known to his patients.

But does the medicine-man believe in the efficacy of his

methods? Strange though it may seem, the answer must be yes. It is true that he uses a certain amount of make-believe and sleight-of-hand, but deep down in his mind is the belief that the sickness could be extracted by the rubbing and sucking and other actions, even though the stones and bones which he produces were never in the patient's body. These, however, are the symbols and expression of what he purports to do and of what the patient earnestly desires. Moreover, there are two important aspects to his work: one is subjective and the other may be called objective by those who possess the faith. In the first case, the thoughtful medicine-man realizes that what he is really doing is restoring the patient's faith in life and his will to live and so helps him of himself to get better. In saying this, I am using the interpretation of a native medicine-man, and not just the obvious interpretation which we would apply to the effects of his methods. In the second case, the medicine-man, by reason of his special "making" or "initiation", believes that he is in touch with unseen powers, totemic and spiritual, which work to effect the cures when he adopts the traditional procedure. He may send out from his "inside" a spirit-snake, a spirit-lizard, or the spirit of a departed person which according to some beliefs may be caught after death and kept by the medicine-man to help him in his profession. Such a familiar may enter the patient's inside to extract the badness or may go after and restore the sick person's wandering soul. But in addition to having spirit familiars, the medicine-man has associations with the departed and with either the heroes of the dream-time or the sky-god, and ultimately, his power comes from these sources. This being so, there is no limit to the curative possibilities of the medicine-man's methods once spirit agents have been brought into operation and the sources of dream-time and sky-world life have been tapped.

It is for these reasons, both subjective and objective, that the medicine-man believes in the efficacy of his methods, and when he is himself sick, he does not hesitate to call in the services of another practitioner. In this way his own will-to-live is strengthened and he receives that supernatural aid which will ensure his recovery.

MEDICINE-MEN AND SPIRITISM

The Aboriginal interpretation of the dream-life, to which reference has already been made, implies that not only may the dreamer visit distant persons or be visited by them, and receive totemic intimations, but he may also come into touch with the departed. This may be the experience of any individual, but in addition, there are in some tribes persons who claim to be mediums and to be able to hold communications with the spirit-world more or less at will, but usually the medicine-men are also mediums. This is only to be expected, because an essential part of their making consists of a spiritual experience in which they see, are possessed by, or are taken away by the spirits of the departed and other spirits too. Ever afterwards, they can, or at least may, get in touch with the spirit- and sky-world, see the spirits of the dead and even of the living. In fact they are believed to partake at times of the nature of spirits; it is said that they can fly through space unseen, and ascertain what is happening at a distance. No doubt, all this is an interpretation of dreams and visions and the psychic experiences referred to in the previous chapter, but it is an interpretation which has an important effect on conduct. It bolsters up the power of the medicine-men, increases their influence and indeed makes them more valuable in society. It makes them links and indeed, channels between the living and the departed, between the incarnate and discarnate spirits, and between this world and the sky-world. To many of us, this may seem a lot of nonsense and mere superstition, but it is a very different matter for a people whose philosophy is animistic and spiritistic. Their life is being constantly influenced by animistic, spiritual and magical forces and unless they had some means of making contact with the latter, life would be continually distracted. But in the medicine-men they have specialists in this aspect of life —men who entered the world of spirits and the supernatural at the time of their making, and unless they have broken some taboo or been deserted by their power, they can still get into touch with that world whenever this is necessary in order to restore the well-being of an individual and his group.

MEDICINE-MEN AND INQUESTS

One of the most important occasions on which these specialists are required is at a death. The group has been emotionally upset by the successful action of some worker of magic; its equilibrium has been disturbed, and cannot be restored merely by the acts of burial and mourning and the recitals of the old myths. The worker of magic must be found and punished, probably killed. But how can he be known, for having worked magically and at a distance, he has left no track and no one has seen him? At least that is what we would think, but we are wrong. We have forgotten the medicine-man. He is able to see the spirit of the "murderer" hanging around the corpse or the deceased's camp, for unfortunately for the murderer, human beings have more than one soul, and not even he can keep control of his spirit-equipment. In this way the medicine-man is able to find an object on which the pent-up feelings against magical and supernatural agents can be vented. A revenge expedition, itself strengthened by ceremony and magic is commissioned to get rid of the worker of evil. When this has been successfully done, social harmony is restored.

There are many forms of inquest, as we shall see in the chapter on Death, and they assist the medicine-man to determine the direction, group and even the name of the murderer. The dying man may also assist by mentioning that he dreamt of the totem of his murderer. Further, the medicine-man's thoughts are guided by his knowledge of social happenings—of the jealousies, quarrels and enmities in existence, and of the social value or worthlessness of likely murderers. These facts, together with the results of the divination, contribute to the content of the medicine-man's vision as he gazes at the corpse, or asks it questions. Sometimes, he does not come to any decision, no doubt for good reason. In such a case, the cause of the death must be found outside the magic-sphere; possibly it was the result of breaking some taboo and therefore was in a sense, self-inflicted. Society adjusts itself to that interpretation, regains its equilibrium and goes on its wonted way.

An examination of these functions of the medicine-man shows that they may all be described as life-giving in nature. He restores life by getting rid of sickness, or by recapturing the straying soul; he is the link with the unseen spirit-world and the sky, from which life is obtained; and he can ascertain the causes of illness and death and so enable the group to readjust itself after the disturbance to its thought and social life which resulted from those events. But this life-giving work of the medicine-man becomes even clearer when we understand the significance of the ritual of his making and the symbols of his power.

THE MAKING OF MEDICINE-MEN

It is difficult to obtain complete knowledge of the initiation of adult males into full membership of their secret life. Judging from fresh bits of information that I acquire from time to time, I doubt whether we have, in any one instance, been admitted into all the secrets of the ritual and knowledge. But if this is difficult, it is more so when we come to inquire into that ritual through which a medicine-man acquires his power. Those who are not members of the profession know little about it, and the more secretive and mysterious the practitioners are with regard to it, the more impressed are both they themselves and others by the wonder of its form and the greatness of its effects.

A medicine-man must have two qualifications: he must have knowledge of method and procedure and also an understanding of the ritual by which he was "made". The former includes the acquirement of skill in sleight-of-hand and ventriloquism, in rubbing and sucking, in examining the bodies of the dead and in conducting inquests, seeing spirits, and in performing the various actions expected of a practitioner. All this he learns from other practitioners who likewise impress on him the significance of the ritual by which he was made and the meaning of the symbols and substances which he will use in his profession. The second qualification rests on the belief that knowledge of what to do is not sufficient; the medicine-man must also have the power with which to do it, and this power cannot be acquired by learning; it is received through a spiritual experience and normally too, a ritual. He must be "made". This can happen in two ways; he may be made by the spirits alone, or by a ritual carried out by other practitioners, which itself leads to a spiritual experience. At least, there seems to be sufficient evidence to permit this distinction, and it is logical enough; in most spiritual or religious groups we find some who are given a recognized position in leadership and influence because of their spiritual powers or experience, even though they have not been ordained or made in the usual way. So it is with the Aboriginal medicine-man. Some have had a striking spiritual experience, the effects of which are recognized by other practitioners as well as by the rest of the tribe. Such an experience may apparently be deliberately sought by sleeping on a grave, or it may be suggested in a dream or in fancies arising when in a state of over-tiredness or when ill. In the latter case, the aspirant then goes where it is likely to come upon him and puts himself in a state of receptivity.

The remarkable thing is that in a tribe or group of tribes the experiences always conform to a set pattern; in other words, the spirits who make the postulant are believed to do so according to a prescribed ritual. Apparently, as soon as an individual shows signs of being a postulant, he is told what experience to expect and he meditates upon it until it occurs in mystic fashion, or else having had and reported some outstanding experience, medicine-men explain what they believe to be its significance and its true and normal form, until he is prepared to believe that he really did experience it in the way they described it. Moreover, in some tribes at least, the form used by the spirits is the same as that used by other medicine-men, and in neither case, could the prescribed happenings narrated have actually occurred, though they could take place in ritual and symbolic manner. It is, therefore, not easy to decide whether even the ritual has occurred, though this is very likely, or whether a vision has been induced by fasting and the endurance of pain and guided by previous instruction and suggestion.

As an example, we may take a celebrated medicine-man of the Unmatjera, a Central Australian tribe, who said that he was made as follows: A very old "doctor" threw some of his magical crystalline stones at him and *killed* him. Some of them went through his head from ear to ear. The officiant then cut out all his inside, intestines, lungs, liver, heart; in fact everything, and left him till next morning when he placed more of these stones in his body, arms and legs, and covered his face with leaves. After singing over him until his body was swollen up, he put more stones in him. He then patted him on the head, causing him to "jump up alive", and made him eat meat and drink water containing magic stones. When he, the postulant, came to, he had forgotten who he was and all the past. He thought he was lost, but he saw the old medicine-man beside him who said: "No, you are not lost; I killed you a long time ago." On his return to camp the people could tell from his strange behaviour what had occurred.

The ritual adopted by the spirits (they belong to the dream-time) in making some of the Aranda medicine-men is similar. The postulant goes to the mouth of their cave, and when they notice him there at daybreak, they throw an invisible lance which pierces his neck from behind, passes through his tongue, making a large hole in it, and comes out through his mouth. A second lance pierces his head from ear to ear. As a result he drops dead and is carried into the cave. The spirits then remove his internal organs and provide him with a new set, together with a supply of magical stones on which his power will depend. He later comes to life again but is for a time insane. When he has partly recovered he is led back by the spirits to his own people. He still remains strange for some days, but eventually recovers and is recognized by other medicine-men who train him in the methods of his profession.

In west-central Queensland the ritual seems to be jointly performed by a mythical water-snake or other nature-spirit and old medicine-men. In one case, the "snake" kills the postulant by pointing, and a few days later, medicine-men remove from his inside the stone or bone which the snake projected into it. He then recovers and becomes a medicine-man. In another example, the postulant is killed and thrown into a waterhole for four days. On the fifth day he is taken out and smoked dry in the midst of several fires; this makes him all right and alive again. He can then be taught.

In the Warburton Ranges of Western Australia, the aspirant goes into a cave where two totemic heroes (the wild-cat and the emu) kill him and cut him open from his neck down the front of his body to the groin. They then take out his internal organs and insert magical substances. They also remove his shoulder- and thigh-bones, which they dry, and before restoring them, insert magical substances in the openings. They cut round the ankles and stuff similar material into those parts, and finally take out and clean the frontal bone, and insert magical substances before replacing it. During all this ordeal, the aspirant is watched by a chief medicine-man who keeps fires alight and in some way controls the young man's experience. Apparently a state of trance is induced, for my informant said that the postulant goes to this cave which is associated with the dream-time and is made to lie down. When he gets up he is given blood to drink and porcupine, emu and wild-cat to eat. As a result he will be able to send the spirit-familiars of these species to do his work.

The insertion of magical substances, such as quartz, and of spirit-familiars, especially snakes, is a constant feature of the rites everywhere in Australia, whether this be done through openings ritually made or by pressing them into the skin, projecting them in by magical passes, or by taking them in food and drink. The possession of such substances in one's inside is absolutely essential, for the medicine-man's powers are associated with, and indeed mediated through, them. Now, these substances possess their virtue because they are derived from the dream-time or the sky-world. Generally speaking, in Central Australia, the former is the case while in south-eastern and north-western Australia, the latter is their place of origin, but in some regions we do not know sufficient about the matter to be sure of their source. In any case, like magic power itself, they are mythical; they are frequently associated with a great mythical water-serpent who is often the rainbow-serpent and like the latter, is in touch with the sky.

This brings us to a wide-spread feature of the ritual outside of Central Australia, namely, that the postulant makes a journey to the sky. This follows on the "death" and is the prelude to receiving power. In the Forrest River region of north-western Australia, for example, the medicine-man takes the postulant up to the sky in the following manner: he assumes the form of a skeleton and fastens on to himself a pouch into which he places the postulant who has been reduced to the size of a very small child; then sitting astride the rainbow, he pulls himself up with an arm over arm action. When near the top he throws the young man out on to the sky thus making him "dead". He then inserts into him some little rainbow-snakes and quartz crystals. I do not know whether he finds these in the sky or down below at the foot of the rainbow, but he can certainly obtain these and other magical substances there. So strong is this belief that ordinary people are forbidden by medicine-men, on pain of death, to enter a waterhole over which a rainbow is passing; if they did enter, they would learn the secret of the medicine-man's powers. Apparently, these objects are supposed to come down the rainbow from the sky to the waterhole. This belief is also well known in New South Wales.

After the operation, the postulant is brought down the rainbow and the old man inserts more magical substances into him, after which he wakes him up. The young fellow then practises going up to and down from the sky on the back of the rainbow-serpent and receives instruction in his profession.

In eastern Australia, the visit to the sky-world brings the postulant into touch with the sky-god from whom his powers are derived. The ritual did not include a killing, so far as we know, but after quartz and other substances were rubbed into the postulant's body, or even before this, he was taken to an actual or ceremonial grave, there to receive an experience. He was then taken up to the sky by means of the medicine-men's magic cord, and also to the foot of the rainbow. In this way he received not only his endowment of magical substances, but also the power to hold intercourse with the dead and to visit the sky-world.

The above outlines of significant features in the rites or trances connected with the making of medicine-men illustrate the point that their work depends on the possession of a power which is of a spiritual and animistic nature. It is derived from the dream-time, the sky-heroes or, in some cases, from great mythical nature-spirits, though even these are said to be transformations of dead persons.

Further, this power comes to the postulant through an initiation ritual, which, whether it be actually performed or not, consists of a death, a rebirth and endowment with new life—a life which is symbolized by new "insides" and magical substances. In other words, the postulant dies to his old life and rises a new person. This explains why he seems so strange when he returns to his people. He now lives on a different plane from them, though in all ordinary relationships there is nothing specially noticeable about him. Some medicine-men are very impressed by their spiritual privileges and responsibilities and feel that the medicine-man should be the perfect man. In eastern Australia he is the *kuradji* or wise man. There may be some scoundrels amongst the medicine-men as some early observers stated—this is true of all professions. But there is a high ideal of conduct for those who have had the ritual and spiritual experience of dying and being restored to life.

To regard them as trouble-makers is to misunderstand them. Granted the animistic and spiritual philosophy of life of the Aborigines, the medicine-men perform, as already stated, a very valuable function in individual and social life. Moreover, their power is not lightly come by, but is "from on high", and can only be retained by the observance of strict rules. They are not a class of impostors. They have behind them the beliefs and faith of the community.

One distinguished student of Australian Aboriginal ritual laid down the principle that whereas there was always a church connected with religion, this was never so in the case of magic. The first point is obviously true with regard to the cult totemism and the rites concerned with the sky-hero. But the facts analysed in this chapter seem to disprove his second point. The beliefs on which magic (black or white) is based are part of the general spiritual and animistic view of life. Black magic provides the explanation of illness and death and the abnormal, while the work of the medicine-man is to set things right again—to restore life and well-being. And though he alone performs the ritual, yet he does it for the whole community. Moreover, the source of his power is the same dream-time or sky-world which is the source of life and well-being for society in general. In fact, the medicine-man is just another link with the eternal, like the members of the totemic cult group, and he is qualified to be this by a ritual of the same type as that which makes the youth a man; he dies that he may become a means of life.

APPENDIX

The Ritual of Making Medicine-Men. The details of the ritual by which medicine-men are made, raise a very interesting problem, for not only is it often based on a pattern of death and "raising", but the manner in which the new life is said in many of the rites to be obtained is most remarkable. An incision is made in the abdomen through which the internal organs are removed to be cleaned before being replaced; through this incision too, other substances of a magical, that is, a life-giving, nature are inserted, and of course, the wound is healed up without leaving a mark, in the same way that medicine-men can heal the incisions through which they take kidney-fat or which have been made by spears in *Kadaitja*. In almost all the rites the magical substances are rubbed along the limbs and breast-bones and in the one from the Warburton Ranges, shoulder, thigh and frontal bones are removed, dried, and put back with the addition of magical material, some of which is also inserted through incisions around the ankles. The drying and smoking of the candidate is mentioned for rituals so far apart as western Queensland and the Warburton Ranges of Western Australia; in the former case, it is definitely said to be a means of restoring him to life. The immersion of the postulant in water for four days in the western Queensland rites as part of his death is also very interesting. Eventually the novice is in all the rites restored to life.

If the procedure carried out on a corpse comprised the making of an abdominal incision, the removal of the internal organs, the cleaning of the inside, the replacement of those organs, together with the insertion of life-giving substances (not only in the abdomen, but also along the limbs and breast and even the ankles), the closing of the wound, and a restoration to life, we should recognize a mummification ritual. The immersion of the candidate and the use of the fire ordeal which, no doubt, was widespread, adds to this impression. But strangely enough, in large areas where this form of ritual for the making of medicine-men exists, there is nothing approaching a mummification ritual used in burial. In eastern Australia, however, from Cape York Peninsula down to the mouth of the Murray, a form of mummification is practised. As we shall see, it consists of three main parts: the drying of the body, which includes often the removal of the outer skin, the carrying of the "bundle"—that is, the dried corpse, for mourning purposes, and finally, its disposal in some prescribed manner. In some cases, the corpse is disembowelled or else the abdomen is opened, so that the intestines can be taken out temporarily to be examined for signs of sorcery. In at least one northern Queensland rite, too, incisions are generally made in the stomach, on the shoulders and in the lungs, and are filled with stones. The purpose is said to be the prevention of the dead person from wandering too far, but apparently it does not stop him reaching the Milky Way. But the classic instance of a type of mummification in eastern Australia is that formerly practised in the Torres Strait, whence the custom apparently spread into eastern Australia. The details of this can be read elsewhere, but it certainly shows a probable origin of the pattern of the rite now being considered.

It is worth noticing that the burial custom of mummification in eastern Australia was normally reserved for most

important men, especially for medicine-men. It was therefore only natural that the ritual of their making, being
like all initiations, one of death and new life, should be
fashioned on this special burial rite. It spread further as
a symbolical ritual rather than in its latter capacity. Public opinion is always conservative in the matter of disposal
of the dead, whereas there was a special reason and mechanism for its adoption in the making of medicine-men,
namely, their secret life. In addition to the recorded instances of this ritual in western Queensland, Central Australia, Victoria and elsewhere, I have come across it in the
far west of the continent, the Broome district and also east
of Laverton, a long way to the south-east of Broome.

In eastern Australia, the home of the dead is in the
sky; mummification, and also some of the other burial rituals, ensure that the deceased reaches there. It is, therefore, appropriate that the medicine-man, whose power and
privileges are closely associated with the sky-world, should
be initiated by a rite which "naturally" admits the initiate
to the sky.

Finally, the procedure in fat extraction is also important
in this connexion. Details concerning the method are hard
to obtain but out of nine procedures in different tribes, the
incision is made in the back in three, in the side in three,
and in the abdomen in two. Packing the wound is recorded
for three tribes, in two of which packing the corpse was
a burial practice. The wound is closed up in each case
(by sewing in one). Such practices seem to be naturally
associated with mummification. The suggestion is strengthened by the accompanying practice in two tribes. In one,
the Buandik of the Victoria-South Australian border, the
operator inserted a stout blade of grass into the nostril and
drew something out. In the Kunganji tribe (east coast,
northern Queensland) the victim's head was pierced with
a bone just above each nostril for the purpose of extracting
the life blood and the tongue. The point is that mummification ritual as practised until recently in the Torres Strait

included the extraction of the brain through the nostrils. The use of a form of ritual without understanding its original purpose is not unusual, and the absence of reports of this custom in other parts of eastern Australia cannot be made the ground for any kind of inference, seeing how lamentably meagre is our information regarding fat taking and the practices of medicine-men and sorcerers in general. But if the details of the operation of fat taking be historically connected with mummification, it is only to be expected that the victim who, for the time being was unconscious, should wake up and live for a time, as was the fact or belief. It is also appropriate that fat taking should be one of the powers of men who were "made" by a mummification type of ritual.

This discussion of the ritual of making medicine-men is not of importance for the understanding of their function in society, but if we had all the facts, including the interpretations held by the medicine-men themselves, we would understand the meaning of those rites. Such meaning is bound up with their history; unfortunately we cannot obtain a satisfactory record of this, but must rely, for the most part, on the distribution of customs. I hope, however, that this discussion will at least show that there is more in these rites and also in the forms of visions, than appears on the surface. They are not just figments of the imagination.

Similarly, for a full understanding of the medicine-man, we should need to examine the rainbow-serpent myth, the beliefs regarding the sky-world to which reference was made in the preceding chapter, and the significance of such substances as quartz and pearl-shell. The colours reflected by them may explain their association with the rainbow and that may be sufficient. On the other hand, there may be some other interpretation of an historical nature.

Chapter XII

DEATH AND WHAT FOLLOWS

DEATH, INQUEST AND REVENGE

Death, a Social Event. Death is probably the most significant and important social event, for it is constantly occurring, though at irregular intervals, and in every case consists of the removal of a member of society from his accustomed place. He can no longer visibly play his role in the various acts of earthly life. Thus, death makes a break in the unity and joint action of the social group or tribe; the latter is weakened and indeed its future is threatened, for the death is a reminder of the fact that all will die, and therefore, as far as the present members of society are concerned, society will cease to exist. Now, such thoughts, if dwelt upon, would lead to apathy and a fatalistic acceptance of everything that occurs. Society must therefore bestir itself. Just as an illness which normally precedes death can be treated and even cured with the result that death is defeated, at least temporarily, so too, the death of an individual, when it does occur, causes a condition of social illness which must be treated at once, or else it will prove fatal to social life and cohesion.

A death is naturally of greatest emotional and practical significance to the immediate relations and neighbours of the deceased person, yet it is also fraught with varying degrees of significance, as already implied, for larger groups, such as the clan or the tribe. Even amongst civilized peoples, the death of an individual affects a town, a state, a religious or other organization. And it is just because death causes these more general effects and distant reverberations, that attitudes, reactions and rituals associated with it become standardized in most, if not in all, societies, guiding both individual and group actions. Of course, the feelings of some mourners occasionally break the customary bounds, or at least, their actions express genuine emotion, but on the other hand, the individual is seldom sufficiently courageous or nonchalant to fall short of the accepted degree or type of mourning. We are all familiar with many of the customs of British peoples, though these are being modified a good deal during recent years. As many as possible of the relations gather round the dying person and take part in the ceremony by which the priest or minister commends and sanctifies the soul of the dying as it passes from this life to the next; later, they are joined in the burial rite by members of the general community according to the social importance of the deceased person or his nearest relations. The accompanying social expressions may consist of meals, wakes, in some parts funerals on a scale calculated to outdo those held by the neighbours, the wearing of black, crape bands and widow's weeds, comparative seclusion for some time, observation of a taboo on marriage for a number of years and a feeling of outraged propriety on the part of many if remarriage seems to occur too soon. Such are some of our rites and customs which are in some form or other practised to-day, even by many who do not believe in them. By these means the relatives and the group react to death and reorientate themselves after it, close up their ranks and face the future as though death were in itself a thing of the past.

Apart from details, this is true also of primitive peoples, including the Aborigines. Amongst them, social and individual behaviour is standardized in the presence of a dying person and death; and mourning is a series of socially sanctioned and expected customs and rites which include not only expression of sorrow and grief, but also taboos, inquest, revenge and burial.

Dying and Death. The scenes around the Aboriginal death-bed have many similar features all over Australia, as the following outlines will show. Referring to a death at Perth about one hundred years ago, Sir George Grey wrote that the dying man's head rested on his mother's knees and her withered breasts now rested on his lips, as she leaned crying over him; other women were sitting round with their heads bent over the wasted frame of the dying man. They were crying bitterly, and scratching their cheeks, foreheads and noses with their nails, until blood trickled slowly from the wounds. The female relatives sang: "My son (brother) again I shall not see in the future." From time to time the women in turn chanted dire imprecations against the sorcerers who were supposed to have caused the death, addressing their words to the men so as to work them up to their duty of taking revenge. As soon as the man died, an old woman started up mad with grief and rage, tore his hut to pieces and poured forth more imprecations against the sorcerers, with the result that the men became very excited and one of them tried to spear one of the deceased man's wives for not having detected the nightly presence of the sorcerers as they consumed her husband's body. The inquest and burial duly followed.

The following is a scene from Central Australia: a man was dying; a loud wail announced that the end was near, and all the men ran to his camp. His hut had already been pulled down. Some women were lying prostrate on his body, while others were standing or kneeling around, digging the sharp ends of yam-sticks into the crown of their heads from which the blood streamed down their faces. They wailed as also did the groups of men who were sitting around. Many men ran up to the dying man and, as the women got up, threw themselves on his body. Another man rushed up, and gashing his thighs, fell down in the middle of the heap of men. He was dragged out by his mother, wife and sisters, who applied their mouths to his wounds. At last all the men got off the dying man whose death, needless to say, had been hastened on. Late in the evening, when he died, the same scene was re-enacted, though more frantically; the men and women rushed about cutting themselves with knives and sharp-pointed sticks; the women battered one another's heads with clubs and then, in less than an hour, the body was carried off to be placed on a platform in a tree, and the whole camp site was deserted.

On the occasion of a death in the Bard tribe, north-western Australia, all present wail and hit their heads until blood comes. The women cry every night for several weeks, and all the mourners put red ochre and grease in their hair, leaving it there to wear off. Further, a man paints his face and body to the waist if his wife or brother-in-law dies, and a woman does the same if her husband dies; she also keeps bands of red and white paint round her eyes for about two weeks. Black paint is used by either a man or woman in the case of the death of a brother, sister, cross-cousin, father's father, son's son, mother's parents and wife's grandparents; but red is used on the death of a father, mother, children, sister's children, mother's brother, father's sister, wife's mother, wife's mother's brother and the spouses of children and sister's children. In other words, black is the mourning colour for members of one's own generation-line which includes grandparents and grandchildren, and such like, while red is the colour for persons of the parents' and children's generation. In the Forrest River district, the members of the deceased person's own generation paint their heads, faces and chests with white clay and charcoal and keep away from the corpse, while those of the other generations do not paint, but approach the corpse.

Such ceremonial divisions have nothing to do with the moieties or other social groups, but in some regions the moiety division orders the signs of mourning and regu-lates the burial duties. Amongst the Ungarinyin the men of the deceased's own patrilineal moiety put the corpse on the tree-stage, and amongst the tribes of north-eastern South Australia, the rule is similar; only the members of the dying and deceased person's matrilineal moiety may normally approach the death-bed or take part in the interment. These persons are painted with red ochre while the members of the other moiety paint themselves with pipe-clay and remain some distance away. In this and the neighbouring part of New South Wales, the widow and her brother or the widower in the case of the death of a married woman, draw attention to their loss by wearing the now well-known "widow's caps", that is, a thick plaster of pipe-clay, up to an inch in thickness, applied directly to the head or over a head-net, and covering the top and back of the head. These caps are put on the grave when the mourning ceremonies have been completed.

In some regions such as this part of South Australia and parts of northern Australia, chants of the dying person's totemic cult clan are sung. This comforts him, reconciles him to his return to the sacred spirit-world, and indeed, prepares him for it. He takes part in the singing as long as he can, and may make appropriate symbolic actions to show his identification with his totemic form; thus he passes to his ancestors in a state of contentment which reassures his earth-bound relations that he will not worry them. In Arnhem Land, the deceased's totem is painted on his body, so that his ancestors will readily know to which totemic spirit-home they must carry his soul. Cycles of totemic songs are sung, the departed is frequently spoken to and then the body is interred in a grave which represents his spirit-home, amidst the announcing of the name of the latter as a request to his ancestors to come and guide his soul to that home.

In north-eastern South Australia, the body is put in the grave very shortly after death and then in the usual rite, the mourners camp near by and the members of the deceased's own moiety and cult-totemic "lodge" sing his sacred songs daily until the totemic cycle has been completed and the grave has been filled in by small daily additions of earth. Sometimes singers who are members of the other matrilineal moiety have to be invited to assist with the chanting, and although they belong to the deceased's own patrilineal cult totem, they must later on be given a present in return for their help.

Without referring further to details observed in particular regions, we may make the following generalizations: the actions of those associated with a dying and dead person are regulated by certain forms of social organization, in particular, the kinship system, generation- or age-levels, moiety, and cult-group. When a person is dying, people watch near by or at a distance, according to relationship rules; they wail or chant, gash and draw blood from themselves, and maybe throw themselves on the sick person. After death, all this expression of emotion is usually intensified and often a state of frenzy is reached; this is not only a sign of real or standardized grief but also of the disturbance of the general sense of well-being; it is, moreover, a reaction to the magical death-dealing forces that are ever about and had just been put into effective operation. As a result of this emotional upset they feel that an attack must be made on someone there and then, more especially on any person present whose relationship to the deceased was such that he could, in some way, have protected him from the evil magic, and obviously failed to do so. An attack may be made on him (or her); this, however, is a ritual matter, and some of those present see that it does not get beyond threats and gestures; the very attack that each mourner makes upon himself, wounding his scalp, face or thighs is probably an expression of this urge to attack and kill the insidious cause of death. At the same time, threats are made by word and gesture against the actual worker of black magic, who will be determined upon later and then dealt with. Gradually the heightened emotions and rage die down and come under control as they become centred in traditional manner on this person as yet unknown, but whose identity will be established.

When this stage has been reached, the body is attended to. It is usually shifted at once to the place of "burial" or preparation for burial, where sooner or later an inquest is held. The various forms of inquest and of burial will be summarized later. Where interment is practised, the grave is dug and usually the body is protected from the surrounding earth by bark or leaves; very often the deceased's personal belongings and weapons are also put in the grave, though sometimes these are burnt with his hut. The grave may, or may not, be filled in at once according to local custom. Also, in some regions, instead of interment, the body may be placed in a tree-stage or, after due preparation, carried round with the group for a period, or cremated. But whatever be the form of disposal of the body, the expressions of mourning and the desire for revenge are much the same everywhere. So, too, is the way in which society tries to separate itself from the spirit of the dead, to speed the latter on its way to its spirit-home, and to avoid any offence which might bring it back.

Aboriginal thinking seems a little confused here, for though at the completion of the burial-rites the spirit has gone to its resting-place, yet it may at the same time be about the camp or in the bush, unless careful precautions be taken. This puzzle is usually explained by the possession of two souls: the real self does go to the spirit-home. This is the eternal dream-time soul which pre-existed and will exist, for a time or eternally, and which, in some tribes, may be reincarnated. Beliefs regarding the fate of the dead vary. There is also another soul which can appear in dreams, which may take up its abode within another person after its owner's death, or may live in the bush and play tricks, scare and even damage its incarnate relations. It is the action of this soul which expresses the deceased person's desire not to leave his former associations, and no doubt, also reflects the latent, if not open, protest of the living against death. On the other hand, it provides the explanation for society's efforts, almost frantic and certainly overloaded, to dissociate itself from the dead. The mourning and revenge customs are faithfully observed so that the deceased will not have any cause to bear a grudge against his group.

But that is not all: everything that was associated with him is destroyed, avoided or purified. His camp and grave are deserted; his belongings destroyed or broken. Though he will no longer need his body as a means of action, yet in some rites, it is weighted down or tied up or the legs are broken so that he will not be able to wander. A zigzag path is followed to and from the grave at the time of burial, or a smoke-screen is passed through so that the spirit of the dead will not be able to follow the mourners. Those who take part in the burial are brushed with smoking twigs, and the wives who are closely associated with the deceased during his life-time, are usually separated from the general camp for a prescribed period. In some tribes certain mourners must not speak for some time, and in all, the name of the dead may not be mentioned for months and even years. In addition, any persons or objects bearing the same name must no longer be referred to by it. Food taboos are observed, and of particular interest are those special ones which are adopted because the food was the deceased's totem or was one of which he was fond, and therefore is associated with him. In all these ways, the deceased, and with him, the thought of death and the gap caused by it, are banished from consciousness. When later, the various taboos on speech and on food have been ritually removed, the widow is remarried or the widower resumes his habitual ways of living, and society regains its equilibrium. Initiation and totemic ceremonies are performed in due season, life is gained from the eternal dream-time, and society, ritually strengthened, bequeaths to the past the associations of death, and faces the future with renewed courage and hope.

The Inquest. The necessity for holding an inquest in almost every case of death arises, as we saw in the previous chapter, from the Aborigines' animistic view of life in general and their magical and personal explanation of illness and death in particular. It is seldom a case of *something* causing a death, but of *someone* doing so. If the death occurs during a fight with weapons, there is no need to hold an inquiry to decide on the someone, though even in this case it is occasionally argued that some person interfered magically with the attacking or defensive powers of the deceased, and is therefore really responsible for the death. His identity might then be sought.

Generally speaking, the holding of an inquest depends on the social value of the deceased. Thus, a magical cause is seldom sought in the case of the death of an infant or young child, though the parents may be very grieved. The child will probably be reincarnated before long. Its death may have been caused by the breaking of some sexual or food taboo by the parents; moreover, in some tribes, newly born infants are frequently put to death, usually for economic reasons. The worker of the death magic is often "discovered" in the case of the death of a woman or very old man, but the inquest is not always followed up with an actual revenge expedition or a demand for settlement of the grievance by a gift of a woman in marriage together with other presents. It depends usually on the temper of the deceased's group and on the existence or non-existence of other grievances against the group of the "murderer" whether revenge is attempted, a gift demanded, or nothing done. If, however, a male dies in the prime of life, not only is an inquest held, but also satisfaction is sought. But in some regions, this does not always lead to a revenge expedition or to the handing over of a woman (instead of the death of the murderer). In this case, the explanation is that the accused man's group has an old grievance against the deceased person's group, and so a meeting is arranged in which the matters are discussed and the two grievances or charges are balanced one against the other. When agreement has been reached, there is a temporary exchange of wives in which the normal social rules regarding the intercourse of the sexes are ignored. This shows that revenge will not be taken and that the men are "brothers", or friends.

There are various methods of inquest, and often several are practised in one tribe. The commonest consists of an examination of the ground around the grave, which was cleaned and levelled at the time of interment. Any hole appearing in this is examined because it might give the direction of the country of the murderer; the medicine-man or other men present decide whether it is significant for this purpose, or is merely an insect hole; in the former case, it was made by the deceased person's spirit coming out of the grave on the side nearest the murderer's country. Sometimes the latter's locality is determined by the direction in which a stick points when it is put in the hole. The tracks made by an insect on the cleared ground are sometimes regarded as indications of the murderer's direction as though they were the tracks of his spirit moving off to his country.

Of course, such a form of inquiry does not specify the particular man, but only his group. The old men must then determine on the basis of old grudges and various happenings who should be selected as the cause of the death, or else, and this is most usual, the medicine-man decides who is the culprit by dreaming of him or seeing his spirit around the grave. Indeed, he may succeed in doing this at the time of the burial and then further inquiry is unnecessary. All medicine-men have this power, though they do not always use it at the time of the death, or if they do, they do not express the results of their spiritual investigations until some considerable time has elapsed, so that they shall be well acquainted with all the circumstances and the likely reactions to any decision which they announce. This postponement of the results of the inquiry or of its conduct is an institution in some tribes, whether the medicine-man acts alone or with some of the elders. For example, amongst the tribes east of Laverton, Western Australia, the grave is not filled in but protected by sticks laid across the top. Some months later when the flesh has dropped away from the bones, the latter are examined for signs of magical choking. Having decided that death was caused in this way, the medicine-man ascertains from the direction in which the smell is travelling from the grave, the quarter in which the murderer lives.

Another form of delayed inquest is associated with a form of disposal of the dead which is practised in the north-western quarter of the continent from Wyndham and Darwin south to about the centre and from the north-west coasts to about the border of Queensland. It consists of tree-stage burial followed much later by a big mourning ceremony and the final disposal of the bones by interment or deposition in a cave. Soon after the death the body is put on a tree-stage, and unless the spirit of the murderer is seen hovering around the body, or unless he is indicated (in some tribes) by the bat, the symbol of death, hovering around him, the determination of the culprit is made later. The details may vary in different tribes, but the exudations from the body are expected to supply the indication according to the tribal belief. Amongst the Bard, rows of sticks, and amongst the Ungarinyin, a circle of stones, is placed under the body. Each stick or stone represents a person who could be held responsible for the death, the definite murderer being indicated by the exudations dropping on or running towards his stick or stone. Amongst the Warramunga of Tennant Creek, Northern Territory, the direction of the flow of the exudation gives the direction of the murderer's group. Vengeance is then taken according to tribal custom modified by practical considerations and the degree of feeling aroused. Magical actions directed towards the murderer's country may be deemed sufficient, even though he does not hear about it. The action, however, satisfies the afflicted group.

Delayed inquest is sometimes associated with another complex burial rite, namely, interment followed by disinterment and a final disposal of the bones. Thus, in the Forrest River district of north-western Australia, and I believe also in some other parts of Northern Kimberley, this form of burial used to be accorded distinguished persons. The body is interred and small stones set up around the grave. These are inquest stones, each representing a possible murderer, and drops of blood are supposed to pass from the buried body to the actual murderer's stone. If this does not happen, the decision remains with the medicine-man. About the time that all the flesh has disappeared from the bones, an important mourning ceremony is held at the grave. The medicine-man is the first to arrive and he does so in a very special manner. He goes up to the sky and then comes down "behind the wind", and sees the murderer poising a spear, and also the dead man walking about. The latter is a sign that the bones are freed from the flesh. The medicine-man informs the dead man's son of the identity of the murderer and either a revenge expedition is sent out, or else an armbone of the dead man or a pearl-shell is sent to the murderer's clan as an invitation to the mourning ceremony as well as an indication of the accusation. The members of this group come with presents and also their weapons and engage in a fight which, my informant said, generally resulted in the death of one or more of the accused clan.

In several tribes of Cape York Peninsula the inquest is conducted on the exhumed body, but this takes place a few days after the interment. In some cases, the bones are removed from the flesh to be made up into a bundle which is to be carried about and mourned over. During this operation a look-out is kept for signs of a magical wound or object. In another, a piece of the flesh with the "splinter" which caused the death, is left in the grave, while the rest of the body is made into a bundle to be carried about until the deceased has told the mourners who "killed" him or her. If necessary, a hair of the deceased is questioned.

This brings us to the method of questioning the dead. There are several varieties. The simplest comes from a north-western Australian tribe: the dead man's hair is pulled in jerks, at each of which the name of a local clan is mentioned, and the group designated at the pull which removes some hair, is guilty of the death. A variation of this method occurs in Dampier Land, north of Broome. The dead person's hair is woven on a spindle into string, and taken out by a group of men into a secluded spot. One of them takes hold of the outside end of the hair-string and holding this up allows the string to unwind in such a way that the long upright stick of the spindle will hit the ground at its lower point. Meanwhile the name of a possible murderer is called, and if the spindle falls over on the ground, this person is considered innocent, but if it keeps on spinning for some time in an upright position, he is guilty and vengeance will be taken. The process is repeated until the murderer is indicated. The names called are those of persons known to be unfriendly to the deceased, or it may be the name of the person dreamed of by the deceased, and mentioned by him just before his death. In such a dream the murderer appears spearing, or in other ways injuring the dreamer who consequently dies.

In many tribes the corpse is asked to indicate his murderer, for the spirit is thought to be near by and able to supply the information. The method formerly used in north-eastern South Australia is a useful illustration:

the corpse was placed on the heads of three men who stood in the right relation to the deceased. After preliminary chanting and tapping of two boomerangs or sticks by the conductor of the inquest, the corpse was asked whether his murderer came from this place or that and a string of names of localities was uttered. At the mention of the correct place, the spirit caused his body to jump off the heads of the bearers. The corpse was then restored and asked in the same way to indicate who was the murderer amongst the persons of the locality. This inquiry was sometimes assisted by information provided by the dying person and of which he dreamt.

Another method of inquiry necessitates a post-mortem examination of the deceased's internal organs. One of the disinterment inquests is similar. Sometimes the dissection of the body is not made solely for the purpose of the inquiry, but is part of the preparation of the body for a later rite. On the Lower Tully River the corpse was kept for several days until it was swollen up. The stomach was then removed through a carefully made abdominal opening and in it was found the "something" with which the deceased had been doomed. In former days on the lower reaches of the Murray River, the medicine-men made an incision in the abdomen, through which they pulled out the intestines and peritoneum for careful examination. During this process the bystanders wailed and gashed themselves. A cicatrice on the omentum would indicate that the death had been caused by sorcery and must be avenged. With the exception of a part of the omentum, the entrails were replaced together with a handful or two of green leaves, and the body was bound up for interment. In some northern Queensland tribes, the viscera are to this day removed and buried; near by an elder male relative of the deceased will have a vision of the murderer.

It is interesting to notice that inquest by examination of the internal organs by means of a surgical post-mortem is

confined to eastern Australia, more especially in northern
and eastern Queensland and the Darling-Murray River
tribes, where it is associated with a form of burial which
may be described as mummification. On the other hand,
inquest by examination of the exudations is connected
with the tree-stage exposure and delayed burial. Examination of the bones of the previously buried body is a custom in the western deserts, while questioning the corpse
is the chief method in north-eastern South Australia and
New South Wales, and the examination of signs on the
ground around the grave is relied on to a very great extent
in the south-west of the continent. Though such a general
distribution does hold, several methods are usually available in each tribe. The medicine-man can always be ap-
pealed to as he has the power to see the spirit of the murderer in an incriminating position, and so may render
unnecessary any other form of inquest. The dying person may give the necessary information which has come
to him through a dream of the actual murderer or of
his totem, or divination with the dead person's hair may
be employed.

The Spirit and the Corpse. The forms of inquest show
that the spirit of the deceased still "animates", controls
or may use the corpse or parts of it. The corpse moves or
jumps off the bearers' heads in answer to the questions
when put in the prescribed manner. The hair gives the
necessary indications when it is pulled or when turned
on a spindle as though it understood, and even the smell
and exudations are controlled. Indeed, it is not until
revenge has been taken or satisfaction obtained, and
the burial and mourning rites completed, that the spirit
finally leaves the body and goes to the home of the head
or its spirit-home. This belief is, of course, an expression
of the urge that something must be done about the cause
of the death, before society can regain its sense of well-
being and return to normal ways. It is not just a matter
of getting over grief, but getting rid of the sense of weak-

ness and danger which was caused by the death. This is not gained by the passing of time alone, but by socially determined action, and the belief in the nearness of the spirit of the dead person and of its interest in the completion of all the rites and duties, provides an incentive and sanction for the performance of those actions by which social equilibrium and well-being are regained.

Divination and Control. The forms of inquest, apart from that of the medicine-man's vision of the murderer may seem to us to depend absolutely on chance, and so to be purely divinatory in nature. But this is not necessarily so. True, the direction of the flow of the bodily exudations, the holes on the ground around the grave, the turning of the spindle, the appearance of a sign on the intestines, are purely matters of chance, but we should remember that the signs have to be interpreted, and this is done normally some days, often many days, after death. By this time, emotions have settled down, at least partially, and the "coroner" or "coroners" have had time to think who the likely murderer could be and what group it would be wise or expedient to implicate in a charge of sorcery. There is no doubt that these and like considerations do control the interpretations of signs, even the movement of the corpse on the bearers' heads when it is being questioned, and also the vision of the medicine-man. There may not always be direct and conscious control or trickery, but unconsciously the spindle is prevented from spinning except when one name is mentioned, the body is jerked off the bearers' heads at the mention of the most likely name, the exudations under the tree and the marks around the grave give the expected indications. Further, in order to avoid complications or because the group was not terribly perturbed by the particular death, the murderer may be reckoned to belong to a very distant tribe, or an unreported magical revenge is deemed sufficient. Sometimes, too, though rarely, no signs are given; that is, no decision is made.

The point is that unless feelings run very high, inquest and revenge are not just governed by chance. The Aborigine has his sense of social order, and does not live on a level of uncontrolled emotion, nor does he give himself up wholly to the whims of chance, not even when he is dealing with death. Perhaps he is not quite consistent in this, but consistency must sometimes be sacrificed or ignored when man is confronted by the big issue of life and death. He is inconsistent, at least, unconsciously so, in not allowing the free play of animistic agencies in specifying the particular person concerned, and in frequently making the decision fit into the social and emotional situation. White folk living near Aborigines do not always realize this, and naturally so, because they form their opinion on the basis of the mere form of the ritual inquest and the interpretation given by the natives. The latter, of course, give the exoteric orthodox theory. But underneath this is its modification by social facts, and it is only intense study and very intimate knowledge which will reveal the extent of such modification.

It is interesting to notice that the inquest sometimes only indicates the group of the murderer and sometimes, too, no more specific identification is sought; this may be left to the act of vague magic which is performed with that group in mind; or the local group as such may be challenged, and it can take up the challenge corporately or hand over to a revenge party, or itself kill, one of its number in order to give satisfaction; this might be done if, for other reasons, it wanted to get rid of this particular person. In any case, just as the inquest and revenge are corporate acts, so, too, is the making of satisfaction, especially when the basis of the accusation is an act of sorcery. The members of a local group are "brothers" and in a sense equivalent; they therefore bear one another's accusations as well as responsibilities and duties.

Revenge and Social Duty. As with the inquest, so with revenge: it is seldom a blind passionate outbreak which sends a revenge expedition against another group of the tribe, or more likely into the country of another tribe, to kill the murderer. Like the inquest, it is socially and traditionally ordered. By the time a revenge expedition is sent out, days, more often weeks or months have passed since the death. The members are then selected according to kinship and moiety rules; magical ritual is performed to give them courage, protection and success; a ceremonial exchange of wives often takes place; and they usually take with them a sacred bull-roarer as an added source of strength. In this way, the emotions and determination of the party are aroused so that the socially necessary duty will be performed. On its successful return, the revenge expedition is ritually received. It is usually successful because the attack is made at dawn, and is irresistible, according to the conviction of all concerned, because of its magical accompaniments. Sometimes when the attack is not so made, the accused person is handed over to the attacking party.

But as already stated, a revenge expedition is not always sent: a magical rite may be performed instead, an invitation to a meeting and fight may be sent, a settlement may be made by the "payment" of a woman, the present death may be balanced against a previous death or other grievance which the murderer's group has against the deceased's group, or, as in some tribes, the initiation, that is a ritual killing of a young member of the former group, may satisfy the latter. This suggests that the endless vendetta is not a general principle of Aboriginal life, nor is the principle "an eye for an eye and a tooth for a tooth" always literally interpreted. Here and there in Australia the reverberations and results following on a death are much greater than elsewhere, but generally speaking, the Aborigines, as I have heard them say, have no desire to exterminate each other's groups, for, if they did, how could wives be found? Grievances must be settled, but the method need not always be by death, even when a death is the matter under consideration.

Thus, this discussion of inquest and revenge shows that in spite of superficial appearance, the Aborigine's social life is controlled by tradition and thought even in times of such emotional disturbance as are occasioned by deaths, and what is more, he knows that the cohesion and future of his clan and tribe would be in jeopardy if this were not so. Incidentally, this should enhance our appreciation of his intelligence. When confronted with the problem of the magical causation of death, the necessity of dealing with the personal agent and at the same time, appreciating tribal and social facts and the task of preserving the cohesion of the tribe, he is able to find a solution, even though it means some inconsistency and the escape from an inexorable logic. For, after all, intelligence is shown by recognizing and solving the problems of life.

BURIAL RITES

There is not space here to examine fully the many interesting forms of burial used in Australia nor to discuss their meaning and possible origins. Reference can only be made in general terms to them, their distribution and significance. The forms are interment, mummification, cremation, platform-exposure and delayed burial, and burial in hollow trees. Some of the rites are composite. Thus, in the Northern Kimberley and north-eastern Arnhem Land, interment, disinterment and final disposal of the bones after a special mourning ceremony constitutes one rite. Likewise, in the north-western quarter of the continent, tree-stage exposure of the body and a later mourning ceremony over the bones, followed by their disposal in the ground, a cave or totemic coffin, constitute the complete rite. Mummification, which is confined to northern Queensland, eastern Queensland and the Darling-Murray River basins, consists of several parts; the body is dried over a fire or in the sun after the internal organs have been removed through an incision and it has been packed, bound up and, usually, painted; it is then made up into a bundle, "the mummy", and is carried around by the mourners until their grief has been assuaged and revenge has been taken; it is mourned over at the various camps and ceremonies may be performed in its presence. It is finally disposed of by interment, cremation or by being put in a hollow tree. In some parts the preparation is complicated by a previous interment and disinterment, and in others by cannibalism, so that the bundle consists only of the bones or the bones and the dried skin. Here interment and disinterment, and also cremation, form parts of a larger rite. There are, however, a few cases of cremation constituting in itself the complete ritual just as interment is practised in most of Australia as a distinct rite. Cannibalism, which was just mentioned, forms a ceremony, not only in connexion with mummification in parts of Queensland, but also precedes the exposure of the body on the tree-stage amongst the tribes on the south-west of the Gulf of Carpentaria and occasionally in the Northern Kimberley; it also forms part of the interment ritual in the north-east of South Australia; parts of the body must be eaten by prescribed relations. A somewhat similar custom is the anointing of the bodies of the mourners with the exudations from the corpse in parts of the Northern Territory as well as in parts of eastern Australia.

Interment which is practised in almost every tribe whether or not some of the other methods are also used, exhibits several variations in detail. Grave mounds are erected in the south-eastern quarter of the continent, namely in parts of eastern South Australia, in New South Wales and Victoria. Elsewhere, this feature is absent. In some parts, (north-eastern South Australia) the grave is filled in gradually during the course of the mourning and ceremonial chanting, and in the central-eastern portion of Western Australia no earth is put over the body, but the bones are later shifted from the original grave and interred near by to the accompaniment of a further mourning ceremony. There are a few examples of the burial of the body in a side-chamber in the grave, and in a limited region of eastern Australia, namely, north-eastern New South Wales and south-western Queensland, as well as amongst a few tribes of the south-western corner of the continent, the trees around the graves were marked with various mythical designs. The same thing was done in the former region in the case of the initiation ground and, no doubt, in both cases symbolized the sky-world significance of both initiation and burial.

It is interesting to notice the wide-spread distribution of the twofold burial of the dead, with the consequent lengthening of the time of the mourning ritual. So persistent is the idea expressed in this custom, that it is not only seen in platform-exposure and delayed burial, in mummification and final disposal of the "bundle", in interment and disinterment and later mourning over the bones or bundle, but it is also seen in the removal of the bones from one grave to another—a form of re-interment which happens in areas outside the northern and eastern regions where the above burials are practised. Such procedures emphasize the significance of the death, and the length of time the society requires to adjust itself to the shock received and the danger incurred.

Social Status and Burial. While every death, except possibly that of a new-born infant is of social significance, the reference to the length of some burial-rites reminds us that deaths do vary in social significance, and that this variation is shown by the type of ritual and the time taken over it. Social status is seldom associated with the Aborigines, but it is certainly present in the sense of social value or importance. In other words, status has to be achieved. Age, knowledge, skill, natural leadership, and physical fitness are means to this end, and once acquired, it is usually reflected in the type of burial accorded. Status, however, can be lost by reaching such an old age that the individual has become useless and is referred to as "close-up dead"—a fact which is also reflected in the burial ritual; less care and time are spent on it and satisfaction may not be sought.

As an illustration we may take the Ungarinyin tribe. Three forms of burial are practised: (i) A little child not more than a few years old, is wrapped tightly in a bark bundle and carried about by the mother for at least some months, after which the bundle is put in a rock-hole. (ii) Children who are too big to be carried about in a bundle, women and very old men are interred. A circular arrangement of stones is placed around the grave. An outer circle of inquest stones may also be placed in position if the group's emotional equilibrium has been sufficiently disturbed, or social grievances justify a demand for satisfaction or vengeance, and if the medicine-man does not "see" the murderer. Women and children are given this second type of burial because, not being initiated and not being channels of the secret tradition, they are not of the same importance as men, while the very old men have lost their value. In spite of this, however, quite a lot of fuss may be made about the death of any of these types of persons, and their spirits do reach the same home of the dead as that which awaits the spirits of men who die in the prime of life. (iii) A complex rite is reserved for the fully initiated men who have not reached the "close-up dead" condition. It consists of exposure of the body on a tree-stage, inquest with the stones under the stage, revenge, and later an important mourning ceremony performed over the bones which are then carried about by the "mother" for some time and are finally put in a cave. There is an alternative method for this class of person, namely, interment with inquest stones around the grave, disinterment some months later, followed by the mourning ceremony and final disposal of the bones. The impression I received was that disinterment had been replaced by the tree-stage exposure form, but probably the inquest stones around the grave reveal the influence of the form of inquest connected with the latter. I did see such graves, though they were said to be very old.

Another good example comes from the lower Murray region: (i) Still-born and unwanted infants were got rid of quietly by cremation. (ii) In the case of a child dying in the normal way, the corpse was made into a bundle to be carried about, then exposed on a platform, and finally the bones were interred. (iii) The body of a "rather aged" person was wrapped up and put on a platform until the flesh had disappeared; the bones were then interred. (iv) Very old women were interred at once or just placed in the fork of a tree, and very old men fared little better. (v) But youths, adults in the prime of life and warriors, that is, the real men of the tribe, received very complex burial ritual which included the main features of all the other forms and a special preparation of the body as well. After the outer skin and hair were removed and the apertures sewn up, the body was anointed with fat and red ochre and dried over a fire. The mummy was then carried about as a bundle to be mourned over. Later on, it was exposed on a platform until only the bones were left; these were then interred.

This principle of status in burial is present in very many tribes. Not only are the more complex and lengthy rites reserved for those considered the more important and valuable members of society, but very often these rites are, I believe, more recent acquisitions than those used for ordinary persons. There are exceptions, but speaking generally, the complex tree-stage exposure and delayed mourning and disposal of the bones in the northwestern quarter of the continent and the various mummification rites in eastern Australia are reserved for the more important persons. This is true, too, of the interment-disinterment ritual which is followed by a delayed mourning ceremony and the final disposal of the bones, or, in the mummification region, by the preparation of the bundle. Cannibalism, too, practised in Queensland as part of burial, was considered a most honourable rite, to be used only for persons of worth. It was incidentally a quick method of preparing the bundle, the flesh being eaten instead of dried. In some tribes, at least, in which interment was the only burial-rite, much more ceremony was observed in the case of those who were deemed of special importance, such as men of much knowledge and medicine-men, than for other persons. For example, in one Victorian tribe, whereas there were several ceremonies in the case of the death of a man, there was none when a woman or child died. The body was merely interred and a fire was lit at the grave. Only the near relations showed sorrow. In other words, society was not concerned.

The important point, of course, is that the Aborigines possessed the concept of social value and expressed it in burial ritual.

The Meaning of the Ceremonies. There is only space to mention this interesting aspect of burial in Australia. Normally, mummification should be practised for the purpose of preserving the body indefinitely so that the spirit will have its fleshly tenement in the next world. In Australia, however, it has been subordinated to another purpose which is contrary in nature, namely, dissociating the spirit from the body. Mummification is used to preserve the body until the period of revenge and mourning is completed; the body is then cremated or exposed and interred, with the result that the spirit is free to go to its home. It will not need the body again. Tree-stage exposure is a very suitable means of gaining this end, for as soon as the flesh has gone, the real mourning ceremony can be performed and the spirit will go to its home. Cremation is likewise a quick means of freeing and disposing of the spirit, but it must be used with discretion, namely for unwanted babies or, in some tribes, a woman killed in a fight, and for the final disposal of a mummy. It would not do to get rid of the body, bones, and all of an important person in this summary fashion until mourning had been duly lengthened and satisfaction for the death had been gained. Interment gains the same end, but unless disinterment is also practised, or the flesh is eaten, or the grave is not filled in until the flesh has dropped from the bones, the mourners cannot be sure that the spirit has gone. They play their part, however, by carefully observing taboos, keeping a fire, food and water by the grave for a stated period, making requests and threats to the deceased not to wander, by weighing down the body and by jumping on the grave; as a result, they hope that the spirit will not worry them, but will go to its home.

All the rites manifest ambivalent emotions towards the dead. The mourners and society still want the deceased in their midst, and so they watch by the grave, carry the body or bones about with them, care for the comfort of the departed, eat his flesh, anoint themselves with the exudations from the corpse, and in some regions hold the most important mourning ceremony months after the death—a kind of "year's mind". On the other hand, they do all this so that ultimately the spirit will leave entirely; they, therefore, add to these attentions quite clear and, at times, even forceful expression of their desire that it should do so. In other words, both the mourners and the tribe want the deceased, but they do not want death, for death disturbs the sense of well-being. But as death cannot be avoided, the thoughts and effects of it must be banished as soon as is possible in keeping with the sorrow of the mourners, and the social value of the deceased.

THE FATE OF THE DEAD

And so we pass to the fate of the dead, to which reference has already been made. In most of eastern Australia and parts of the west and north-west, the spirit eventually goes to the sky, as the culture-heroes before him have gone. In the greater part of the Northern Territory, north-western Australia and Cape York Peninsula the spirit returns to its spirit-home in which it pre-existed, or else it becomes identified with its totem, or lives near an important centre of the hero of its cult totem. In some beliefs, the spirit-home is beyond the sea or on an island, and in one Central Australian group there is even a belief in a final destruction of the spirit by a convulsion of nature. The spirit referred to in these beliefs, is the primary pre-existent spirit and not the spirit double or a secondary spirit, which may hang around its former associates for good or ill. Reincarnation is believed in by some tribes either for all persons or at least for children who die young. Some of their spirit-beliefs are remarkably involved, and are frequently inconsistent, but after all, the same is true of our own beliefs regarding this subject. For our own part, we have not yet reached a conclusion apart from faith, the rationalization of which leads to much argument. And in spite of the spiritual powers of the medicine-men, the Aborigines have also failed to find a path through the valley of the shadow leading to a haven where they would be. They therefore make, by ritual and belief, adjustments to the fact of death, which enable them to carry on.

THE CYCLE OF LIFE

To the Aborigine, life is a cycle, though whether it is continuous or not, he does not always dare to say. Found by his parent in a spiritual experience, he is incarnated through his mother and so enters profane life. But a few years later, through the gate of initiation he partially re-enters the sacred dream-time or sky-world which he has left for a season. After passing farther and farther into it, so far as the necessities of profane life allow, he dies, and through another gate, the transition rite of burial, he returns completely to his sacred spirit state in the sky, the spirit-home or totemic centre, perhaps to repeat the cycle later, perhaps to remain, perhaps to cease to be. In the case of a woman, the central part of the cycle does not exist—except in so far as she is the means of incarnation for sacred pre-existing spirits.

There are some interesting symbols of this return to spiritual existence. In north-western Australia, the individual's spirit came by way of a waterhole associated with the spirit of fertility or life; initiation gives him conscious knowledge of the source of his life, and after the final mourning ceremony his bones are put in a cave near by. In some of the desert areas, a hair-belt made from the deceased's hair, which contains something of his spirit, is finally returned to the cave or waterhole of the mythical serpent, from which the spirit issued for incarnation. In north-western Arnhem Land, the bones are finally placed in a totemic coffin and so identified with the totem and, therefore, with the source of life in man and nature. Finally, in parts of eastern Australia, the young fellow passes at his initiation to the sky-world which is symbolized on the initiation ground by the marked trees, and when he dies, his burial-ground is likewise marked to symbolize the sky-world from which all life is believed to come and to which he now returns.

There we leave him—his cycle complete, and whether the wheel turns again or not, he does not know, and neither do we. In the meantime, we must realize that we are interfering with his cycle and for the most part are failing to replace or improve it. Let us hope, however, that in honestly trying to understand him, his way, beliefs and hopes, we may learn to help him so that he may with success adjust himself to the great changes which have come upon his world. He speaks to us from the long past-time and yet his language, as expressed in his social order and spiritual attitude, is not so very different from our own. Our cultures are different in some ways, but they are also alike in many, and fundamentally both he and we are social personalities, finding life a task which we both try to perform in our various ways, and a problem which we shall ever try to solve.

Chapter XIII

EPILOGUE: THE ABORIGINES ON THE MARCH

THE PAST

THIS book has been written because it should be the desire, as it is the duty, of non-Aboriginal Australians to understand the Aborigines. Historical circumstances have brought both together in one great land, so that our task is not merely to understand the Aborigines in themselves, but also in relation to ourselves, and indeed, also ourselves in relation to them. Nor is this just a matter of the past. For a century and a quarter it seemed to many that the cry of the Aborigine was, or should be: "I must decrease; you [the white man] must increase," and that, therefore, the problem of the Aborigines would disappear with them. Now, however, as a result of the readjustment of those that remain—some fifty-odd thousand full-bloods—and of improved official policies and administration, the Aborigines seem likely to increase, rather than decrease. In addition the mixed-blood Aborigines, a continuing core of about 30,000 apart from those who become "lost" or assimilated in the general Australian community, are becoming more and more a positive factor in the relations between the full-bloods and ourselves. To appreciate the present Aboriginal problem, we must survey, at least briefly, the history of racial contact in Australia since 1788.

PHASES OF ABORIGINAL-EUROPEAN CONTACT

Pauperism and Clash. The first European settlements, from Port Jackson in 1788 to Port Phillip, Moreton Bay,

Swan River and Adelaide during the next fifty years were intensive. The number of "invaders" immediately or very soon far outnumbered local Aboriginal tribes, and "usurped" the most fertile parts of their countries in order to establish themselves securely. This meant a complete undermining of the Aborigines' way of life. Free movement over their "own" country for food-gathering, and for social and ceremonial purposes was denied them at many points, and before long in most directions. At first, they did not realize this, and made tentative approaches to the newcomers as sojourners with whom goods and services could be exchanged. Permanent settlement, however, left them dispossessed, with only two courses open—pauperism and clash. The former was unintentionally encouraged by the official gifts of trinkets, clothes and, when possible, food, as well as by unofficial gifts, including alcohol, sometimes in exchange for the favours of native women. Such parasitism led quickly to depopulation.

Clash was almost unavoidable as farms and grazing became established. The Aborigines, logically from their point of view, collected and speared respectively the farm produce and cattle which the white man regarded as his own property. Resenting this, the latter sought or adopted forceful measures to punish and deter the natives, who, in his eyes, were thieves.

The official policy, enunciated in England, and sincerely adopted by governments in Australia, ruled that the Aborigines were British subjects, and as such should not be treated as enemies. Clashes between settlers and them were to be matters for regular legal processes. Moreover, every effort was to be made to win the Aborigines' friendship, and especially from 1820 to 1840, to bring them the blessings of civilization and Christianity.

"*Pacification by Force.*" As settlement spread along the coasts and inland, away from the continued oversight of governors and higher officials, the settlers felt unable to wait for official action. In some cases their outposts were raided, stores taken, shepherds killed, cattle and sheep speared and crops pilfered. In self-protection they banded together and organized punitive expeditions to teach the natives a lesson—often by shooting indiscriminately. This method of "pacification by force" grew up particularly during the decades from 1840 to 1880, receiving indirect recognition from the Legislative Councils and later the Legislative Assemblies established during that period. The "frontier" pastoral interests were represented in the Legislatures; and pastoralists and settlers were not prevented from dealing with their local Aboriginal problems as they deemed best, on the spot and immediately, if circumstances prevented them from applying and waiting for official action.

Justifications were given for this policy. The settlers on the interior and northern frontiers in contact with the Aborigines, claiming to know them best, asserted that they could not be civilized. Indeed, all attempts in this direction had failed. They were "too primitive". Moreover, the settlers were lawfully opening up the country and considered that they should be protected from the depredations of the natives. For such reasons they objected strongly to the interference of humanitarian societies, which were inspired by Wilberforce, Buxton and others in far-off England. Fear and ignorance also played a part: the settlers on the frontiers were few and scattered, and were outnumbered by the Aborigines, whom they did not understand.

Thus, force and punitive expeditions became an institutionalized way of dealing with the Aborigines, and lingered on in the sparsely settled central, north-western and northern parts of the continent until the 1930s.

Aboriginal Adaptation—Intelligent Parasitism. The Aborigines, on their part, learnt that they could not rid their various tribal countries of the white man, nor take his possessions with impunity, for they came off worst when faced with either guns or courts. They therefore gradually adapted themselves to the white man, with his flocks and herds, as a permanent factor in the environment. Fortunately, they could do this in the outback and north because settlement there was both slow and sparse. They had time to learn from their own clashes or from those of tribes farther in, the futility of force, and to sum up the position. Moreover, there seemed to be room in most regions both for the settler and his herds, and also for the tribes. The Aborigines realized too, that the settlers and managers of properties were dependent on them for labour and, in some cases, for sexual partners. Here then was an opportunity to obtain by peaceful means some of the white man's goods, such as tobacco, sugar, tea, flour and iron. They provided labour for him, and did just sufficient work to enable him to carry on his property and to give them the articles they desired in return for that labour, and also for associating with their women. From their point of view, this was a policy of Intelligent Parasitism.

No advance could be made through it either for them or for the country, but it was a *modus vivendi*. Many of the settlers concerned have recognized the position quite well, summing it up in the picturesque phrase that they were "just working for the Blacks". They were right. This situation, which still prevails here and there, was not peculiar to the small settler on the frontier. It also prevailed on many of the big stations. The manager or owner regarded, and still regards, the local tribe or clans as "his Blacks", while they summed up each new owner, manager or stockman to see how they could best get what they wanted from him with as little interference as possible to their own domestic and tribal affairs. Their position, however, was servile. In the course of a couple of generations station Aborigines had woven station activity and certain European goods into their social and economic organization and into their psychology without upsetting the fundamentals of their social behaviour or beliefs. The country was still their geographical and spiritual home, so that, except temporarily in individual cases, they were wholly dependent on employment on the station for their material and psychological well-being.

This rather unsatisfactory situation can only be changed by employment within a money economy and by education. Pastoralists have opposed both these measures, correctly realizing that their patriarchal hold on "their" natives would be loosened if government made them effective.

Protection Policies. To return to the more closely settled regions, we find that as early as 1843 some sentimental regret was expressed for the tribal remnants. A writer in that year wrote in the *New South Wales Magazine*: "I wish to see our means applied to rendering the current of events by which the grave is closing on our sable brethren, smooth and regular." "Smooth the Dying Pillow" became the comfortable rationalization to justify the passing of a "stone age people" confronted by civilization. Gradually, however, people in the growing cities and large towns, who knew nothing of frontier conditions, realized that the Aboriginal problem was not simply an expression of some sociological or biological laws. They heard of atrocities on the frontier. They saw the pitiable plight of tribal remnants and of mixed-bloods on the outskirts of towns. They were disturbed. The Aborigines should surely be protected and treated benevolently. Moreover, from 1870 onward, anthropologists, pursuing their new field of knowledge, became especially interested in the Aborigines. L. H. Morgan, E. Tylor and James Frazer abroad, and L. Fison, B. Spencer, W. E. Roth and A. W. Howitt at home showed that the social organization and religious system of the Aborigines were complex and full of interest. The Aborigines were indeed, human. Here was an additional reason for showing them kindness. But nothing more could be done, as the failure of earlier civilizing and missionary efforts had shown.

Consequently, policies of protection were drawn up and

put into operation in State after State, with the object of protecting the Aborigines from abuses and of providing the remnants around towns with some rations, blankets and medicine. Victoria instituted its policy in 1860; South Australia in 1880; Western Australia in 1886; Queensland in 1897; New South Wales in 1909; and the Commonwealth for the Northern Territory in 1911. These policies were negative. The underlying theme was that the Aborigines were inevitably doomed to pass away, even on the stations. The only hopeful note struck during all the years of protection was that if groups could be kept on inviolable reserves and left to themselves (missionaries and anthropologists possibly being admitted), they would continue in their wonted way and so survive.

Actually, this plan arose from pessimism. It implied that the Aborigines could not play a useful part in Australian life and survive. Moreover, to admit missionaries (and no government would seriously consider refusing this), meant that the Aborigines' way of life and thinking would be changed. In addition, even if such reserves could be kept inviolable, in spite of the discovery, for example, of valuable minerals in them, the plan was doomed to failure. The Aborigines have always shown an irresistible urge to migrate to the nearest white stations and settlements, once the local natives have seriously declined in numbers. They move out to see and share in this new world, of which they have heard. They are fascinated, even to the extent of their own uprooting. Inviolable reserves, therefore, have been a protection from outsiders, but not from their own urges.

Protection policies not only failed to ensure the survival of the Aborigines; they also failed to protect them from harsh treatment. Atrocities, protests and inquiries were frequent. Every now and then some white man, generally fairly new in the frontier regions, and scornful of the mutual adaptation worked out there, acted in a high-handed manner, which resulted in resentment and clash. Or the same result was caused by an Aboriginal young man trying to presume on a white newcomer, before the latter's character had been summed up. Further, the attitude was deeply entrenched amongst most white settlers, stationmen and townsfolk that the Aborigines were an inferior race, to be used or abused, and at best to be regarded paternally as amiable adjuncts to one's station.

Positive Policy. Observations during field-work in 1927–30 convinced me that the only way to change this attitude, to prevent unfortunate clashes, to break through the stalemate of a parasitic adaptation, and possibly to ensure the survival of the Aborigines, was to work out and implement policies based on the conviction that they need not die out. Efficient health services, education and improved conditions of employment would have to be essential features of such policies.

At this time, too, Australia was becoming conscious of its responsibility for peoples of primitive culture in its territories. It had accepted a mandate from the League of Nations to administer the former German New Guinea in such a way that the peoples of that region would eventually be able to stand on their own feet in world relationships. Missionary, humanitarian and League of Nations Union groups and some sections of government were studying the implications of the mandates principle.

Attention became focussed on the Aborigines, for whom Australia had, at least, a moral mandate. Reports of unfortunate happenings in the centre and north did not pass unheeded. Moreover, systematic anthropological research was in progress, and anthropologists, returning from the field, emphasized the humanity, courtesy and intelligence of the Aborigines. They also threw light on problems arising out of the contact of white and black.[1] As a result,

[1] Following on a recommendation of the Pacific Science Congress held in Australia in 1923 and the representations of the Australian National Research Council, the Department of Anthropology was founded in the University of Sydney in 1925,

conferences, representations, commissions of inquiry, speeches, public meetings and avid newspaper interest became the order of the day in the early 1930s.

In 1936 the various governments bowed to an informed public opinion, and began to give a positive aspect and content to Aboriginal policies and administration. The title of Protector or Chief Protector of Aborigines was changed in the Northern Territory and three States to Commissioner, Director or Superintendent of Native Affairs; and the idea of development and welfare was written into, or implied in, amended Acts and Ordinances. Citizenship became the goal and assimilation the process. Commonwealth social services were extended, with prescribed limitations, to Aborigines and persons of part-Aboriginal descent, and methods were devised to exempt even full-bloods from all Aboriginal Acts, Ordinances and Regulations, provided that they were living independently in the general community.

Great advances were made in the course of a decade. In 1944 I published a small book under the title *Citizenship for the Aborigines*, discussing principles to be observed and methods to be followed in reaching that goal. To have written such a book in 1934 would have been unrealistic, for the task then was to supersede the ineffective and negative phase of protection, retaliation and injustice, and above all to convince public opinion and authority that there was a future for the Aborigines. Ten years had seen

---

and both teaching and organized research was begun in 1926. The research was made possible by generous grants to the National Research Council from the Rockefeller Foundation and the Carnegie Corporation. The Council's Committee on Anthropology, with the Professor of that subject as its chairman, organized the research. By 1936 nine trained anthropologists, two linguists and one psychologist had spent about two years each in their several fields. In addition, several short expeditions had been made from the universities of Sydney and Adelaide (where a Board of Anthropological Research had been formed in 1926) under the auspices of the Australian National Research Council. Research has gone on almost continuously since 1936.

a veritable revolution in governmental attitudes and public interest. Moreover, the impetus then gained has not abated. Opportunities for education and vocational training are being increased; health services have been extended to Aborigines everywhere; employment conditions have gradually but surely been raised; and, above all, prejudices have been combated.

ABORIGINES AND THE WAR—AND AFTER

The Second World War played no little part in maintaining this impetus. For a few years northern regions of Australia, particularly the Northern Territory, were the scene of much military and Air Force activity. The Aborigines got to know men of the Services. They worked for them both casually and in labour units. They were treated justly as persons performing necessary tasks. They appreciated the Services' attitude and responded quickly to the routine of work, hygiene and camp life generally. In so doing they showed that they were intelligent beings capable of working efficiently and of appreciating civilized services and amenities (hospitals, hygiene, canteens, films, huts and schools). Moreover, the very camp-setting of this experience related it to their own way of life, and suggested that a blend of the old and new was possible. They were still able to maintain the essential structure of their social and ceremonial life, and no attempt was made to change their philosophical and religious heritage.

Therefore when, after the war, government, especially in the Northern Territory, began to implement its positive policy by establishing settlements to provide oversight, housing, training, schools, work, wages, canteens and hospitals, the Aborigines were ready to co-operate. They had become familiar with similar institutions and had begun to gain an intelligent appreciation of at least some aspects of the white man's way of life. There have been delays in providing adequate staff and buildings, and the full-bloods in and on the borders of the reserves still tend to move about a good deal for their own social and ceremonial occasions, and so interfere with settlement routine. But as the settlements become better organized, with regular activity, the Aborigines will more and more fit these occasions into the time-table of seasonal work, school and settlement life generally. In any case, Aboriginal reserves are already beginning to function, not as human preserves, but as preparation centres for life in the larger world.

In the more inaccessible parts of the Northern Territory and the neighbouring States a policy of government-mission co-operation is being developed in the spheres of health, welfare and education. Generally speaking, too, the main missionary bodies recognize that these are essential services which they can render at once, but that Christian conversion is a process which will only come slowly as the Aborigines relate their interpretation of Christianity to their own changing background of culture, of social and economic life.

Western Australia experimented for a quarter of a century with State-run buffer Aboriginal cattle stations. Queensland and South Australia have conducted for some decades large settlements and stations for mixed-blood and detribalized Aborigines. Employment as well as amenities and social services are provided for most of the wage-earners within the settlement. A thin but constant stream of individuals move from these into the general community. Victoria has one, and New South Wales nearly twenty small settlements, which are community centres under the guidance of a manager-welfare officer. He helps the men get employment in the surrounding district. In New South Wales houses are also provided on small reserves for mixed-bloods who are living almost independently of official supervision. About five thousand live on the settlements and reserves in that State, but over six thousand are fending for themselves in the cities, towns and country districts. Many of them live in unsatisfactory conditions on the outskirts of towns and on the banks of rivers, but they prefer to do so rather than to be subject to even a mild degree of specific supervision, such as prevails on a settlement. This same problem exists in all States. Its solution is being sought through the tactful work of welfare officers and through schemes for better housing.

THE PRESENT PICTURE

Aboriginal Australia to-day presents a complex picture. A few thousand full-bloods remain living all or part of the time in their former traditional, semi-nomadic way. These are mainly in Arnhem Land and in the west-central arid regions, but they are gradually settling around government or mission stations. Another generation will see a great change in their habits and attitudes.

The great majority of full-bloods, however, are either living and working on stations or around towns and mines. In many cases they are only tribal remnants, usually clinging to their old tribal country or its neighbourhood. But though these may be regarded as relatively detribalized, they still speak their own languages and observe as far as possible their social rules. Further, wherever possible, they tend to retain or revive their ceremonial life, though in a modified form. This provides a sense of solidarity and continuity in a changing world.

A third type is made up of full-blood remnants and part-Aborigines, scattered and completely—or almost completely—detribalized. The full-bloods associate freely with mixed-bloods and tend to be absorbed through miscegenation with the latter, particularly with the darker castes. This mixed type of full-bloods and part-Aborigines is found on government settlements, on some mission stations, and scattered about in small groups camping in the vicinity of pastoral properties and country townships, generally in districts associated with their Aboriginal ancestors. Some degree of Aboriginal culture is usually retained, but this varies a great deal. In some parts it is very marked in group relationships and social behaviour; it also lingers in vague beliefs about the soul and about the cause and treatment of illness; in the part-time use of a native language; and in an urge to pursue a semi-nomadic life. This third type, especially when nomadic, is not yet orientated towards assimilation.

A fourth group consists almost wholly of mixed-bloods, mainly quadroons and lighter. These are definitely seeking or hoping to be assimilated. They strive on the one hand to have as little as possible to do with Aborigines or part-Aborigines living on settlements and reserves; and, on the other hand, to become unobtrusively absorbed in the general community. The number of light-caste folk who have realized this aim during the past fifty years must be considerable, but at any one time the number is not great. Cities and large towns provide the best opportunities for this transition, small country towns the least, especially if there is an Aboriginal settlement or camp in the vicinity.

THE PROCESS OF ASSIMILATION

The future of the Aborigines, whether full-blood or other, lies within the general framework and current of Australian economic, political, social and religious life. The old order is passing, and a new order is being entered through a process of assimilation; but the rate varies according to the types of Aborigines and their geographical position. Probably, too, assimilation will be achieved in the various spheres of Australian life in the order given: firstly, in the economic sphere, for their services and contributions are needed. Secondly, in the political sphere, for they all have both State and Commonwealth franchise already in three States (New South Wales, Victoria and South Australia), and all full-bloods and mixed-bloods have the Commonwealth franchise everywhere; moreover, Australian-born wage-earners and taxpayers cannot be long denied political rights. Thirdly, social assimilation will come slowly, hindered by differences in appearance and some customs, and by prejudices on the part of many in the general community, especially of those who equate assimilation to miscegenation (or intermarriage); this, of course, is logically correct, but in practice it is exceptional, and will remain so for generations. Fourthly, religious assimilation is retarded by social prejudices and by doctrinal difficulties: a mission to Aborigines does not regard them as part of parochial or circuit pastoral work along with, and in the same way as, white residents. Further, neither full-bloods nor part-Aborigines will enter fully into our religious life until they can relate it to the social life which they lead or adopt. In other words, religious assimilation will wait on social assimilation. Moreover, philosophical and doctrinal changes have to be worked out from within, and cannot be hurried.

In addition to this differential rate of assimilation, as it could be termed, other difficulties arise in the process—the result of historical and psychological factors. Aborigines, especially of the second and third types mentioned above, who have been in close touch with ourselves, frequently mistake employment and missionary interest, and the material and physical advantages associated with these activities, as symbols of entry into the white man's way of life. Eventually, however, they realize that his is a world different from their own, that they are not being admitted to it, and that they are not sure that they want to become part of it.

As a reaction, there has been a definite move to strengthen, or to recapture, at least some of the social and spiritual elements of the Aboriginal past.[2] This is quite marked amongst the part-Aborigines of the third group, even amongst those who have been in close contact with the white man, his towns and activities, for two and more generations. In parts of New South Wales they carry out, in modified form, old initiation and burial rituals. In some

[2] I have been watching this movement since 1936. See above, Chapter VII, first section.

districts, in spite of being literate in English, amongst themselves they use the local native language or a mixed talk of English and what has survived of their own tongue. This provides a section of life from which the white man is excluded, and which gives them a feeling of solidarity.[3] Some groups too, welcome non-denominational religious sects, in which the emotional element is strong. Moreover, they are asking for their own Church. This tendency is especially strong in the eastern coastal region. Religious conventions have been held from time to time in southeast Queensland, at Tuncester near Lismore, and at La Perouse (Sydney). Part-Aborigines come from near and far. Living together for days as a big group and emotionally stimulated in common by the singing and by the preaching (of their own leaders), they express and feel their unity as a distinct people facing their problems in their own way.

The Group Aspect of Assimilation

Generally speaking, therefore, mixed-bloods regard themselves as a separate group in the community, though they are not yet organized or politically conscious. Significantly, too, they think of themselves as Aborigines and are not ashamed of the fact. Indeed, it is from amongst them, including those consciously seeking assimilation, that individuals and groups have been arising for nearly two decades to become vocal on behalf of the Aborigines as a whole. They form associations with various titles, which last a few years, disappear and are replaced by others. They talk of their rights. They proclaim against injustices, some of which, though formerly facts, have been righted.

[3] Bandjelang, the language of the far north-coast of New South Wales, was studied in 1945 as a living and functioning language by W. E. Smythe. It is now reported (1953) that a large number of the mixed group at Brewarrina, in the far north-west of New South Wales, is using the local language—a recent revival.

And they protest against the treatment of the Aborigines up north. True, they are often ill-informed and sometimes misguided, but their action is a sign that they are realizing their existence, and, indeed, their solidarity as a group. The Aborigines, wherever they are, and of whatever noticeable degree of caste, are one.

It may seem strange that part-Aborigines in New South Wales, for example, who have full citizenship rights,[4] should openly or tacitly be interested in such movements, or share in the attitudes expressed in them. But after all, they do realize that they are an out-group, and as such are regarded as a caste lower in status than the "white" citizen. They have felt the prejudice which puts them into the worst houses in a country town, the overcrowded parts of a city, the worst seats in a picture theatre and, in many towns, their children into separate schools. They are diffident. They are shy. They feel deprived of something—and they are, for they lack full community life in the context in which they find themselves. Therefore they listen with interest, though not always with comprehension, to demands for their rights, for what amounts to reparations for all that has happened to the Aborigines since 1788. Land, houses, rations, amenities—all these things, they dimly feel, should be theirs, but without effort on their part, and without supervision if they are provided with them. Only very slowly do they learn that rights imply responsibilities, and without the latter are of little worth. The main task of the State Aboriginal or Native Affairs Departments is to help the Aborigines realize this fact.

Further, both as cause and effect of this development of a sense of Aboriginal oneness, the part-Aboriginal popu-

[4] In this State, all discriminatory clauses in Aboriginal Welfare Legislation were removed in 1963, including the prohibition on possessing and drinking alcoholic beverages. The results have been gratifying. Secret and "defiant" drinking has ceased. All persons of Aboriginal descent in New South Wales are eligible for all social services, irrespective of place of residence.

lation is apparently reaching at least a temporary, stationary position as regards colour and caste around the quadroon—three-eighths "degrees". Studies of various mixed groups have shown that the reproduction and survival rates of these castes are comparatively high, as compared with the true half-caste and darker. Further, there is a definite concentration of marriages or continuous mating within the half-caste—quadroon section of the mixed-blood community. Octoroons whose rate of survival is high are relatively few in number, and must often find marriage partners in darker castes, for marriage with white persons is rare. It is often desired, but is hindered by a social-colour bar.[5] These facts of marriage and survival make more obvious the existence of a distinct Aboriginal people in Australia. The shade of colour and features become the symbol of distinction and of "belonging".

If this is so in the case of mixed-bloods, it is even more so with regard to the full-bloods of central and northern Australia, those of the second type. Whatever be the wording of legislation, whether or not we avoid in it the term Aboriginal and substitute native or ward, the fact remains that for decades or even generations to come, those full-bloods and near full-bloods will regard themselves as Aborigines, and see no reason why they should not do so. Moreover, this will be the case whatever the degree of citizenship status or economic position accorded to them.

Aboriginal Citizenship the Goal

This attitude and its consequences should neither be ignored nor discouraged. These "true" Aborigines are *not* going to become "white" in all but skin colour in the foreseeable future, though they can and will become worthy

[5] A. P. Elkin, "Position and Problems of Aboriginal Mixed-Bloods in Australia", *Proceedings of the Seventh Pacific Science Congress.* New Zealand, 1949, vol. vii, pp. 629–37. M. Reay, "Mixed-Blood Marriage in North-Western New South Wales", *Oceania,* vol. xxii, no. 2, 1951, pp. 116–20.

Australian citizens. To become the latter does not imply that they must turn their backs on their own history and culture. That would mean "wandering in the wilderness", with consequent social disintegration. We would do well, therefore, to encourage them to keep their language, each group literate in a regional lingua franca; to develop their own art, poetry and music where this still flourishes; to retain their ritual in modified form; and to cherish the essence of the doctrines enshrined in their mythology. For in the process of change they will need this heritage as a source of moral strength and courage, and as firm ground for further advance.

Indeed, this is already being sought. One tribe and the remnant of another in the far north have recently revived certain advanced initiation rites and degrees of the nearly extinct local tribes. They were doing so as a means of inculcating tribal discipline and pride, and also self-control and circumspect behaviour in the contact situation. The two men being raised to these degrees had been acting irresponsibly, and here was an attempt to ensure Aboriginal prestige. The elders considered that the white man's official treatment of such persons was not efficacious. In other words, they were aware of the contact situation and were trying to cope with the behaviour aspect of it. This action is a sign that the Aborigines appreciate the significance of the problems arising out of contact with ourselves, and that they will meet these out of their own cultural heritage, rather than out of ours, at least for decades to come. Fortunately there are still Aboriginal headmen in some regions who have the "tribal" authority to lead in such circumstances. Likewise there are part-Aborigines who are trying to set an example in circumspect behaviour, so that the Aborigines in general, and themselves in particular, will gain the respect of the general community. They are ashamed of, and condemn, unseemly behaviour on the part of other mixed-bloods, and may even try to avoid such persons lest their own reputations be sullied.

To sum up: Although there are numbers of families which have taken their place unobtrusively and timidly in the general community, and although hindrances to assimilation are officially and legally being removed and aids to it provided, yet assimilation is not a simple linear process by which individuals become citizens in fact and daily life as well as in law. Indeed, an ambivalent attitude is rising towards assimilation. Although the Aborigines more and more want to be a part of Australian life in their own right, they want to reach this goal as Aborigines. Prejudice against them, their own slowness and difficulty in appreciating what citizenship entails, and the "pull" of their background culture on full-bloods and part-Aborigines alike, is giving rise to a group-consciousness with an emphasis on Aboriginal tradition and solidarity.

Moreover, there is no sign that the mixed-bloods will disappear in the near future through miscegenation with whites, nor that the full-bloods in the north and centre will either die out or be subsumed in the mixed-blood group. In other words Australia has and will have the Aborigines as a distinct element in its total population, more distinct, for example, than southern Italians.

This may seem like resistance to assimilation. Actually it is an inevitable part of the process. For assimilation does not mean necessarily intermarriage with the main stock— marriage is a matter of individual choices, not of policy —nor the reduction of every group to the same cultural pattern. There are sub-cultures and lesser cultures in every society. Eventually the Aborigines may become as other Australians in all things except physical features. The nearer goal, however, is that while still Aboriginal in many social and spiritual aspects of life, they will become full and responsible citizens sharing in our general economic and political life, and not offending against essential features of our social behaviour.

Out of their treasures, old and new, the Aborigines can

enrich Australian life. Whether they do so or not will depend on white Australians as much as on themselves.

Note. For further reading on the subject of this chapter, see A. P. Elkin, *Citizenship for the Aborigines* (1944); "Reaction and Interaction: A Food-gathering People and European Settlement in Australia", *American Anthropologist*, vol. liii, 1951, pp. 164–86. Marie Reay and Grace Sitlington, "Class and Status in a Mixed-Blood Community", *Oceania*, vol. xviii, no. 3, 1948, pp. 179–207. P. M. Hasluck, *Black Australians* (1942), for a history of opinion and policy in Western Australia from 1838–97; E. J. B. Foxcroft, *Australian Native Policy: Its History* (1941) (especially valuable for Victoria). R. M. and C. H. Berndt, *From Black to White in South Australia* (1951).

ADDITIONAL READING

THE following books and articles will be found helpful by those who desire to increase their understanding of the Aborigines. In addition to having a general knowledge, it is wise to acquire also detailed knowledge of one or two tribes. The classic book is *The Native Tribes of Central Australia*, by B. Spencer and F. J. Gillen, published in 1899. This was revised by the former and published in 1927 in two volumes with the title *The Arunta*. It should be read, for it gives a sound picture of the social, ceremonial, magical and economic aspects of the life of that tribe. Though it is full of detail, it is not difficult. There is another monograph on one tribe, *A Black Civilization*, by W. L. Warner (1937), which deals with a tribe in northeastern Arnhem Land. It is a very complete and sound sociological study, and should be read, but it is an advanced book. In 1939 Dr Phyllis Kaberry gave us a much needed and well-written book on *Aboriginal Woman, Sacred and Profane*, based principally on her field research in Eastern Kimberley, north-west Australia. A related study for an adjacent region has been provided by Catherine H. Berndt's *Women's Changing Ceremonies* in northern Australia (1950). A. P. Elkin, *Aboriginal Men of High Degree* (1946) is a study of medicine-men. *Kunapipi* (1951) and *The Djanggawul* (1952) by R. M. Berndt are studies of two religious cults in Arnhem Land, and *Sexual Behaviour in Western Arnhem Land* (Viking Fund Publication No. 16, 1951) by R. M. and C. H. Berndt, deals with the social organization, marriage and rituals of the area. *Art in Arnhem Land* (1950), by A. P. Elkin and R. M. and C. H. Berndt, is concerned mainly with the bark-paintings and wooden figures of that region. So, too, are *Art, Myth and Symbolism* by C. P. Mountford (Records of the American-Australian Expedition to Arnhem Land), published in 1956; and the beautifully produced and illustrated *Un Art a l'Etat Brut,* by Karel Kupka (La Guilde du Livre), 1962. Several other studies have appeared recently: *The Tiwi of North Australia,* (1962) is a short, general monograph on the Melville and Bathurst Islanders near Darwin; *An Adjustment Movement in Arnhem Land* (1962), is a study of culture change on Elcho Island, Arnhem Land; and three important books for advanced readers: in 1960 *Classification of Kin, Age Structure and Marriage amongst the Groote Eylandt Aborigines,* (an island off the east coast of Arnhem Land); and in 1962, *Kin and Totem* by J. Falkenberg, and *Desert People* by M. J. Meggitt, being studies respectively of the social organization of the Murinbata tribe in the Port Keats district, south of Darwin, and of the Walbiri tribe of north-western Central Australia.

Spencer and Gillen's *Northern Tribes of Central Australia* (1904), B. Spencer's *Native Tribes of the Northern Territory* (1914), and A. W. Howitt's *Native Tribes of South-East Australia* (1906), contain much useful information which will be found of interest and value, though they are compendiums of observations (sometimes not quite reliable) rather than aids to our understanding. H. Basedow's *The Australian Aboriginal,* like N. W. Thomas's *The Aborigines of Australia,* is very superficial, but the former, especially, is interesting from the point of view of the physical anthropology and food-gathering activity of the Aborigines. Mrs L. Parker's *The Euahlayi Tribe* (1905) and John Mathew's *Two Representative Tribes of Queensland* (1910) are light but sound contributions to our knowledge of those tribes. Those two old works, Brough Smyth's *The Aborigines of Victoria* (2 vols, 1878) and E. M. Curr's

The Australian Race (3 vols, 1886) consist of contributions by many correspondents, hardly any of whom were trained observers, and so do not take us very far into Aboriginal life. The same is the case with J. D. Woods's *The Native Tribes of South Australia* (1879). Somewhat different is L. Fison and A. W. Howitt, *Kamilaroi and Kurnai* (1880); it contains interesting material about the Kurnai, as well as theoretical discussion of social organization. W. E. Roth's works, *Ethnological Studies in North-west Central Queensland* (1897) and a series of ethnographical bulletins published by the Queensland Government, are sounder, though like many anthropological works of the period, savoured too much of the spirit of the collector and compiler of interesting social and religious exhibits, and too little of the student of a people's life.

Many articles have been written during the past seventy and more years on the Aborigines, but few people have ready access to these. The reader is advised to concentrate especially on *Oceania,* a quarterly journal, published by the Australian National Research Council, Sydney, from 1930 to 1954, and now by the University of Sydney. Professor Elkin has been Editor since 1933. It is devoted to the study of the native peoples of Australia and the Pacific and contains for the most part only the results of the original field-research amongst those people. Since 1926 a great deal of such research has been carried out under the auspices of the Australian National Research Council, which has administered grants made for that purpose by the Rockefeller Foundation of New York, and later by the Carnegie Corporation.

More than half of almost every number of *Oceania* consists of articles on the Aborigines written from the point of view of this book. The chief contributors and the regions of their researches have been: Miss U. McConnel and Dr R. L. Sharp, Cape York Peninsula; Professor W. L. Warner, north-eastern Arnhem Land; Dr C. W. Hart, Bathurst Island; Dr W. E. H. Stanner, Miss O. M. Pink, Mr T. G. H.

Strehlow, Dr H. K. Fry, Dr M. J. Meggitt and Dr Marie Reay, Northern Territory; Dr Phyllis Kaberry, Dr A. Capell and Dr R. Piddington, north-western Australia; Mrs Caroline Kelly, south-eastern Queensland; R. M. and Catherine Berndt, South Australia and Northern Territory; J. H. Bell, M. Calley, Marie Reay and Ruth Fink, New South Wales; and Professor A. P. Elkin, north-western Australia, South Australia, Arnhem Land, eastern Queensland and New South Wales.

In addition, some of the articles have been reprinted in monographs. *Oceania* Monograph No. 1, *The Social Organization of Australian Tribes,* by Professor A. R. Radcliffe-Brown: This gives a general introduction to the subject and also a brief outline of the social organization and totemism of the main groups of tribes as far as this was known in 1930. Professor Radcliffe-Brown had previously laid the foundations for a systematic study of Australian kinship and social organization in the reports of his fieldwork in the central coastal region of Western Australia and the Lower Murray and Darling regions of South Australia and New South Wales. The reports are entitled "Three Tribes of Western Australia" (*Journal of the Royal Anthropological Institute,* vol. xliii, 1913) and "Notes on the Social Organization of Australian Tribes" (*Journal of the Royal Anthropological Institute,* vols. xlviii, 1918, and liii, 1923). In this work he was both following on, and running parallel to, R. H. Mathews, who published a long series of articles (1900–10) on the structure and totemism of many tribes—especially in New South Wales. *Oceania* Monograph No. 2, *Studies in Australian Totemism,* by Professor A. P. Elkin: This includes a detailed study of totemism in some north-western Australian tribes, and also two general studies on Australian totemism. *Oceania* Monograph No. 3, *Studies in Australian Linguistics,* edited by Professor A. P. Elkin: Two articles deal respectively with "The Nature of Australian Languages" and "The Structure of Australian Languages", while the others are concerned with particular languages of north-western Australia. *Oceania* Monograph No. 7, *Aranda Phonetics and Grammar* (1942), by T. G. H. Strehlow: This is the most complete study of an Australian language yet published. *Elementary Grammar of the Gumbainggar Language, North Coast, N.S.W.* (1948), by W. E. Smythe (Monograph, No. 8), is a comparable piece of work, and most praiseworthy because only a few of this tribe are still living. The same author has prepared a grammar of the Bandjelang, a language still spoken on the far north coast. Two special *Oceania* reprints have been issued: "Kinship in South Australia", (1940), by A. P. Elkin, and "A Preliminary Report of Field-Work in the Ooldea Region, Western Australia" (1946), by R. M. and C. Berndt.

Recent *Oceania* Monographs include No. 9, by A. P. Elkin and Trevor A. Jones, *Arnhem Land Music (North Australia)*; No. 10 by W. E. H. Stanner, *On Aboriginal Religion (Murinbata Tribe; Port Keats District, Northern Territory)*; and No. 11 by A. P. Elkin, *Religion in South and Central Arnhem Land*. A Series of *Oceania Linguistic Monographs* is also in progress; this includes so far No. 1, *A New Approach to Australian Linguistics*, by A. Capell; No. 4, *An Introduction to the Western Desert Language*, Australia, by W. H. Douglas; and No. 7, *Some Linguistic Types in Australia* (a continuation of No. 1) by A. Capell.

INDEX

ANCHOR BOOKS

ANTHROPOLOGY AND ARCHAEOLOGY

ANCHOR BOOKS

Sociology (continued)